CANADA
Portraits of Faith

Endorsements

"a magnificent coffee-table book…beautiful and substantive"—*World Magazine*

"surprisingly informative…handsome"—*Vancouver Sun*

"interesting and beautiful…elegant and thoughtful"—*Alberta Report*

"visually stunning and intellectually powerful"—*Edmonton Sun*

"striking…astonishing…a beautifully crafted coffee-table book"—*Faith Today*

"colourful and attractive…tales of faith, courage, and achievement"—*Christian Week*

"This remarkable book should be found in every library, every classroom, every pastor's study and in the offices of every professional, teacher, and politician. It should also be found in every home whose inhabitants care about the impact of Christianity on this country in earlier times."
—*BC Christian News*

"*Portraits of Faith* provides accurate insights into the lives of many Canadian heroes. This publication will encourage us all to inspire our children."
—Eric Lowther, member of Parliament

"I'm very excited about your *Canada: Portraits of Faith* project…one after the other, every successive generation of Canadian men and women has taken up the burden of moulding their country into an even better place to live and raise a family. Now it's our generation's turn to take up this noble task."
—L'hon. Jean J. Charest, C.P., leader of the Quebec Liberal Party

"A magnificent contribution to Canada's Christian heritage…captures the essence of those immortal souls whose vision and commitment strengthened the fabric of their nation."
—Chuck Swindoll, president of Dallas Theological Seminary and Bible teacher for Insight for Living

"An exciting book that needs to be read by every Canadian. *Portraits of Faith*'s commitment to graphic quality and historical integrity will establish it as both an art book and a history book."
—Rev. David Maines, host of 100 Huntley Street and president of Crossroads Ministries

"An exceptional and magnificent book. Marshall would have loved it."
—Corrine McLuhan, widow of Marshall McLuhan

"Examines our history for evidence of the profound impact Christian faith had on our nation, Canada. This creative production helps us all see that, as King David said, 'Blessed is the nation whose God is the Lord.' Canada's strength is in relation to her understanding and dependence of God. *Canada: Portraits of Faith* points us in that direction, and for that I am most grateful."
—Dr. Brian C. Stiller, president of Tyndale College and Seminary

"An attractive coffee-table book…reflect[ing] our cultural diversity…very well done indeed."
—*The Beaver,* Canada's national history magazine

Edited by
Michael D. Clarke

This book was made possible through the generosity of many individuals, families, ministries, and businesses. Thank you.

Published by
Home School Legal Defence Association of Canada
#2-3295 Dunmore Road, SE
Medicine Hat, Alberta T1B 3R2
Telephone: (403) 528-2704
Fax: (403) 529-2694
E-mail: info@hsldacanada.org

THIRD EDITION

Printed in Canada by Friesens

Editor:	Michael D. Clarke
Academic Review Board:	Bob Burkinshaw, Ph.D.
	John G. Stackhouse, Jr., Ph.D.
	Marguerite Van Die, Ph.D.
Copy Editor:	Howard Brandt
Proofing:	Curtis Gillingham
Art Director:	Cindy Clarke
Graphic Design:	Tim McAlpine, McAlpine Design Group Inc.
Digital Photo Editing:	Bob Fugger

Canadian Cataloguing in Publication Data
Clarke, Michael D., 1963–
Canada: Portraits of Faith

ISBN 0-9681835-0-6
1. Canada—Biography.
2. Canada—Biography—Portraits.
3. Christianity—Canada.
4. Canada—History.
5. Canada—Art—Portraits.

Distributed in Canada by
Home School Legal Defence Association of Canada
#2-3295 Dunmore Road, SE
Medicine Hat, Alberta T1B 3R2

Dedication

For Cindy, Travis, and Natasha—my family, my support, and my priority. Thank you for your prayers, love, and encouragement.

Preface to the Third Edition

At the time Canada patriated its constitution in the early 1980s, Prime Minister Pierre Elliot Trudeau reminded Canadians that

> The golden thread of faith is woven throughout the history of Canada from its earliest beginnings up to the present time. Faith was more important than commerce in the minds of many of the European explorers and settlers, and over the centuries, as successive waves of people came to this country, many in search of religious liberty, they brought with them a great wealth and variety of religious traditions and values. Those values have shaped our laws and our lives, and have added enormous strength to the foundation of freedom and justice upon which this country was built... It was in acknowledgment of that debt that the Parliament of Canada later gave its approval during the Constitutional Debate to the statement that Canada is founded upon principles that recognize the supremacy of God and the rule of law. Faith played a large part in the lives of so many men and women who have created in this land a society which places a high value on commitment, integrity, generosity and, above all, freedom. To pass on that heritage, strong and intact, is a challenge worthy of all of us who are privileged to call ourselves Canadians.

It is in this spirit that the Home School Legal Defence Association (HSLDA) has commissioned the third edition of *Canada: Portraits of Faith*. As even Trudeau—a proud secularist—realized, the most pervasive religious, cultural, and ethical influence upon Canada is clearly the Christian religion.

Prominent historians and a plethora of studies continue to remind us that Canadians know very little about their past. What little historical knowledge exists comes primarily through the processed filter of our public school system, with people of faith all too often profiled in a negative light. This lack of contextual and accurate historical fact needs to be corrected.

Modern-day Canada, however, is losing its moral moorings, and it seems as though many of Canada's leaders have forgotten the faith-based roots from which our country has grown. The psalmist could easily have had twenty-first century Canada in mind when he penned Psalm 88:12: "Wonders cannot be found in the midst of darkness. Righteousness cannot be done in a land of forgetfulness." We seek to assist in remedying this situation by making this book available to Canadian families.

History is about people. This book portrays fifty-two individuals, many of whom are not profiled in today's history books. It is hoped that their stories will inspire Canadians of our generation and of our children's generation to courageously apply the principles of faith to help Canada truly be a nation "founded upon principles that recognize the supremacy of God."

Dallas K. Miller, Q.C.
Executive Director and Senior Counsel
HSLDA of Canada

Table of Contents

Academic Review Board

It has been our privilege to participate in *Canada: Portraits of Faith* as members of an academic review board. As Canadian historians, we believe that it is important that the public have access to accurate and credible historical research on Canada and Canadians. Too often historians are content to write only for their colleagues. It has thus been exciting for us to review a work written by a group of historians for what we hope will be a considerable audience of interested Canadian readers.

As historians of religion, moreover, we are especially pleased to support a project that takes seriously the role Christian faith played in shaping and motivating the lives of leading Canadians. Seldom are modern Canadians exposed to the contributions of Christians to our society. That both the subjects of and the contributors to this work represent a wide range of backgrounds makes this an unusual effort. The editor has not included only those whose beliefs and expressions are closest to his own or to anyone else's. He has instead sought a diversity representative of the range of Christians in Canada.

Our role as academic reviewers has been to ensure the historical accuracy and credibility of each biography. We have been concerned that none of the authors engage in writing hagiography: the turning of people into saintlike idealizations by ignoring their shortcomings. Thus, not everything written here about every subject is entirely laudatory. We have striven to ensure that it is as accurate and as balanced as possible, given the limitations of space, and that it provides a clear picture of the person's contribution to Canada and of the faith that motivated him or her.

Bob Burkinshaw (chair), Ph.D., Trinity Western University
John G. Stackhouse, Jr., Ph.D., Regent College
Marguerite Van Die, Ph.D., Queen's University and Theological College

Acknowledgements

The individuality and style that each author has brought to this book is only matched by their common desire to faithfully tell their subjects' stories. The writers are commended for their dedication to excellence.

This book's academic review board—Bob Burkinshaw, John G. Stackhouse, Jr., and Marguerite Van Die—individually and collectively reviewed each submission to ensure that the rigours of academic scrutiny and historical authenticity were met. Their thoughtful critiques and helpful suggestions were immensely beneficial. Howard Brandt and Curtis Gillingham were often given unrealistic deadlines and still had the work returned to me—early.

Sincere gratitude is also extended to all who assisted in locating paintings and photographs. The employees of the public institutions and government agencies cited throughout the book were exemplary in their efforts.

Some thirty photographers were employed to capture some of the finest portraits ever painted by Canadian artists. Their talent reveals the talent of the painters. On the acquisitions end, Michael Solowan, even when told no image of the subject existed, diligently acquired two illustrations of each subject.

My wife, Cindy, has a unique knack for knowing what looks best and of seeing the finished project when it is still in the idea stage. Her contributions to the design and style of this book reflect her passion for excellence. Tim McAlpine exceeded all expectations in assimilating this vision onto the page.

Don Kornelsen said, "Let's do it," and he maintained his determination to see this book become a reality.

Above all, I acknowledge the saving grace of my Heavenly Father and thank Him for directing me to begin this project some three years ago. May *Canada: Portraits of Faith* bring glory to Him.

A Note on the Illustrations

"A tangible object," proclaimed C. W. Jefferys, the dean of Canadian historical artists, "cannot lie or equivocate so successfully as a word."

Canada: Portraits of Faith has as its highest mandate to communicate truth and excellence. It attempts to chronicle Canada's history through the written word and to support what is written with unequivocal tangible objects from among our nation's most precious resources—the arts.

There exists no exhaustive database from which images can be culled simply by typing in a subject's name. Finding the artwork that graces *Canada: Portraits of Faith* involved galleries, archives, and museums from coast to coast. While some of the images featured hang in our nation's most prominent buildings, others, long thought lost, were found in the attics of subjects' relatives and in the basements of institutions that doubted if they even had them anymore. Many of them thus have never before been published. I thank everyone contacted for giving their fullest cooperation in locating these extraordinarily fine illustrations for this book.

The paintings featured in *Canada: Portraits of Faith* are the works of among the finest portrait painters this nation has ever produced. Each projects the individual talents of its artist and the aesthetic conventions of its period. Observers cannot help but be immensely appreciative of each painter's skill in providing posterity with such an invaluable legacy: an admirably accurate reflection of each subject's image.

The transition from the painter's to the photographer's studio corresponds closely to the emergence of Canada from colonial dependence to national awareness. In addition, photography, unlike painting, is an essentially democratic process. It is so by virtue of its being a mechanical and eminently reproducible craft. Yet, photography is also an art; photographers, and especially portrait photographers, use conventions and artifice to enhance their subjects. The photographs included in the gallery that is *Canada: Portraits of Faith* are drawn from all the stages of photography's development, from daguerreotype to celluloid. Moreover, all of the colour illustrations in *Canada: Portraits of Faith*, both photographs and paintings, have been reproduced from originals using high-definition photographic technology.

Exodus 35 provides an account of the commissioning and the empowering of Bezalel to create the artwork for the tabernacle. It is worth noting that this artisan, Bezalel, is the first person in the Bible to be described as "filled … with the spirit of God." Hopefully, the illustrations that complement each of the biographies in *Canada: Portraits of Faith* offer the reader an opportunity not merely to put a face to the name, but, more importantly, to reflect on how God used painter and cameraman alike to capture in the image created God's unique purpose for each subject.

Introduction

"The history of the world," wrote Scottish essayist and historian Thomas Carlyle in 1841, "is but the biography of great men." Later that year, American essayist and poet Ralph Waldo Emerson would echo: "There is properly no history, only biography."

Nowhere is an endorsement of biography as history stronger than in the Bible. Much of the Bible emphasizes and records the historical relationship of man with God, as epochal events focus on man's belief or disbelief in God.

The Bible, thus, offers the archetype for a study of history. History, it suggests, far from being the concern only of ivory-tower academics, is a study of life and of faith from which we all can learn. To know merely the who, what, where, and when of history—in this case, Canadian history—without knowing the why, without understanding the beliefs that made men and women act as they did, is to leave us with an uninspired and potentially uninspiring heritage.

Nonetheless, much of what is written about the prominent people in Canada's history fails to ask the crucial question: Why? Why did these men and women live as they did? Why did they take risks and make sacrifices? Why were they moved to great acts? Surely, why is a question that should and must be explored in classrooms nationwide as a key to understanding our past and to providing a blueprint for building our future.

To teach faith and its companions compassion and character today, we must illuminate the faith, the compassion, and the character that marked the men and the women of our past. Ignoring the role of faith in the lives of so many great Canadians overlooks an essential ingredient in the remedy for our present-day cultural malaise.

The purpose of *Canada: Portraits of Faith* is to showcase how faith helps to shape our nation. It is a book about people—Canadians who share a common commitment to the Christian faith. *Canada: Portraits of Faith* traces the golden thread of faith that God weaves into the fabric of a country as He directs and inspires its people.

This is not a book to be read at one sitting. It should be savoured page by page. Each portrait, or biography, offers an inspirational journey into the past to be either poured over or browsed through, but above all enjoyed.

*Quis nescit, primam esse
historiae legem, ne quid falsi
dicere audeat?
Deinde ne quid veri non audeat?*

(Who does not know history's first law to be that an author must not dare to tell anything but the truth? And its second that he must make bold to tell the whole truth?)

—Marcus Tullius Cicero (106–43 B.C.), *De Oratore*, II, 62

For inquire, I pray thee,
of the former age
and prepare thyself
to the search of their fathers.
Shall not they teach thee, and tell thee,
and utter words out of their heart?

Job 8:8,10

Thomas Faed (1826–1900)
Sunday in the Backwoods of Canada
1859, oil on canvas, 106.7 x 144.8 cm
Courtesy: The Montreal Museum of Fine Arts, Gift of Lord Mount Stephen
Photographer: The Montreal Museum of Fine Arts

Artist unknown
Saint Jean de Brébeuf
Oil on canvas, 61.0 x 50.1 cm
Courtesy: Musée de la civilisation, dépôt de: Oeuvres de la Maison Dauphine inc.
Photographer: Pierre Soulard

inset: C. W. Jefferys / detail of *Martyrdom of Brébeuf and Lalemant, 1649* / C. W. Jefferys Estate

The Giant of the Huron Missions
Jean de Brébeuf
1593–1649

"His desire was to die for Jesus Christ."

Michael Solowan

Jesuit priest Jean de Brébeuf, the giant of the Huron missions, was a hero and a martyr. His unbridled commitment to God's work among the Huron resulted in his canonization by Pius XI in 1930 and, in 1940, his being proclaimed the patron saint of Canada by Pius XII. For Brébeuf, Jesus Christ was the sole reason for living and, indeed, for dying, as he reveals in his diary:

> My God, my Saviour, I take from thy hand the cup of thy sufferings. I vow never to fail thee in the grace of martyrdom, if by thy mercy, thou dost offer it to me. I bind myself, and when I have received the stroke of death, I will accept it from thy gracious hand with all pleasure and with joy in my heart; to thee my blood, my body and my life!

Death held no fear for Brébeuf; for him, it meant life with God forever. Fifteen years before his death, he told his Huron friends that "it is in God alone that my heart rests, and, outside him, all is naught to me."

Jean de Brébeuf was born in 1593 in Condé-sur-Vire in Lower Normandy, France. He grew to become a giant of a man, physically and spiritually. Tall and broad shouldered, Brébeuf would live up to his Huron name, *Echon*: "he who pulls the heavy load."

When Brébeuf was twenty-four, he entered the Jesuit novitiate in Rouen, France. Although he later became known as the most robust of the Blackrobes—as the Jesuits were called by the natives—poor health shortened his studies and brought his early ordination into the priesthood, in 1622. Brébeuf then remained at the College of Rouen for a time, where he held the office of steward, before eventually being chosen for the missions in New France. He sailed for Quebec from Dieppe in spring 1625. After a brief missionary apprenticeship among the Algonquin, Brébeuf was assigned by his superior, Father Charles Lalemant, to Huron country (near modern-day Midland, Ontario), where the sedentary Huron were deemed more desirable candidates for evangelization than the nomadic Algonquin. Three years later, he was forced back to France. Brébeuf, however, returned to Huronia in 1634 and, except for one brief stay in Quebec, remained there to his death.

Lalemant chose Brébeuf to work among the Huron primarily because of Brébeuf's talent for languages. Indeed, Brébeuf's ability to communicate with the Huron and the ease with which he assimilated into their culture endeared him to the Huron. Brébeuf composed the first dictionary and grammar of the Huron language, translated prayers into Huron, and wrote the *Huron Carol* in an attempt to give an indigenous interpretation of the nativity.

Other Brébeuf writings include two contributions to *Relations de Jésuites*, in 1635 and in 1636. In them, Brébeuf reveals a desire to thoroughly understand the culture of the Huron. They remain a significant contribution to Huron ethnography. Along with Samuel de Champlain, Brébeuf is one of the most important witnesses of this period of first contacts. Like the other Jesuits, however, Brébeuf viewed Huron country as a "stronghold of Satan" and viewed the dances and native ceremonies as pagan.

The Jesuits nonetheless pinned their greatest hopes on the Huron mission, seeing it as a prototype for native evangelization and a model for other missions. The work of conversion, however, advanced very slowly, the result, in Brébeuf's estimation, of the Huron's immorality and attachment to customs and the prevalence of epidemics. Unwittingly, the Europeans had brought diseases unknown to and against which the Indians had little immunity. After smallpox broke out in 1637, the natives—rightly attributing the scourge to the Europeans—tore down crosses and vandalized the chapel. The few members of Brébeuf's flock deserted their newly embraced faith.

Amid beatings and attempts on his life, Brébeuf remained steadfast. In a letter to priests in France who were considering joining the mission, he wrote:

> Your life hangs by a thread. Of calamities you are the cause—the scarcity of game, a fire, famine, or an epidemic ... you are the reasons, and at any time a savage may burn your cabin down or split your head.... "Wherein the gain," you ask? There is no gain but this—that what you suffer shall be of God. So if despite these trials you are ready to share our labours, come; for you will find a consolation in the cross that far outweighs its burdens.

Father Ragueneau, another of Brébeuf's superiors, is known to have commented, "I find nothing more frequent in Brébeuf's memoirs than the expression of his desire to die for Jesus Christ."

Heedless of entreaties for him to flee, even when the weakened Huron faced attack from their traditional enemies, the Iroquois, Brébeuf remained with the Huron, ministering to them as they awaited the approaching war party. With the Huron greatly outnumbered, the outcome was inevitable.

Brébeuf's death ranks among the most atrocious martyrdoms in the annals of Christianity. The few Huron prisoners who escaped provided Jesuit scribes with eyewitness accounts of how he was killed. The Jesuits later confirmed their stories by examining Brébeuf's body.

Brébeuf was stripped naked by the triumphant Iroquois. His fingernails were torn from his fingers, and he was then beaten with sticks and bound to a stake. He exhorted his fellow captives to suffer patiently and promised heaven as their reward. His feet were severed from his legs so that he could not smother the fire that was lit at the base of the stake. Then, as the Iroquois taunted him, boiling water was slowly poured over his head in a mockery of baptism. Still, Brébeuf continued to preach. Next, they drew red-hot hatchets from the fire and placed them under his arms, on his loins, and around his neck. Brébeuf did not cry out. In a rage, strips of flesh were cut from his limbs, roasted, and devoured before his eyes. Brébeuf, the prized captive of the Iroquois, seemed insensible to pain, further enraging the Iroquois, who took pride in their ability to torture. As he continued to pray aloud, his captors cut away his tongue and lips and thrust a glowing iron shaft down his throat. With the torture entering its fourth hour, Brébeuf was scalped. Seeing him near death, they laid open his breast and devoured his heart and drank his blood, thinking that they might imbibe some portion of his courage.

Brébeuf's ministry among the Hurons lasted fifteen years. Sadly, he never lived to see the abundant harvest of his apostolate. It is in his death that his life is best understood and that his work bore its greatest fruit. Conversions, which for many years were few in number, grew to number in the hundreds and even thousands in the years following Brébeuf's martyrdom. The dispersion of the Huron spread the Christian faith among the native peoples of the Great Lakes. And these converts formed the Christian communities that the Jesuits were to found among the Iroquois and the natives of the west. Brébeuf's death, like his Saviour's, led others to eternal life.

Attributed to Hugues Pommier (1637–1686)
Portrait de madame de la Peltrie
oil on canvas, 72.0 x 59.7 cm
Courtesy: Collection Ursulines de Québec
Photographer: François Lachapelle

inset: National Archives of Canada / C-69278

Marie-Madeleine de Chauvigny de La Peltrie

1603–1671

"To devote herself to the service of Indian girls."

Françoise Deroy-Pineau

Marie-Madeleine de Chauvigny was born in 1603 into an affluent and noble family in Alençon, France. Her brothers had died in childhood, and her father wanted his daughters to marry aristocracy. At nineteen, after a brief experience in a religious order, Marie-Madeleine married the Chevalier de Gruel, the seigneur of La Peltrie, despite her desire for the cloistered life. This marriage lasted just five years, ending with de Gruel's death, and producing one daughter, who died in infancy.

Marie-Madeleine, widowed at twenty-five, inherited her husband's estate. Beautiful and rich, she was sought by many suitors, usually at the design of her father. Her desire, however, to involve herself in works of charity did not, in her opinion, reconcile with remarriage. Instead, she devoted herself to serving the less fortunate and to zealously practicing virtue. She eventually sought solitude to avoid her father's unrelenting matchmaking.

In 1636, while reading the *Relations des Jésuites*—a series of letters written by Jesuit missionaries in New France—Marie-Madeleine discovered where to invest her fortune and her energies. She felt that the appeal on behalf of missions was directed specifically at her: "Alas, my God! If the superabundance of some of the ladies of France were employed in this holy work [founding a convent of teaching nuns in Quebec], what a great blessing it would bring!"

She was, nonetheless, tentative in pursuing this vision and then became ill. Feverish and near death, she had a dream in which Saint Joseph—the earthly father of Christ—encouraged her to go to New France. She promised, in return for her recovery, to do so and to build a house in New France under his patronage and to devote herself to the service of Indian girls. The next day, her bewildered physicians remarked, "Madame, you are healed. Surely your fever has left for Canada."

It was the French custom at this time to bestow gifts on educational institutions—but not on the other side of the Atlantic. Furthermore, a journey to New France was unheard of for someone as affluent as Marie-Madeleine. Her family threatened to intervene and to have her confined because of what they perceived as her unstable mental state. They even went to court to get control of her estate. To outwit them, she contracted a marriage of convenience with Jean de Bernières, a well-respected man with a reputation as a mystic. The marriage protected her and enabled her to win legal proceedings to reclaim, unchallenged, her great wealth, which was compounded when her father died.

Through the Jesuits, Marie-Madeleine met MARIE GUYART DE L'INCARNATION, who likewise had a vision to go to Canada. They became close friends. When Marie-Madeleine was unable to find space for their baggage on ships leaving for New France, she chartered a vessel and loaded it with provisions and furnishings at a cost to herself of 8,000 livres. She and Marie de l'Incarnation were joined in their venture by nineteen-year-old Charlotte Barré, who, as Mother Saint-Ignace, would become the first professed nun in the Quebec convent. Within three years of their arrival in Quebec, in August 1639, the La Peltrie fortune inherited by Marie-Madeleine had erected a three-storey stone convent that was by far the most imposing structure in Canada at the time.

Marie-Madeleine daily demonstrated her zeal for ministering to the natives. She undertook the most menial duties and assisted those whom others deemed unworthy. The love of Christ, she felt, was demonstrated through merciful service. Her kindness and humbleness attracted a large group of Indian girls that followed her around the compound. Marie-Madeleine and the Ursulines tried their best to teach them, and the convent was always filled, but few of the native children were converted. "Of a hundred girls who have passed through our hands, we have scarcely civilized one," lamented Marie de l'Incarnation.

In 1641, Marie-Madeleine met a new arrival to Quebec. JEANNE MANCE was also inspired to found a hospital on the island of Montreal. The Iroquois were a constant threat, and the large island was inhospitable; even many natives had abandoned it. But Marie-Madeleine, sensitive to Jeanne's faith, supported her and participated in her almost utopic vision. When PAUL DE CHOMEDEY DE MAISONNEUVE arrived, Marie-Madeleine accompanied him and Jeanne before the governor of Quebec City to defend the idea of Montreal as a strategic centre for the future.

In spring 1642, Marie-Madeleine participated in founding the new centre. She spent two winters in Montreal and experienced firsthand the constant threat of invasion from the Mohawk and other Iroquois. Together with Jeanne Mance, she made plans to go further afield to reach the Huron. To prepare, Marie-Madeleine set up camp with the Montagnais at Tadoussac. There, she readied the provisions, the canoes, and the rowers who would accompany the Jesuits and their friends along the shores of the Great Lakes, where she intended to found a school. Many tried to discourage Marie-Madeleine in her ventures. Nothing, however, neither the threat of invasion nor natural dangers, seemed to frighten her. Finally, a Jesuit convinced her to stay in Quebec to help her friend Marie de l'Incarnation.

Back at the mission, Marie-Madeleine moved into a house next to the Ursuline convent. (This building today serves as the Museum of Marie de l'Incarnation.) When the novitiate was opened in 1646, Marie-Madeleine sought the privilege of becoming an Ursuline nun. However, she found that she could not embrace the monastic life while retaining her fortune. Although she continued to live in the cloister, where she served as a seamstress and observed all of the rules of convent life, she maintained her secular dress. Because she was not a nun, moreover, she was able to sponsor numerous native girls, bequeathing the money for their education with the Ursulines. Eventually, however, the teaching convent and the hospital founded by the sisters became a mission not to the natives but to the French settlers.

In November 1671, Marie-Madeleine contracted pleurisy. When she died, Marie de l'Incarnation referred to her as "a saint," echoing the sentiments of those whose lives she had touched. In accordance with Marie-Madeleine's last wishes, her heart was given to the Jesuits as a token of the respect and affection that she felt for them.

Alessandro Bottoni (unknown)
Vénérable Marie de l'Incarnation
1878, oil on canvas, 99 x 75 cm
Courtesy: Collection Ursulines de Québec
Photographer: François Lachapelle

inset: National Archives of Canada / C-8070

Marie Guyart de l'Incarnation

1599–1672

"One of the greatest of Catholic mystics."

Françoise Deroy-Pineau

Commanded by a vision, Marie Guyart—better known as Marie de l'Incarnation—arrived in 1639 in what would become Quebec City. By 1642, Marie, an Ursuline nun, had established the first school and built a convent in New France.

Marie was born in 1599 in the French town of Tours into an industrious family of craftsmen and bakers. As a child, she spent hours talking with God and would stand on a chair and repeat sermons that she heard in church. At age seven, she saw the Lord Jesus in what she later described as a mystical dream. "Do you want to be mine?" he asked. "Yes," she replied. Marie's affirmation was to be a lifelong commitment.

Against her wishes, her parents arranged her marriage at seventeen to a man in whom she had no interest. Two years later, she was a widowed young mother. She discouraged all further suitors, lived with her father, and earned a living as an embroiderer.

Although Marie's desire to become a nun remained unabated her worldly affairs kept her from withdrawing into a cloister. She was urged to remarry to reestablish her financial situation, but she chose instead the reading of works of piety and conversing with God.

In her diary, Marie tells of a unique spiritual experience on the morning of March 25, 1620, when an irresistible force descended upon her. In a moment, the eyes of her spirit were opened and all her faults and imperfections were revealed to her with "a clearness more certain than any certitude." She saw herself immersed in Christ's blood. After confession, she was completely changed, and committed to prayer. She studied the Gospels, meditated on the life of Christ, and practised the sacraments at her local parish church.

Marie left her father to help her sister and brother-in-law in their shipping and conveying company. They made her the company manager because of her knack for administration. At the same time she became deeply involved in benevolent works in Tours.

Her son, Claude, had entered college at age twelve, a separation that was heart-rending for Marie. She sought the advice of her priest and waited for divine guidance. In January 1631, she asked her sister to care for her son and entered the novitiate of the Ursulines of Tours. Distraught, Claude tried to storm the convent with a band of schoolboys. Amid the uproar, Marie overheard him crying; "Give me back my mother, give me back my mother." She would later say of her decision to leave her son that "no human explanation can justify such an action," she was obeying divine commands.

Marie took her vows in 1633 as Marie de l'Incarnation. Like many other nuns, Marie had read of opportunities to create religious communities in New France in *Relations des Jésuites* (published in English as *Jesuit Relations and Allied Documents*), and she prayed fervently for the Catholic work in the colony.

While Claude continued his schooling with the Jesuits in Rennes, Marie rose to become the assistant mistress of novices and an instructor in Christian doctrine. In yet another dream, however, God took her to a vast country full of mountains, valleys, and heavy fogs. "It was Canada that I showed you," said the Lord, "you must go there to build a house for Jesus and Mary."

Marie interpreted the dream to mean that she must go to New France to evangelize the natives and to build a convent and a school. Socially and culturally, such a project was unheard of in her day. She knew that it would draw strong opposition, especially since she lacked social status But her passion grew. She spoke with key individuals within the French Catholic reform movement and, surprisingly, succeeded in convincing them to fund the project.

In addition, Marie found herself increasingly aligned with *Compagnie des Cent-Associés* (the Company of One Hundred Associates), which, already at work in New France, assisted her in getting the bishop of Tours to allow her to pursue her vision. In May 1639, she set sail from Dieppe accompanied by two other Ursuline nuns and one of her main lay supporters, Marie-Madeleine de La Peltrie.

After three months at sea, they disembarked at the future site of Quebec City, then a community of a few dozen inhabitants. Marie threw herself wholeheartedly into the demands of the new country, striving to be of service through teaching native girls and to save souls through sharing the Gospel.

Marie's letters overflow with picturesque stories describing the "children of the woods," whom she often referred to as the "delights" of her heart and with whom she recommended that the nuns "use affection." Her work among adult Indians was equally passionate. She catechized them and regaled them with *sagamité* (a dish of corn meal and meat). She studied Indian languages under the Jesuits and mastered them to such a degree that she wrote Algonquin, Iroquois, Montagnais, and Ouendat dictionaries and a catechism in Iroquois. She wrote prolifically, and her correspondence—over 12,000 letters—is an invaluable document of colonial history.

At age fifty-one, Marie was as active as ever—high atop scaffolding, for example, supervising the reconstruction of the convent when fire destroyed the original in 1650. Tenaciously, she disagreed with Quebec's bishop Laval and his attempts to control Quebec's Ursulines. She vigorously opposed him and openly challenged his authority over the religious community. Not until after her death was the bishop of Quebec able to impose his rule on the Ursulines.

Claude, meanwhile, continued to be her delight. He had joined the Benedictines of Saint-Maur in 1641 and by 1668 was the assistant to the superior general. Just before dying, Marie sent him an affectionate message: "Tell him that I am carrying him with me in my heart." She passed away in 1672 after a bout with hepatitis.

Bishop Laval, with whom she had sparred for so long, eulogized her. "We consider as a special blessing the acquaintance which it pleased God to give us with her.... She was dead to herself to such a degree, and Jesus Christ possessed her so completely, that one may assuredly say of her, as of the Apostle, that it was not she who lived, but Jesus Christ in her, and that she lived and acted only through Jesus Christ."

Marie de l'Incarnation is considered to be one of the greatest of Catholic mystics. She was beatified by Pope Jean-Paul II in 1980.

Artist Unknown
Jeanne Mance (1606–1673)
Lithograph, 9.7 x 8.0 cm
Courtesy: Musée des Hospitalièrers de l'Hôtel Dieu de Montréal

inset: National Archives of Canada / C-69277

Jeanne Mance

1606–1673

"The will of God is my God."

Françoise Deroy-Pineau

Jeanne Mance, a nurse from a small French town, founded the first hospital in Montreal and cofounded the settlement with Paul de Chomedey de Maisonneuve. Saintly, womanly, courageous, idealistic, yet vastly practical, Jeanne had a rich character in which exceptional qualities were graciously blended. Her primary passion was revealed in a letter:

> "There is nothing in the world that I would refuse to do to accomplish the divine and all-loving will of God. [God's will] is the only desire and love of my heart. Therein is my passion, all my affections, my only love, and my sole paradise. In a word, it's my God; the will of God is my God. The good pleasure of my God is my God."

Jeanne was born in 1606 in Langres, in the Champagne region of northeastern France. During her youth, she witnessed the death of almost half her town from war and epidemic. As a result, she dedicated her life to extending the healing hand of Christ by becoming a nurse during the Thirty Years' War.

In 1639, Jeanne was thirty-three, unmarried, and unaffiliated with a religious order when she heard of Marie-Madeleine de Chauvigny de La Peltrie, a wealthy widow and layperson who had left for New France with three Ursuline sisters. Among the sisters was Marie Guyart de l'Incarnation. Jeanne was intrigued by the vision these women had of founding a school for native girls.

Through acquaintances, Jeanne met Angélique de Bullion, an intriguing and wealthy woman who wanted to fund a hospital in New France—if Jeanne would oversee its founding. Jeanne felt the call to go and sought counsel from her priest and the Jesuits. After much prayer, Jeanne's priest, too, felt that she must go to Canada, "that it was infallibly Our Lord who wanted this association" with the wealthy lady. Madame de Bullion was delighted with Jeanne's decision and gave her a purse of over 40,000 livres.

Jeanne joined the founders of Ville-Marie as their nurse, treasurer, and supervisor of provisions. In May 1641, she set sail for New France.

On May 17, 1642, she joined Maisonneuve and the other settlers in the founding of Montreal. Jeanne cared for her fellow colonists under a makeshift tent and organized the first temporary dispensary. Although a few Algonquin had dared to pitch their tepees near the fort, they soon departed, fearing Iroquois attacks. Jeanne wanted to seek out the Huron and to care for them where they lived, on their terms, but was unable to do so because of Madame de Bullion's insistence that she be directly involved with establishing the first hospital in Montreal.

In June 1643, some forty Iroquois attacked six colonists who were at work in their fields. Three colonists were killed and the other three were carried off to the Indian camp. Of the latter, one escaped to Ville-Marie, where. despite his terrible wounds, he was able to tell of the fate of his companions: "carved up, scalped, and killed at the stake in a barbaric fury."

Construction on the hospital, the Hôtel-Dieu, began in 1645 under Jeanne's supervision. The building measured sixty feet by twenty-four feet and was made of logs. Subsequently, it was clapboarded and solidified in wood. The hospital's chapel was built of stone. Ornaments and pictures, statues and sacred vessels were sent from France for the chapel. Later, Jeanne would import furniture, clothing, utensils, medicines, and domestic animals from France.

On three different occasions, Jeanne was required to return to France. From 1649 to 1650 she had to convince Parisian sponsors to maintain their support amid France's difficult political and social climate. From 1658 to 1659 Jeanne, accompanied by her friend Marguerite Bourgeoys, again returned to France, to care for her broken arm and to recruit nuns to work in the Hôtel-Dieu. In 1662, another trip was needed to set in place the legal structure necessary for the ongoing transfer of resources to Montreal. On each of these occasions, Jeanne conducted delicate negotiations concerning new funds and the arrival of future hospital workers—the *Hospitalières de la Flèche*—in New France. Her recruiting efforts increased the membership in the Société Notre-Dame de Montréal, a society devoted to improving the Catholic Church in New France, from eight to thirty-seven, of whom eight members were women.

In Montreal, Jeanne faced floods and harsh winters, inconsistent administrators and supporters, and intestinal disorders. Of particular concern was the ever-present danger of attack. Sister Marie Morin, Ville-Marie's first historian, recalled: "The Iroquois have now turned entirely against us. They encircle us so closely and their attacks are so sudden and frequent that there is no safety for us. They kill our people and burn down our houses … our hospital is far from being secure, and we have had to place a strong garrison to protect it." Jeanne narrowly escaped capture several times and often found herself in the heat of battle.

Amid the turmoil, Jeanne planted gardens of medicinal plants that were the perfect treatment for scalp and other wounds related to climate and conflict. She also welcomed orphans and was a constant resource to the inhabitants of the city—men and women, adults and children, French and native.

After more than thirty years of tending to the sick and the wounded of New France, Jeanne saw the colony at Ville-Marie grow strong and secure. Wearied, however, by the excessive demands of a new administration that seemed oblivious to the challenges facing the pioneers and to the unique role played by women, Jeanne Mance died in obscurity in June 1673.

Eventually, Jeanne has come to be recognized as a remarkable individual who participated in the transformation of an inhospitable island into a prosperous city. Her journey, much like the city's development, extended into new frontiers—political, interracial, economic, geographic, and spiritual. Through caring for the physical bodies of those she encountered, Jeanne also nurtured the social body of the settlement. The bonds woven together through her service provided cohesion for a new society.

Donald Kenneth Anderson (1920–)
Detail of *The Founding of Montreal*
oil on canvas, 26.5 x 39.5 cm
Courtesy: Confederation Life Association / Scarborough Christian Academy

inset: C. W. Jefferys / detail of *Maisonneuve Carrying the Cross to Mount Royal* / C. W. Jefferys Estate

Paul de Chomedey de Maisonneuve

1612–1676

"Bring about the glory of God and the salvation of the Indians."

Dominique Vinay

Paul de Chomedey de Maisonneuve was a noble soldier with a desire to make redemption accessible to the native people of New France. His efforts were part of the Counter Reformation prevalent in seventeenth-century Europe to strengthen and spread Roman Catholicism throughout the world. This religious impulse led to the creation of Montreal in 1642, with Maisonneuve its first governor. Maisonneuve, along with a group of affluent Catholic mystics in France, were moved by visions to build a missionary centre in the wilderness with the intention of converting the natives.

Maisonneuve was born and baptized in Neuville-sur-Vanne in the province of Champagne in 1612. His family was deeply religious, well-known, and well respected. As was the custom, Maisonneuve's military career began early: he became a soldier at thirteen. Maisonneuve's inclination toward a role in the New World took root as he was recovering from a war wound received in Arras (Flanders). His long recovery proved to be a time of enlightenment, sparked by his reading of Paul Le Jeune's *Account of What Happened in New France on the Great Saint Lawrence River*, wherein the Jesuit priest describes his evangelistic mission to a Montagnais tribe in Tadoussac. Aware that a handful of English citizens had recently crossed the Atlantic in the *Mayflower* to establish a devout Protestant society in the New World, Maisonneuve reasoned, "Why not attempt the same on French and Roman Catholic land?"

At thirty years of age, Maisonneuve retired from soldiering and went to Paris to seek employment. There, he met Jesuit Charles Lalemant, the procurator of the Canadian mission in France. Lalemant informed Maisonneuve of a project to create in Canada a station for the evangelization of the natives led by Jérôme de La Dauversière, a friend of Lalemant's. La Dauversière had founded the Société Notre-Dame de Montréal and was in charge of acquiring the island, appointing a governor, and financing the colony. A meeting was arranged, and La Dauversière, finding Maisonneuve to be "a gentleman of virtue and heart," appointed him the governor of the new colony.

Maisonneuve's mission was to establish a Catholic settlement at Montreal for evangelization and colonization. He summarized it in four points: evangelize the Algonquin, teach them agricultural skills, provide them with medical assistance, and educate them.

Maisonneuve and his recruits left for New France in two ships on May 9, 1641. Accompanying him was JEANNE MANCE, the nurse and treasurer of the contingent, and some fifty men and women who were promised free land. Fall storms delayed their plans for the settlement of Montreal, however, forcing them to winter in Quebec City.

The colonists and the governor of Quebec City and their governor called their missionary intentions a "crazy plan." The money and effort, they felt, would be better spent on Quebec City than in trying to evangelize Algonquin. They especially warned of attacks from the Iroquois. But Maisonneuve was resolute: "Nothing shall turn me one inch from my mission. Those who send me want me in Montreal, and it is my honour to fulfill their wish. Should each tree of the island be changed into an Iroquois, I would go."

On May 17, 1642, Maisonneuve founded Ville-Marie on the island of Montreal, naming it after the Virgin Mary to whom he entrusted the protection of the colony. Mass was celebrated, and Father Vimont, the superior of the Jesuits in Canada, sermonized: "You are a grain of mustard seed that shall rise and grow until its branches overshadow the earth. You are few, but your work is the work of God." A description of the day relates that "They sang hymns of joy and thanksgiving to God. After stepping out of a boat and putting his feet on the soil Monsieur de Chomedey dropped to his knees to adore God. They all sang psalms and hymns to the Lord."

The purpose of the colony was to "bring about the glory of God and the salvation of the Indians." Maisonneuve would be its governor for twenty-three years.

Meanwhile, La Dauversière published a book on Ville-Marie, *The Purpose of Montreal*, that raised support for the project in Paris. Written in 1643, it describes the settlement shortly after its founding: "There is a chapel there that serves as a parish, under the title of Notre Dame.... The inhabitants live for the most part communally, as in a sort of inn; others live on their private means, but all live in Jesus Christ, with one heart and soul."

The settlement, however, was nearly destroyed by a flood in its first winter. On Christmas Eve 1642, the Saint Lawrence River overflowed. After consulting with the chaplains, Maisonneuve promised that he would carry a cross to the top of Mount Royal if the waters that were already surging against the gates of the fort subsided without causing serious damage. He put his promise in writing; had it read publicly; and then placed a cross, at whose foot was the written statement, on the bank of the overflowing river. After much prayer and invocations for the Virgin's protection, the waters subsided. Two weeks later, Maisonneuve carried a cross through the bush to the top of Mount Royal. Today, an illuminated cross marks the spot.

Soon, a few Algonquin made contact with the settlement, which offered them food and protection. By 1643, however, Indian attacks were endangering the mission. Warring Iroquois forced Maisonneuve to return fire, first with thirty men against two hundred Indians, then with an organized, permanent defense. France, comparing persecuted Ville-Marie to the early church, sent new recruits. Maisonneuve was a revered leader who governed wisely and kept order in the growing colony. He ordered brawlers to pay the medical bills of their victims and slanderers to praise each other in public.

Over the years, Maisonneuve was recalled to Paris many times to discuss how best to preserve Montreal's religious purpose amid growing economic interests. He took part in the powerful Communauté des Habitants assembly to save Montreal from becoming only a relay for the fur trade market, arguing that "money leads to perdition." He also led fund-raising drives and recruited homesteaders in France. On one of these trips, he and Jeanne Mance were successful in getting funds and 120 new settlers. Among the latter was MARGUERITE BOURGEOYS, Montreal's first teacher and the first of its nursing sisters.

In France, however, the Société Notre-Dame de Montréal weakened, lost directors, and went bankrupt. La Dauversière, insolvent and ruined, died. And Ville-Marie's future was entrusted to Louis XIV.

Maisonneuve was recalled to France permanently in 1665. Although he had lived in Ville-Marie for twenty-three years, he never became a landowner, choosing instead to dedicate himself to his religious cause. Back in Paris, he lived in a secluded cabin that he built, and remained humble and discreet until his death in 1676.

Elmina Lachance (1864–1937)
Marguerite Bourgeoys à la Première École de Ville-Marie
oil on canvas, 67.5 x 52.0 cm
Courtesy: The Marguerite Bourgeoys Museum, Montreal

inset: Léopold Massard (1812-1889) / engraving / Marguerite Bourgeoys Museum, Montreal

Marguerite Bourgeoys

1620–1700

"I gave myself to God."

Patricia Simpson

"All I have ever desired most deeply and what I still most ardently wish is that the great precept of the love of God above all things and of the neighbour as oneself be written in every heart." So wrote Marguerite Bourgeoys, who left the security of a seventeenth-century French bourgeoisie life to serve the early pioneers in New France. She assisted in bringing the gospel to the natives, established schools, taught vocational and domestic skills to women, helped the poor, and founded the Congrégation de Notre-Dame de Montréal.

Marguerite was born in the city of Troyes, the ancient capital of the province of Champagne, in France, on Good Friday 1620. She was baptized in the parish church the same day. Her father was a master candlemaker and an official in the city mint, giving the family a respected position in the community. At the age of twenty, while taking part in a religious procession, Marguerite was touched by an experience of grace so profound that she felt herself transformed. Late in life, she wrote, "I gave myself to God in 1640."

Marguerite began working among the poor in Troyes with other young women who were organized and directed by the sisters of the Congrégation de Notre-Dame de Troyes, a cloistered teaching community. They met regularly, prayed together, taught the children of the poor, dressed simply, and were known as the extern congregation. Marguerite had previously declined to join them because she thought of herself as rather flighty, liked to be chic, and didn't want to be seen as sanctimonious. She was to become not only a member but also the prefect of the Congrégation de Notre-Dame, whose number swelled to four hundred under her leadership.

In 1652, Marguerite met PAUL DE CHOMEDEY DE MAISONNEUVE, who had founded the settlement of Ville-Marie on the island of Montreal in Canada in 1642 for the express purpose of carrying the gospel to the Amerindians of the New World. Its organizers, a group of devout men and women in France who financed, recruited, and planned the settlement, believed that, just as other Christians had left the Mediterranean world to carry the gospel to their ancestors in northern Europe so they were now responsible for reaching the aboriginal peoples of North America. They hoped life in the settlement would reflect that of the early Christian church as described in the Acts of the Apostles. Maisonneuve, in France to seek more recruits for the tiny, fragile settlement, happened to visit his sister Louise, a cloistered nun in the congregation of which Marguerite was the prefect. When Maisonneuve said that it would be a long time before Montreal could support such a convent of cloistered teaching nuns, Louise suggested that he take Marguerite to teach the children.

The decision to go to Montreal was not easy for Marguerite. It meant leaving the poor of Troyes, and it also seemed to mean abandoning the idea of a community dedicated to honouring the life of Mary, the mother of Jesus. However, she eventually found peace with the idea and arrived in Montreal in November 1653.

During her first five years in Montreal, she lived in the governor's house within the fort. Marguerite worked closely with Maisonneuve and with JEANNE MANCE, the foundress of the Hôtel-Dieu hospital. In 1658, Marguerite opened Montreal's first school. Later that year, she made the difficult journey back to France and returned with four companions to help in her work. Three would remain with her and would become the first members of the Congrégation de Notre-Dame de Montréal, dedicated to imitating the life of Mary, particularly Mary's visitation and her work in the early Christian church. They were later joined by other women from France; by the daughters of French settlers; by Amerindian women; and even by women from the American colonies, who, brought to Montreal as captives by the Amerindians, chose to stay there, became Catholics, and joined the congregation.

Led by Marguerite, these women taught the children of the French settlers, first in Montreal and then in the villages coming into being along the Saint Lawrence. They also received into their convent young women who had come to marry. The *Filles du Roy* (King's Daughters), as these young women were called, were recruited by the royal government in France and given a dowry on condition of going to New France to marry. After they married, Marguerite visited them in their homes to teach them to read and to perform for them whatever services were required. Marguerite, who greatly valued the role of women in the family and in society, saw in these women the future of Canada. She welcomed them, helped them adjust to their new conditions, and later supported them in their efforts to raise families.

In 1676, Marguerite and her followers began teaching Amerindian girls in what was called the Mountain Mission. Although the transmission of the Christian faith was the most important part of their mission, they also taught reading, writing, arithmetic and the skills needed to earn a living. Because they considered the last such an important responsibility in the teaching of the poor, they even opened a vocational school for the teaching of older women. All of this education was offered free of charge. Marguerite wanted her community to be self-supporting, and her members worked hard not to be a burden to the settlement. They lived a poor and simple life close to the ordinary colonists.

The Congrégation de Notre-Dame de Montréal achieved civil recognition when Louis XIV granted letters patent to Marguerite in 1671. In 1676, it received ecclesiastical recognition. In 1693, an aging Marguerite resigned as the superior of the Congrégation de Notre-Dame de Montréal. She lived long enough to see, in 1698, its Rule of Life approved, permitting the sisters to pronounce their vows publicly for the first time.

Marguerite Bourgeoys died in Montreal on January 12, 1700. A local clergyman wrote to a friend: "Never were there so many ... as there were this morning at the funeral of this holy woman. If the saints were canonized today as they were in olden times, tomorrow we would be saying the mass of Saint Marguerite of Canada." Almost three centuries later, in 1982, Marguerite was, indeed, canonized into sainthood.

Eva Scott (flourished 1979)
Detail of *Henry Alline—Eighteenth-Century New Light Evangelist*
1983, oil on canvas, 88.8 x 117.8 cm
Courtesy: Acadia Divinity College
Photographer: Acadia University

inset: Detail of Eva Scott's *Henry Alline—Eighteenth-Century New Light Evangelist* / Acadia Divinity College

The Father of the New Lights
Henry Alline
1748–1784

*"Go forth, and enlist my fellow-mortals to
fight under the banners of Jesus Christ."*

Jack Bumsted

Henry Alline grew up in a strict Puritan home in Falmouth, Nova Scotia. In 1775, when he was twenty-seven, he became a preacher, firm in his belief that God had called him to spread the gospel throughout Nova Scotia. He started the New Light Movement, which became wildly popular. He was a fine singer and a fiery speaker whose preaching sparked a religious revival called the Great Awakening.

Alline was born in Newport, Rhode Island, to William and Rebeccah Clark Alline. His father was a miller who responded in 1759 to the Nova Scotia government's advertisements for settlers. The family arrived in Falmouth, near Windsor, in 1760 and received one thousand acres of land.

Although young Alline had attended school in Newport, he received no further formal education in Nova Scotia. Yet he still became proficient in French. Life in a remote farming village saw Alline spend most of his free time in youthful recreation and in studying the Bible and the small number of religious writings available to him in rural Nova Scotia.

While the political turmoil that would become the American Revolution swirled around him, Henry Alline dealt with his own internal conflict. His concern for the state of his soul consumed him. In his writings, Alline confessed that he was the "chief contriver and ringleader of the frolics" of his contemporaries and that he "would act the hypocrite and feign a merry heart."

As the American crisis escalated, Alline—now in his mid-twenties—wrote that his chief concern was his "carnal mirth." Alline found partial release from his inner turmoil through conversion in 1775, when "redeeming love broke into my soul with repeated scriptures with such power that my whole soul seemed to be melted down with love."

This experience, however, did not resolve all of Alline's problems, for he had become extremely suspicious of the traditional teachings of the New England Puritanism in which he had been raised. He was particularly critical of the picture of a vengeful rather than a loving God and of the insistence on the preordained election of the saints. Moreover, although Alline felt called to go forth and preach the gospel to others his upbringing told him that only those with formal educational credentials were allowed to become ministers.

Alline wrestled for a year with the inconsistencies between his own theology, developed on the Nova Scotia frontier, and traditional New England doctrine. His internal dispute paralleled the confusion in Nova Scotia resulting from the outbreak of armed rebellion in New England. Soon after his conversion in March 1775, he wrote that "the prejudices of education and the strong ties of tradition so chained me down, that I could not think myself qualified for it, without having a good deal of human learning."

He rejected an offer of a commission in the Nova Scotia militia, deciding that his only commission should be one "from heaven to go forth, and enlist my fellow-mortals to fight under the banners of Jesus Christ." On April 18, 1776, a day set aside by the Nova Scotia government for "fasting and prayer"— perhaps not entirely coincidentally the first anniversary of the battle at Lexington that began the war—Henry Alline decided upon a public preaching career. He had successfully rejected New England and Nova Scotia in favour of offering to others what he had found: a spiritual assurance that rejected and transcended the tribulations of the secular world. In times of civil war, many responses were possible.

God brought the planters to Nova Scotia to shelter them "in this peaceable corner of the earth," preached Alline. Many New Englanders in Nova Scotia associated the coming of the American Revolution with the judgement of God. The use of natural disaster imagery became common code in Nova Scotian religious circles to avoid having to refer directly to the political conflict.

For the first three years of his brief career as an itinerant preacher, Alline focused his efforts on the region around the Bay of Minas, including the Chignecto area that was so involved in the American invasion of 1776. He sometimes also made occasional and controversial forays to the south-coast fishing communities.

Alline's principal opponent and critic was Jonathan Scott (1744–1819), the pastor of the Puritan Church at Jebogue (Yarmouth), who saw in Alline's anti-Calvinist emphasis on free will a dangerous alternative to New England theology. For Scott, Henry Alline was as radical and revolutionary as any rebel firebrand.

Apart from Scott, only local supporters and opponents paid much attention to Alline's theology or to the movement of Christian pietism and rejuvenation that he began. Anglican clergyman Mather Byles recorded in his journal for 1784 a visit to Yarmouth, during which a Yankee shoemaker asked the visitor's opinion of "Allan's [sic] treatise," saying, "he begun it, but finding it was not right sound doctrine he hove it by again." Many were put off by Alline's unorthodox theology, but at least the common people were reading him.

Not until well after Alline's death did the authorities in church and state really begin to recognize the dangers of the levelling egalitarianism Alline espoused. He deliberately denied that "earthly dignity, the esteem of man or a conspicuous station in the world" made a man of God, insisted that political leaders would have no special privileges on the day of judgement, and emphasized that Christ had commanded his followers "to salute no man by the way.' For those who shared his vision and spiritual experience, Alline insisted on withdrawal from "this ensnaring world" on the grounds that "you have no continuing city here."

In his own way, Alline was a populist leveller. He traveled the countryside singing hymns, regarding music as a way to attract and hold an audience—as well as a useful vehicle on the road to salvation. Alline, in fact, composed more than five hundred hymns. One, written in 1781, reveals Alline's deepest desire: "Ye sons of Adam lift your eyes, / Behold how free the Saviour dies, / To save your souls from hell! / There's your Creator, and your friend, / Believe and soon your fears shall end, / And you in glory dwell."

To the Atlantic region he left a legacy of evangelism and revivalism—his followers were called New Lights. His theological ideas, however, would make their greatest impact among the Free Will Baptists of the United States and the Baptists of Maritime Canada. In a period of political confusion, Alline offered an alternative to public declarations of political allegiance. In the process, he founded in Canada an enduring tradition of evangelical pietism. Alline died of tuberculosis in 1784 while on a preaching tour in the United States.

Annie Bentz (unknown)
Barbara Heck (1734–1804)
ca. 1932, oil on canvas, 90.2 x 68.6 cm
After original by John Barnes, 1773
Courtesy: John Street Methodist Church, NYC

inset: reprinted from *The Story of Methodism* (Toronto: William Briggs, 1894).

The Mythological Mother of Methodism
Barbara Heck

1734–1804

"Speak the word of God that all might be saved."

Elizabeth Gillan Muir

*I*n August 1760, Barbara Ruckle Heck, twenty-six years old and recently married, arrived in New York City from Ireland on board the ship *Pery*. The voyage had taken sixty-three days. Just before leaving Ballingrane in County Limerick for the New World, Barbara had married Paul Heck, a neighbour. Emigrating with them were at least twenty-four friends and relatives, including her cousin Philip Embury, a Methodist lay preacher. Historical focus has dwelt not on Embury, but on Barbara, who within a century became widely revered as the mother of Methodism in the United States and Canada.

Many of the first Methodists to come to the United States quickly lost their religious fervour. Lacking churches, they indulged in secular pastimes, such as cardplaying. One day in 1766, Barbara confronted some cardplayers and seized their cards, which she threw into the fire. She then begged Philip Embury to speak the word of God that all might be saved. Philip, who had become a teacher, did as he was asked after some hesitation. He initiated the first Methodist class in North America, and two years later opened the first Methodist chapel. Barbara was an active member, and it was said that her motivation often found expression in a favourite hymn: "All Hail the Power of Jesus' Name."

Around 1778, Barbara and her family fled the Revolutionary War, entering Canada at Montreal. By 1785, they had settled in the township of Augusta in Grenville County in Upper Canada along with several of their friends. Barbara belonged to the first Methodist class in Upper Canada, formed in 1788 and led by a descendant— probably her son, Samuel.

Barbara died in 1804 at age seventy. After her death, she became a model of female spirituality. She was credited with beginning the first Methodist class and later the first Methodist church in North America. Monuments were built to her, halls named after her, and countless articles written about her. It was reported that when Barbara died, she was found in her chair with a smile upon her face and her husband's German Bible lying at her feet. Pages of this Bible were sent to individuals anxious to retain some memento of the venerable lady who helped establish Methodism in North America.

Barbara Heck's story is part historical accuracy and part legend. Early records either do not name the woman who destroyed the cards or make no mention of a woman at all. One account suggests that one woman entreated Philip to preach, while another helped found the first church. But some time after her death, Barbara was credited as the sole woman involved, thereby becoming the foundress of American Methodism.

For a period of seven years, from 1859 until 1866, controversy raged in the Canadian Methodist newspaper the *Christian Guardian* as to what had taken place in New York City the day the cards were burned and over the role Barbara had played in the beginning of Methodism in North America. In a sense, however, what is factual is unimportant, for Barbara is the stereotype of the devoted Canadian woman that was promoted by mainstream Methodists in the 1800s.

Prominent Methodists were inspired by her story. The Canadian itinerant minister and editor of the *Christian Guardian*, EGERTON RYERSON, described a visit to two of Barbara's surviving children in 1839: "O my heart burned within me when I heard them converse about their sainted mother … I almost envied them the privilege of being thus related to the Founder of American Methodism."

American Methodist centennial celebrations in the 1860s emphasized Barbara's contribution and embellished her story. In 1865, the American Methodist Ladies' Centenary Association asked ministers' wives to canvas all ladies for a donation of up to one thousand dollars to build a residence at the Evanston Biblical Institute in Illinois as a memorial to the "Foundress of American Methodism." Historian Abel Stevens devoted thirty-seven pages to her in an 1869 publication, *The Women of Methodism*. In his account, Barbara is credited with issuing a request for the first minister, convening the first congregation, meeting the first class, planning the first Methodist church building, and "securing its completion."

By the 1890s, Barbara was being described alternatively as a prophetess who came to the United States "under divine impulse," a new Deborah rescuing the nation a modern Abraham setting out under God's command to an unknown land, a Christ-like figure sitting calmly in a boat while her children "nestled in terror at her feet" en route to Canada, and the leader of a loyal British Protestant remnant escaping the tyranny of the American Revolution. By 1934, there was even a story that she was of royal birth of the House of Guelph and a descendent of Elector Frederick III.

That same year, to commemorate the bicentenary of Barbara's birth, a dedication hymn was written and placed in the American Methodist Hymnal:

O happy one who found in youth the joy of Christ's reality,
Then sailed the seas to share that truth through waiting world's immensity!
We yearn to have Christ own our land, its wealth, its life, its art, its trade.
As age on age our dreams expand may these at His dear feet be laid.
O mother dear, strong Pioneer of faith that knows no dark defeat,
Lead us that we, like you, may rear,
New shrine where Christ's true hearts may meet.

Barbara had evolved from a young eighteenth-century Irish immigrant to the United States to become the foundress of Methodism in North America. In the late nineteenth and early twentieth centuries, she evolved further to become the symbol of the ideal United Empire Loyalist woman. Over the decades, the details of her story were altered to fit mainstream society's changing perception of women.

The one constant, however, was the passive role that she adopted toward preaching the gospel. In the 1800s, this model of a submissive, but spiritually devout woman was upheld by mainstream Methodism as an example of how women should conduct themselves. A Methodist woman "never presumed to *preach*." Instead, she spent her time "in visiting awakened persons from house to house … in prayer meetings … in collecting the poor and neglected of her own sex" and reading them a sermon. Barbara Heck was thus important as a model of faith for women to follow in earlier times.

Attributed to William Valentine (1798–1849)
Rev. William Black
oil on canvas, 40.9 x 36.2 cm
Courtesy: Owens Art Gallery, Mount Allison University, Sackville, N.B.
Photographer: Bob McLean

inset: C. W. Jefferys / National Archives of Canada / C-69290

The Apostle of Methodism in Atlantic Canada
William Black
1760–1834

*"Never did hunter pursue game with greater zest
than Black in his passion for the souls of men."*

Don Chapman

William Black's life roles have variously been described as itinerant preacher, pioneer evangelist, revivalist, apostle, bishop, and superintendent. His rigorous, lifelong "pursuit of souls" and desire to establish the Methodist Church in the Maritime colonies left an enduring legacy. At the time of Black's death of edema in 1834 at his Halifax home at age seventy-four, the Methodist Church in Atlantic Canada consisted of more than six thousand members in three districts, with forty-four circuits and about fifty ministers and local preachers.

Black was born in November 1760 in Huddersfield, West Yorkshire. He immigrated in 1775 with his parents to the Isthmus of Chignecto in the colony of Nova Scotia, where the family settled near Amherst. It was a turbulent time, in England and in the colonies. The Acadians had been recently expelled from the region the Black family now called home. The industrial revolution and its associated human dislocations were changing English life dramatically. American colonists were discontented, and revolution was at hand. And a religious revival in England and in the colonies, led by Wesleyan Methodists, was challenging the established church.

Lacking a structured religious community in Nova Scotia, Black's early religious influence came from his mother, Elizabeth Stocks. Elizabeth, however, died shortly after the family's arrival. Looking back on his years as a teenager, William confessed to a rather idle lifestyle: "In the fall of 1776 some people came among us, and raised all the disaffected.... It was our usual custom at this time to sit up whole nights at cards and dancing.... we would run to watch the flash of the fire from the guns; and as soon as it was over, return again to waste our time in sin and vanity."

Three years later, Black experienced conversion and began his religious calling. The circumstances of his conversion were typical of the Methodism of the period: an awakening within the earnest atmosphere of a class meeting to one's sinful state and a need for forgiveness. As one biographer wrote, "Mr. Oxley provided the setting [his home], John Newton [author of *Amazing Grace*] ... gave out a hymn, and William Wells was present to offer a prayer. Young William, for some time under deep conviction of sin, found peace one night in the spring of 1779."

On the verge of his nineteenth birthday, William involved himself in the conversion of family members, friends, and neighbours. In the following thirty years or so, until illness forced his retirement in 1812, he would fill the dual roles of evangelist and church organizer.

Following the Wesleyan model, Black was an itinerant preacher. He travelled a vast and generally sparsely populated area by whatever means possible, in fair weather and in foul, dependent for food and shelter upon the kindness of those with whom he came into contact. Contemporaries remember him as "A model itinerant ... Never did hunter pursue game with greater zest than [Black] in his passion for the souls of men. His sermons had ever in view the conversion of sinners, and he often employed his pen in writing to individuals about salvation." Black had a dream of undertaking formal religious instruc-

tion, but his commitment to the field prevented this. Consequently, the first decade of his ministry was conducted without his having received ordination or his being able to dispense the sacraments.

Black kept a journal of the early years of his working life. Interestingly, however, he was reluctant to make a permanent record of his sermons, even when encouraged to do so, evidence of his self-effacing nature. His journal entries reveal that a key ingredient of his success was that he cared deeply about each person he met. He was a man of the people, and he drew energy from his ability to have a positive influence upon them.

Black also corresponded extensively with John Wesley, the founder of Methodism. In the early years, essentially alone in his ministry, Black was directed by Wesley to be in contact with and to seek support from the Methodist Church in the new United States.

For the most part, Black's religious knowledge was gained through individual study. He often read on horseback, in the fashion attributed to Wesley. Black read widely and was familiar with the biblical texts in Greek and Latin despite his limited formal schooling in religion. As one historian put it, "Of systematic theology he knew but little, and this is no cause for regret in view of the work to which he was called. The Nova Scotia churches of that day had been fed on the dry husks of a lifeless orthodoxy."

Black often crossed paths with the celebrated New Light preacher HENRY ALLINE. He frequently grieved over Alline's efforts to break up the Methodist societies that he, Black, had formed. One day, his patience exhausted, Black wrote of Alline in his journal: "O Satan, a wicked man could not have served thy purpose so well!"

Black was married in Boston in 1784 to Mary Gay. After the wedding, he "had the honour of laying the foundations of Methodism in that city, the first Methodist preacher who appeared in New England after the visit of Charles Wesley."

At the 1789 Methodist Conference in Philadelphia, Black was ordained as a deacon and as an elder. From that point until his retirement, he was considered the superintendent of the region that now includes Nova Scotia, New Brunswick, and Prince Edward Island.

Black's efforts were not confined to Nova Scotia. On Prince Edward Island, he preached the first Methodist sermon; in New Brunswick, he was also a Methodist pioneer. Black's most celebrated evangelistic achievement was his work in establishing Methodism in the colony of Newfoundland late in the summer 1791. A one-month visit by Black resulted in Methodism becoming a main religious influence on the island. Black's journal entry focuses on feelings as he preached a departing sermon: "We had to tear ourselves from each other. It was a most affecting time. They wept as if for an only son. Blessed be God, there is a world of love, where we shall not weep for the departure of a friend, or the absence of a brother."

William Black, the first Canadian Methodist evangelist, revered and remembered by tens of thousands as Bishop Black, left a legacy of faith and perseverance that echoes still in Atlantic Canada.

J. W. L. Forster (1850–1938)
The Reverend William Case (1780–1855)
oil on canvas, 130 x 95 cm
Courtesy: The United Church of Canada / Victoria University Archives, Toronto
Photographer: Steve Boyko

inset: The United Church of Canada/Victoria University Archives, Toronto / 76.002 P / 937N

The Methodist Father of Indian Missions
William Case

1780–1855

"I would freely spend my life among them for Jesus' sake."

William Lamb

On November 18, 1808, William Case confided to his diary, "O, if I could but speak their language I would freely spend my life among them for Jesus' sake." It was a decisive moment. The young Methodist circuit rider had just preached to a number of tribal chiefs gathered in council with government authorities at Stoney Creek in Upper Canada (Ontario). That expression of his yearnings proved to be a prophecy of his future and the articulation of a divine calling.

There were several such turning points in Case's life. He was born during the American Revolution and grew up in the tidewater area of Swansea, Massachusetts, where the family probably attended Hornbine Baptist Church near their farm. His uncle, Isaac Case, became a Baptist preacher in Maine, with some missionary forays into New Brunswick. William received a good education and did some teaching as a young man. Around 1800, the family moved to Chatham, New York, just east of Albany. There, in the boisterous atmosphere of frontier life he faced some new temptations. As John Carroll, his biographer, delicately stated it, "his amiable heart and handsome person exposed him to some dangers from which he did not wholly escape." It was there, too, that he heard the gospel from Methodist preachers. Grace prevailed, and Case's life found new hope and direction. Years later, Case simply stated, "I was converted in February, 1803." He was then twenty-three years of age. Soon, he volunteered for missionary service in far-off Upper Canada. Except for five years on New York state circuits, he remained in Canada for the rest of his life.

Another turning point came as the result of a letter he sent in 1810 to his Methodist bishop, Francis Asbury. It was a report of a deep and widespread revival on his circuit in the southwestern part of Upper Canada. Asbury deemed it worthy to send to England, where it was published in *the Methodist Magazine*. From then on, Case ceased writing in his personal diary and wrote an increasing number of reports for the Methodist press, becoming a religious journalist.

A third crucial event came at a camp meeting near Ancaster in 1823. Among those who responded to the gospel invitation were a brother and sister of mixed Ojibwa-white race, Mary and PETER JONES. Case, who had often visited in the home of their father, saw the import of that moment and cried, "Glory to God, there stands a son of Augustus Jones of the Grand River, amongst the converts; now is the door opened for the work of conversion among his nation!" And he was right. He realized that indigenous missionaries who understood native culture and spoke native languages must accomplish the mission to native peoples. His role would be that of administrator, coach, and encourager. He would also supervise the translation of scriptures and hymns into native languages, not an easy task considering that these tongues had scarcely been written down. Peter Jones, meanwhile, would become the vanguard of a team of some sixteen native evangelists who would have a powerful impact chiefly on the many Ojibwa tribes scattered from Kingston to Lake Superior. These peoples were then at a low point, crippled by disease, despair, and alcohol following the recent invasion of white settlers.

During the 1820s and 1830s, over a thousand native converts were baptized. Many tribal groups requested that teachers be sent to them. In response, Case led several fund-raising tours to cities in the eastern United States. The Americans were enchanted with the testimonies, scripture recitations, and singing of the new Ojibwa Christians in Case's entourage. They responded with money, clothing, and other supplies, and many wanted to "adopt" the children by paying for their education. Such was the case with Adam Steinhauer of Philadelphia, who offered to support ten-year-old Sowengisik if he adopted the European name of his deceased son, Henry. HENRY BIRD STEINHAUER, as the lad became known, proved a brilliant scholar (even learning Hebrew); teacher; and ordained Methodist preacher and led mission work on the prairies.

Case, meanwhile, was greatly respected by his fellow ministers. He was appointed to many responsible positions, including presiding elder (district superintendent) and the secretary of the conference. In 1828, when the Canadian church separated from its American parent body and formed the Methodist Episcopal Church in Canada, Case was elected to its top position of general superintendent for four years. But he is most remembered for his work as the superintendent of Indian missions.

Case had a sweet singing voice with which he often captivated audiences. He loved the camp meeting songs and the hymns of Charles Wesley. "The Garden Hymn" became a sort of signature song for him, a verse of which he often used as an invitation:

Amen, amen, my soul replies,
I'm bound to meet you in the skies,
And claim my mansion there:
Now here's my heart, and here's my hand,
To meet you in that heavenly land,
Where we shall part no more.

Case was forty-nine when he finally married. Earlier, he had recruited Hetty Hubbard and Eliza Barnes (see ELIZA CASE) from Massachusetts to work as missionaries with the Indian women. A rivalry developed between the two women that was partially relieved when Case married Hetty. Alas, two years later she died, leaving a six-month-old daughter. Eliza became Case's second wife and partner until his death in 1855.

What proved to be Case's final year was a significant one for them. With the permission of the conference, they travelled across the province renewing acquaintances with those to whom they had ministered for half a century. Case was invited to deliver a Jubilee sermon to the conference in celebration of his fifty years of ministry. Eliza and William posed for a photographer in Belleville for a portrait that became widely circulated. In October 1855, William Case died as a result of injuries received when he was thrown from his horse. He was buried, as he had wished, in the Indian cemetery on the Alderville Reserve, north of Cobourg.

Mrs. WILLIAM CASE

J. W. L. Forster (1850–1938)
Mrs. William Case
oil on canvas, 84 x 70 cm
Courtesy: The United Church of Canada / Victoria University Archives, Toronto
Photographer: Steve Boyko

Female Missionary and Preacher
Eliza Case
1796–1887

"The very gates of heaven were opened to our souls."

Elizabeth Gillan Muir

The best-documented Canadian female preacher in the Methodist Episcopal tradition is Eliza Barnes Case. She was a dynamic and energetic missionary teacher who came to Canada from the New England states in the 1820s and later married WILLIAM CASE, the superintendent of Indian missions. Historians have chronicled her preaching in a number of places after her arrival in Canada and her leadership in at least one revival.

Eliza Barnes was born in Boston, Massachusetts, in November 1796. Little is known of her until she began work as a missionary at the Canadian Methodist Indian missions when she was about thirty years old. In her career as a committed and energetic teacher and preacher, Eliza became one of the most effective and best-known workers with the native Indians in southern Ontario.

In her first years as a missionary, she travelled from mission to mission, supervising Indian women, organizing benevolent societies, and teaching children and adults. She made at least one trip annually to the United States to raise funds and make reports.

The year 1829 is typical of Eliza's constant activity. In February, she travelled north with male missionaries on an exploratory trip to Holland Landing to discuss establishing a mission on Snake Island in Lake Simcoe. In March, she set out on a two and a half month tour of the New England states to raise funds and to arrange for the translation of biblical materials. By the middle of May, she was back in Upper Canada working at the Rice Lake Mission, near Peterborough, and two months later she began a mission tour of Lake Simcoe and Lake Huron. In September, she was at the Grape Island Mission, near Belleville. In October, she went to York (now Toronto) to collect supplies for the Credit River Mission, and in December she organized a benevolent society for the Indian women at that mission.

One of Eliza's main activities was the organization of native women's Dorcas societies to raise money to spread Christianity among the Indians. These groups made items such as moccasins, gloves, straw hats, and brooms. Eliza obtained the materials the women needed to produce these goods and then took the finished products to city bazaars, where they were sold.

Of all her skills and accomplishments, though, contemporaries were most impressed by her preaching ability. At that time, however, it was generally not acceptable for women to preach. The Canadian Methodist newspaper the *Christian Guardian* noted in 1829 that a woman preaching was an "eccentric effort," out of her proper "sphere." Ladies "preach the precious gospel by sewing gloves and moccasins, knitting mittens, making baskets and brooms," it was later pointed out in another Methodist paper, the *Christian Advocate*. Yet, Eliza's preaching successes were well received and well documented.

Like all early Methodists who experienced conversion and felt God's grace and forgiveness, Eliza had a passionate need to share her religious convictions. She was an assertive and forceful woman. She had grown up in the more liberal atmosphere of the United States, where women had more freedom to speak out in public than they did in Canada. And she did not hesitate to proclaim her theology with fervour and eloquence and preached extensively in both countries until 1830.

Eliza created a sensation preaching in York and began at least one great religious revival in the area. The prominent Indian missionary PETER JONES wrote about several of her preaching triumphs, including one occasion at Yellowhead's Island in Lake Simcoe where she caused a "mild Pentecost ... the very gates of heaven were opened to our souls, and the spirit of God descended upon our hearts." Jones saw a footpath appear "like a blaze of fire," and the whole camp "manifested the presence of God."

The Canadian Methodist educationist and temperance worker LETITIA YOUMANS reported that Eliza already had a reputation as an effective speaker when she came to Canada from the United States, and that she was greatly sought after for camp meetings and services in private homes. Letitia recorded the reminiscences of one woman whose doorway had become the pulpit for one of Eliza's sermons. The inside of the house was filled with women, while the men stood in the large yard in front. Eliza's text was from Ezekiel's vision of the waters, and the woman recalled that, "When the preacher [Eliza] spoke of the spread of the Gospel, and quoted in raptured accents, the waters were still rising ... I fancied I could still see the waters of life flowing in until the earth was filled with the glory of God."

In an era when women were considered to be the weaker sex, Eliza tangibly dispelled the notion. Travel from mission to mission was hazardous, and on one occasion she was thrown from a wagon. Later, a boat in which she was travelling almost capsized in a gale on Lake Couchiching. For a time, she lived with another missionary teacher, Sally Ash, in a cramped seventeen-foot-square bark schoolhouse where they also taught twenty-five girls how to read, sew, knit, and braid straw. The structure caught fire, and Eliza narrowly escaped. That summer, she lived in a wigwam on an island because of a virulent fever on the mainland.

Eliza's days began at five o'clock in the morning in winter, at four in the summer. She and other female missionaries were in charge of weekday schools for girls and instructed women in the evening. On Sundays, there could be as many as six sessions—prayer meetings, preaching services, and classes.

The hard work, long hours, and primitive living conditions notwithstanding, Eliza had an opportunity to share and to live out her faith in a salaried position, an unusual alternative for a woman of that time.

Eliza stopped preaching abruptly and settled down in the early 1830s, just before she married William Case. A number of male ministers had objected to Eliza preaching, and William, at first, had refused to sit on the platform with her when she was speaking.

After her marriage, Eliza continued teaching household and "domestic science" at the missions where she and William lived. By the time she died at the age of ninety-one, Eliza had contributed greatly to the spread of Christianity in Canada and the United States. Her faith served as a dynamic model for the women of her era and continues to do so today.

Matilda Jones (active 1825–1859)
Kahkewaquonaby: Reverend Peter Jones (1802–1856)
oil on ivory, 11.3 x 8.7 cm
Courtesy: Victoria University Library, Toronto
Photographer: Steve Boyko

He Stands People on Their Feet
Peter Jones
1802–1856

Donald B. Smith

"Saul-like stature, broad shoulders, high cheekbones,
erect bearing, sleek jet-black hair, and fine intellect."

Peter Jones was born in a wigwam at Head of the Lake (present-day Hamilton) in 1802. His father, Augustus Jones, was an American surveyor who had come to Upper Canada—as Ontario was then known—fifteen years earlier. There, he met a Mississauga woman named Tuhbenahneequay who became Peter's mother. Since Augustus already had a Mohawk wife and family, he could not continue to live with his Mississauga companion and their sons John and Peter.

Tuhbenahneequay raised John and Peter with the help of her parents and other band members. The boys learned the religion and customs of their mother's people, and young Peter (known in Ojibwa as Kahkewaquonaby, "sacred feathers," and in Mohawk as Desagondensta, "he stands people on their feet") earned the reputation of being an excellent hunter.

The late eighteenth and early nineteenth centuries proved difficult for the Mississaugas. From approximately five hundred individuals in the late 1780s, the Mississaugas at the western end of Lake Ontario had declined to about two hundred by the early 1820s from smallpox and from alcohol abuse. The War of 1812 also led to great devastation when a major battle occurred at Stoney Creek in 1813 between the British and the American invaders. And game declined because of the increased settlement in the area immediately after the war.

When Tuhbenahneequay's band appeared on the point of disintegration, Augustus Jones intervened. In 1816, he took his Mississauga sons to live with him and his Mohawk family on the Grand River, thirty miles to the west. Peter benefited from two years of schooling in small one-room schools. Augustus taught his sons how to farm and to care for poultry and livestock. Peter also learned the carpentry skills needed to build houses and barns.

At his father's request, he was baptized into the Church of England in 1820. He later confessed that the ceremony had meant nothing to him. He consented to it only because, as he later wrote, "I might be entitled to all the privileges of the white inhabitants." He hoped eventually to enter the fur trade as a clerk, but a visit to a Methodist camp meeting in 1823 changed the direction of his life.

Peter attended the five-day gathering in Ancaster Township at the request of his half sister Polly. Here, Peter became a convert, his soul touched by the preaching of evangelical Christians. At the end of the meeting, the Reverend WILLIAM CASE, seeing Peter rise to his feet in acknowledgment of conversion, cried out with joy: "Glory to God, there stands a son of Augustus Jones of the Grand River, amongst the converts; now is the door opened for the work of conversion among his nation!"

Jones devoted his life to teaching his people about Christianity. Fluent in Ojibwa and knowledgeable about their culture, he made the new faith comprehensible. By the end of summer 1825 the young native evangelist had converted half his band. Moreover, he and his non-Native Methodist missionary allies had successfully convinced the governor of Upper Canada to construct, using the Mississaugas' funds, a permanent village on the Credit River. There, the Methodists taught religion and farming. By the end of 1826, almost all of the remaining Credit River Mississaugas had become Methodists, with converts looking to Peter Jones for direction.

Over the next two decades, Jones evolved his plan of how to help the Upper Canadian Ojibwas. Jones believed that by accepting Christianity and a settled agricultural way of life the Ojibwa could survive and prosper even amid the steadily growing settlement. In 1826–27, the Mississaugas established an agricultural village that quickly became the envy of other Ojibwa communities. Peter's older brother, John, became the schoolmaster, and he and Peter translated the Bible into Ojibwa.

News of the Credit River mission spread throughout Upper Canada. To raise funds for this and the other Methodist Indian missions that followed, Peter Jones went on speaking tours throughout the colony and later to the United States and Britain. The highlight of his foreign trips came in 1838 when he was granted an audience with Queen Victoria at Windsor Castle, where he made a great impression. An Irish clergyman described him as a man of "Saul-like stature, broad shoulders, high cheekbones, erect bearing, sleek jet-black hair, and fine intellect."

In 1833, Peter married Eliza Field, the daughter of a wealthy English soap and candle manufacturer. They had met and fallen in love during his first missionary tour of Britain in 1831. Eliza helped Peter copy the scriptures and Methodist hymns into Ojibwa, taught the Mississauga girls to sew, and instructed them in religion. She also strengthened him in his resolve to fully Europeanize the Credit River Mississaugas.

Although Jones's work to protect the remaining land base of the Ojibwas met with strong support, a number of Mississaugas—perhaps as many as half of those at the Credit River mission—opposed his attempts to erase so much of the remaining Ojibwa culture and customs. He nonetheless persevered in his attempts to introduce European-style discipline for the children, to promote residential schools, and to govern by vote rather than by consensus.

The Methodists' emphasis on Europeanization alienated many Ojibwas in other communities, helping to check the Methodist advance in the mid-1830s, by which time approximately two thousand Indians in Upper Canada had joined the church. Splits among the Methodists also hurt their missionary work; for seven years in the 1840s the Methodists in Upper Canada divided into two separate conferences. Increased competition from the Anglicans and especially from the Roman Catholics further weakened the Methodists' outreach.

Peter Jones's declining health in the late 1840s and early 1850s removed him from serving as the Methodists' leading native missionary. He died at Brantford in 1856, survived by his wife, his aged mother, a half sister, and four sons. The Venerable Archdeacon Nelles visited Jones shortly before his death and shared his observations in a note written to Jones's longtime friend EGERTON RYERSON: "Mr. Jones ... enjoys great peace of mind, and I believe truly trusts that Saviour whom he has so often pointed out to others as the only refuge and hope of poor sinners. May my last end be like his."

Abridged from "Peter Jones" by Donald B. Smith, from ENCYCLOPEDIA OF NORTH AMERICAN INDIANS, edited by Frederick E. Hoxie. Copyright © 1996 by Houghton Mifflin Company. Reprinted by permission of Houghton Mifflin Company. All rights reserved.

Artist unknown
John Strachan
ca. 1827, oil on canvas, 17.7 x 15.2 cm
Courtesy: Trinity College Archives

inset: Trinity College Archvies / P1051/0001

Faith and Loyalty United
John Strachan
1778–1867

*"Remarkable for self-sacrifice, devotion, downright honesty,
resolute firmness, and unflagging industry."*

John Moir

Few individuals influenced Canada's early development more than John Strachan. He was the first Anglican bishop of Toronto and the founder of Ontario's school system and of three of its universities—McGill, Toronto, and Trinity College. Strachan's activities from the first day of the nineteenth century until his death at age eighty-nine in 1867 were centred in Ontario. His impact as an educator, a legislator, and a religious leader, however, extended to eastern Canada and later helped to shape the western provinces. His long, active, and multifaceted sixty-seven years in Canada earned him admirers and enemies, even after his passing.

Strachan was born in Aberdeen in 1778. He was the youngest son of a quarryman, who was a member of the Episcopal Church of Scotland, and of a pious mother, who belonged to a Presbyterian secession body. His mother wanted him to become a minister, but after his father was killed in a blasting accident Strachan began teaching to earn his university tuition. In 1799, he arrived in Kingston, Upper Canada, to tutor the children of Richard Cartwright, a prominent loyalist who, with Anglican missionary John Stuart, inspired Strachan with admiration for British political and religious institutions.

Strachan's early years in Canada contributed greatly to his Canadianization. Canada offered Strachan the best opportunities for advancement. He obtained the Anglican rectorship of Cornwall in 1803 and started a school there for the children of leading colonial families. Four years later, he married Canadian-born Ann Woods, and in 1812 he became the rector of St. James Church in the tiny provincial capital of York (Toronto). Strachan was also the principal of York's grammar school and the chaplain to its legislature.

In 1813, York was captured and sacked by Americans. Strachan's stand against the pillagers convinced him that his life's mission was to make Upper Canada a loyal British and Christian colony. To achieve these goals, he joined the province's executive council, or cabinet, in 1817, and its legislative council in 1820, and in 1823 he became the president of the province's education board.

By the 1820s, many of Strachan's former pupils—the so-called family compact—were in positions of political power. With their support, he exerted his influence on behalf of the Church of England and of British constitutionalism. Believing that every nation required an established church, he worked to strengthen Anglicanism's preferred status, including its monopoly of the Clergy Reserves—almost two and a half million acres set aside in 1791 "to support the Protestant religion."

From his position of privilege, Strachan defended the rights of the establishment and disparaged rival dissenters as uneducated, disloyal, and fanatical. In 1826, Strachan was publicly challenged by EGERTON RYERSON, who defended the province's Methodists and launched a vigorous attack on the political churchmanship that Strachan typified, including the tendency to reduce the church of Christ to a tool for political preferment. Arguing that there was no basis in Scripture for formal ties between church and state, Ryerson insisted that Strachan's proposals degraded Christianity by obscuring and perverting its spiritual mission. The interdenominational strife that ensued forced Strachan to resign from the executive council and political activities in 1835.

Meanwhile, the growing Church of England in Upper Canada had long needed a local bishop, and Strachan was consecrated in 1839 at age sixty-one. Theo-logically, Bishop Strachan belonged to the High and Dry school, which relied on the Book of Common Prayer as a corrective for excessive ritualism and evangelicalism. He also rejected ecclesiastical colonialism and strengthened his church by introducing synodical government by clergy and laity. His ambitions for a state church, a completely integrated education system, and a universal polity of loyalism were, however, never achieved.

More than a century after Strachan's passing, Canadians view him as either a saint or a scoundrel. To Strachan's pupil and successor as bishop, A. N. Bethune, he was "a fast friend, a man of prayer" who disliked pretence. Another longtime acquaintance said that Strachan had many opponents, but no enemies. Even Ryerson, an early opponent of Strachan's politics, called him "as thoroughly Canadian as any native of the country" and "remarkable for … self-sacrifice, devotion, downright honesty, resolute firmness, and unflagging industry."

To many opponents, though, Strachan was a dishonest "demon" and a "hypocrite." He was depicted as proud, arrogant, autocratic, reserved, and possessed of or by, an iron determination. William Lyon Mackenzie nicknamed him "the Governor's jackal," and in an age that required thirteen loaves in a baker's dozen as proof of a baker's honesty Strachan was considered "His Majesty's Baker." Strachan's occasional dictatorial lapses, moreover, were widely publicized.

Strachan, however, disdained popularity and said that he would defend to the death his unpopular beliefs. Those who could not, or would not, share his convictions were stigmatized as ignorant or wrong or both. He has been vilified as ambitious, manipulative, and even devious, yet his efforts were always directed toward a single goal: building a Canada loyal to the best political, religious, and educational traditions of Britain—goals to be achieved, he thought, by the Anglicanization of Canadian society. And in private life he was a loving husband and father and a caring and generous friend.

Strachan, a born organizer, was not so much an original thinker as a synthesizer of others' best ideas, a man who informed himself fully before forming a judgement that, for him, was henceforth etched in stone. Physically slight, Strachan was nonetheless energetic and a workaholic who demanded as much effort from everyone else. At eighty-one, he travelled more than one thousand miles (three-quarters by stagecoach) and confirmed over sixteen hundred persons in forty-four churches in thirty days.

Any brief evaluation of John Strachan and his place in Canadian history is complicated by his wide-ranging interests and enigmatic character. Throughout his life, he was consistently fearless: facing invading Americans and cholera epidemics. Although supposedly an archconservative, he introduced student government at his Cornwall school and recommended a five-and-a-half-day workweek so that a labourer's life could contain more than physical toil. Strachan was a mediocre sermonizer, but he published some ninety pamphlets of speeches and homilies and one arithmetic textbook. He was, in the Scottish phrase, a 'lad o'pairts'—educator, politician, and churchman. A father of universities, the first architect of Ontario's education system, the first bishop and primary formative influence in the Anglican diocese of Toronto, John Strachan was, above all, a remarkable Canadian and a faithful Anglican.

J. W. L. Forster (1850–1938)
George Brown
oil on canvas, 121.9 x 91.4 cm
Courtesy: *The Globe and Mail*
Photographer: Steve Boyko

inset: National Archives of Canada / C-26415

A Truly Loyal Subject
George Brown
1818–1880

"The man who made the union feasible."

Vincent Marquis

The life of George Brown combines tragedy and heroism. Brown made Confederation possible for Canada through self-sacrifice. By a simple but magnificent gesture, he threw away personal ambition to better serve his country. Although history portrays him as a statesman who failed to attain the power and position that seemed his political heritage, as a publisher, journalist, and editor he was a man of superior influence.

George Brown was born into a devout and reform-minded evangelical Presbyterian family near Edinburgh, Scotland, in 1818. In 1837, the Browns immigrated to New York City following a business setback. In New York, George's father, Peter, became successful in dry goods merchandizing and in newspaper publishing.

Peter Brown and his son conjectured that there was no greater evil than government interference in church affairs. They also believed that personal integrity and morality were essential ingredients for any man seeking public office. According to the Browns, individuals were entitled to full freedom of conscience and expression and to the full protection of the law. Government must not encroach on basic freedoms, and vigilance among the free citizenry was always necessary to curb the tendency of governments to go beyond their proper limits.

On visiting Upper Canada on business in 1842, George Brown wrote to his father, "The country is young. There are few persons of ability and education. There is no position a man of energy and character may not reasonably hope to attain." On the invitation of Scottish Upper Canadians to publish a religious newspaper, the Browns moved to Toronto in 1843. The *Banner* expressed "Presbyterian interests and upheld Reform principles" on all great public issues.

In 1844, George launched his own newspaper, the *Globe*, in Toronto, Upper Canada's fastest-growing city. Within a year, it was the colony's leading newspaper, and the *Globe*'s young publisher had become the colony's most successful and powerful journalist. By 1847, Brown's paper had become the official newspaper of the Reform (which later became a major component of the Liberal Party of Upper Canada). The *Globe* fiercely defended the values George Brown had grown up with.

Accused by opponents of advocating godlessness because he stood for separating educational institutions from the control of sects or denominations, Brown replied (with regard to the proposed Anglican controlled King's College in Toronto in 1847) that the young should learn their Christianity at home from their parents. Professors in colleges should nonetheless "teach every science as Christians ought, both in the mode of doing it, and by the example they set before the students."

When Brown was first elected to the Canadian Parliament in 1852, he came to the capital in Quebec as a friendless outsider. He had gone into opposition to the Liberal government of Francis Hincks because of its numerous compromises of Reform principles. Gradually, he won the support of the majority of Canada West's electors and of the Reform members of Parliament and became their official leader. Reform, however, had lost power to the Conservatives, led by John A. Macdonald.

For Brown, politics was a civic duty. In government, high principle alone should direct one's course. When engaged in affairs of state, Brown was virtually humourless, but always passionately intense, a merciless debater, and a relentless juggernaut of logical argument and moral persuasion. He maintained a reputation for incorruptibility and throughout his life maintained a strong belief that biblical morality should govern public life.

Macdonald on the other hand was urbane, suave, casually anecdotal, disarmingly charming, a master of the political game, a good administrator, and a great handler of men. For him, politics was the art of the possible rather than a quest for the ideal.

In 1861, Brown lost his seat in Parliament. He believed that his political career was over. He concentrated instead on improving the *Globe*. In addition, he pursued his Christian ideal of public service by helping fugitive American slaves in Canada and by promoting temperance. On a visit to Scotland in 1862, he married Anne Nelson. They shared a happy marriage and a warm Christian home with their children.

Brown reentered Parliament in 1863. He stood for representation by population, for the federation of the two Canadas, and for acquiring the Hudson's Bay lands of the west. By 1864, he again led Reform, this time against a shaky Macdonald-Cartier government.

In May 1864, Brown chaired a parliamentary committee studying ways to amend Canada's constitution to break the east-west deadlock that paralyzed effective government in Canada. The Macdonald-Cartier government fell, and another fruitless election loomed. Swallowing his personal antagonism to Macdonald and believing that God had provided him and his colleagues with a once-in-a-lifetime opportunity to change the course of history, Brown offered to stake his career on an attempt to form a coalition with his opponents if they would agree to resolve the constitutional impasse once and for all. Thus, the Great Coalition was formed to seek a federation of all the colonies of British North America or, failing that, a federation of the two Canadas.

Brown's role in the subsequent Charlottetown and Quebec conferences in September and October 1864 was significant, as was his contribution in promoting Confederation in the *Globe* and in numerous speeches. Although recent historians have often neglected Brown's role, it was crucial. As his definitive biographer has explained: "The active force that drove the question of union to the point of decision, opened the way to decision through the constitutional committee, and then made the crucial move that transformed a blank wall of deadlock into vistas of nationhood was George Brown—in all this, the real initiator of Confederation."

Brown lost his seat in the Conservative sweep in the 1867 election. He retired as Liberal leader in September 1867. Alexander Mackenzie, his friend and the new prime minister, named him a senator in 1874. From 1875 to 1880, Brown concentrated on personal affairs. He was instrumental in the formation of the Presbyterian Church of Canada in 1875.

On March 25, 1880, a disgruntled ex-*Globe* employee shot Brown in the leg. The wound became gangrenous, and Brown died on Sunday, May 9, to the sound of church bells summoning worshippers to meet with God. Lord Monck, governor-general in the Confederation years, termed Brown "the man whose conduct in 1864 had rendered the project of union feasible."

Despite the accolades, throughout his life Brown had remained humble. He had refused the lieutenant governorship of Ontario in 1875 and a knighthood in 1879, preferring always to remain, simply, George Brown of the *Globe*—which for him was distinction enough. As the Presbytery of Toronto testified: "By his pure life and conversion he commended the religion of Christ. He was sustained … by his trust in God, and in the blood of the Redeemer."

June Forbes (1921–1961)
Egerton Ryerson
oil on canvas, 127 x 96 cm
Courtesy: Victoria University, Toronto
Photographer: Steve Boyko

inset: National Archives of Canada / C-014235

The Father of Canadian Public Education
Egerton Ryerson
1803–1882

"To make men Christians."

Goldwin French

*I*n midlife, Egerton Ryerson shifted from Methodist minister to civil servant and established a system of public education in Ontario that became a model for other English-speaking provinces. By the age of forty-one, he had served as a revivalist preacher, acted as the chief debater for the Methodists, learned five languages, been the editor of a prominent newspaper, received an honourary doctorate, and been appointed the superintendent of education for Upper Canada.

Ryerson was born into a prominent United Empire Loyalist family that was among the first settlers in Upper Canada's Long Point region. His early years were spent working in the fields on his father's farm, with intermittent attendance at the district schools in nearby Vittoria and Hamilton. His teachers and his voracious reading equipped him to become a highly effective speaker and writer—skills that would be indispensable in the years to come.

His father wanted him to remain on the farm, while others encouraged him to become an Anglican clergyman. Ryerson considered becoming a lawyer, but, along with his mother and brothers—four of his five brothers also became Methodist ministers—he was caught up in an evangelical revival. On his twenty-second birthday, he wrote: "I have decided this day to travel in the Methodist Connexion and preach Jesus to the lost sons of men." Ten days later, he preached his first sermon, and in 1825 he became a circuit rider, as the horse-riding, black-frocked itinerant Methodist preachers were called. From a circuit, Ryerson was assigned to an Indian mission. He was ordained in 1827 and remained a Methodist minister for the rest of his life.

Ryerson believed that his primary task was "to make men Christians—Christians in heart and life, in temper, word and work." Almost immediately, he made a name for himself by defending the Methodist cause against the Reverend John Strachan. As the leading Anglican clergyman in Upper Canada, Strachan had laid exclusive claim on behalf of the Anglican church to the Clergy Reserves—the tracts of public land set aside for the support of Protestant clergy. Ryerson's skillful rebuttal of Strachan's claim impressed his fellow Methodists. Thus, when the newly independent Methodist Conference decided in 1829 to publish a newspaper, the *Christian Guardian*, Ryerson became the editor and continued to defend the equal rights of all denominations. Although he preached frequently, after 1829 Ryerson served his church and his community primarily as a journalist (he was the editor of the *Guardian* intermittently from 1829 to 1840); educator; and as an educational administrator.

In 1841, he became the first principal of Victoria College in Cobourg. In his inaugural address, he stressed that the college would have a balanced curriculum, infused with "the fundamental principles of Christian theology." Ryerson further stated that "youth should be furnished with right *principles*, as well as with right *knowledge* … the *first* requisite is the religious and moral knowledge of right and wrong: the next is an acquaintance with the history of mankind."

In 1844, he was appointed the superintendent of education for Canada West (Ontario). He began with "the prospect of seeing … every child of my native land in the school going way … and of witnessing one comprehensive and unique system of education from the a.b.c. of the child up to the matriculation of the youth into the provincial university … which would present an aspect of equal benignity to every sect and every party upon the broad basis of our common Christianity." He achieved his goal when the Legislative Assembly of Ontario passed the School Act of 1871 and universal education became an accomplished fact, resulting in a well-ordered school system in which elementary education was free and compulsory attendance would soon become the norm.

The role and the curriculum of the grammar schools had been redefined, and the foundations of a free secondary school system also had been laid. The students used textbooks in which Christian values and loyalty to the constitution were included (Ryerson wrote the textbook *First Lessons in Christian Morals* in 1871). And they were taught by instructors who met improved certification criteria. Despite Ryerson's conviction that Christian ideals could be taught on nondenominational lines, he had reluctantly concluded that it was politically impossible to prevent the growth of Roman Catholic schools and had helped to enact legislation defining their position within the provincial system. Ryerson, moreover, a tireless and methodical administrator, developed his department into "the first effective social service bureaucracy" in Ontario. In 1876, the Department of Education became a ministry, and Ryerson retired from the superintendency, his work completed.

From 1874 to 1878, he was the first president of the General Conference of the Methodist Church of Canada. As a Methodist minister and as a civil servant, he clearly articulated the values that he believed should shape the development of Ontario and Canada and strove to put them into practice. Ryerson believed that the inhabitants of his province and, indeed, that all British North Americans had the right to civil and religious liberty, that church and state should be kept separate, and that all citizens should be free from religious discrimination. Such convictions led him to play an active part in the protracted church-state controversy in Ontario. His liberal position on this issue was balanced by his attachment to Britain and the constitution. Ryerson stressed as well that factional politics degraded government and that free and independent legislators were a vital necessity in the political system.

Ryerson's last years were devoted largely to the completion of a two-volume history, *The Loyalists of America and Their Times*. His autobiographical *The Story of My Life* was published posthumously in 1883. His enduring legacy, however, was the Ontario school system—a system that enabled every child to acquire essential knowledge and skills and to experience a climate of opinion informed by the Christian and British values of Ontario society and that "would become … a model for most of English-speaking Canada."

Egerton Ryerson died in February 1882 in Toronto. Ontario united with Methodism in honouring his life and work. His conviction was that he had tried, "however imperfectly," to serve God. As a minister, polemicist, writer, and tireless civil servant, he had sought tenaciously to inculcate in his community a fuller understanding of the import of its political, cultural, and religious traditions and a firm commitment to perpetuate them through its schools and colleges. In so doing, he was faithful to the spirit of Methodism and exemplified the authority and the meaning of Christian commitment.

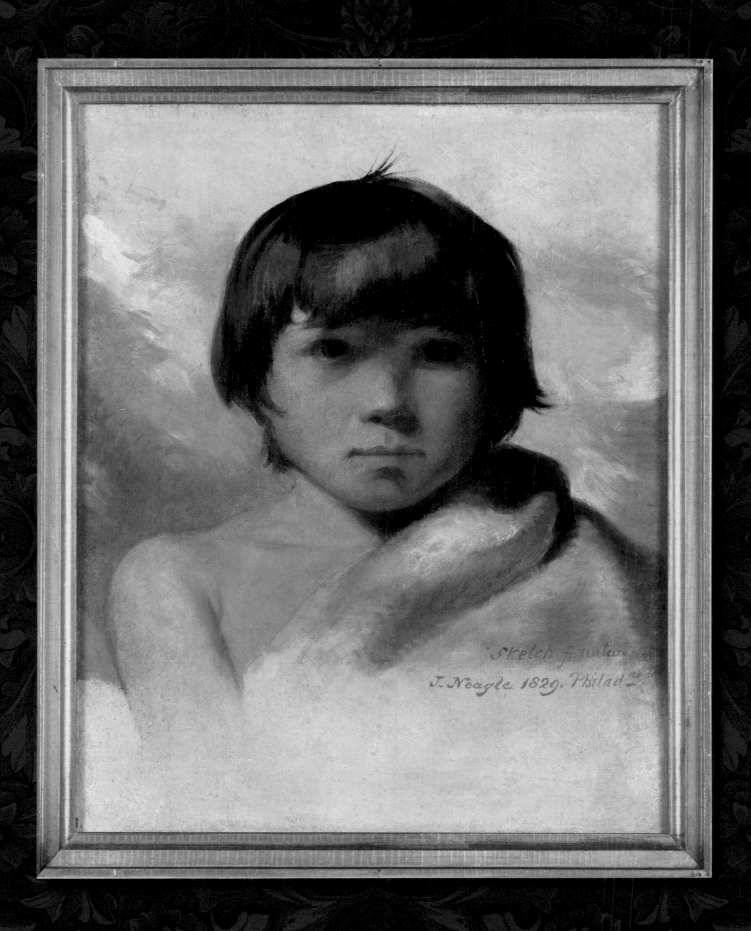

Within the painting:
Sketch fr. nature
J. Neagle 1829. Philad.

John Neagle (1760–1829)
An Indian Boy: Shahwahnekshih (Henry Steinhauer)
oil on canvas, 51.0 x 40.5 cm
Courtesy: Glenbow Collection, Calgary, Canada
Photographer: Glenbow Photography, Ron Marsh

inset: Glenbow Archives, Calgary / NA-352-4

The Man of God Who Taught Peace
Henry Bird Steinhauer

1818–1884

"He worked to make the Bible relevant."

Gayle Simonson

Early in the nineteenth century, the Methodists in Upper Canada worked extensively among the native people. Mission schools were established "to win souls for God." One of the Methodists' highest priorities was to train native leaders who would then minister to their own people. They had many successes, but perhaps none was more devoted to his work, to his people, and to his God than Henry Bird Steinhauer.

Steinhauer was born into an Ojibwa band. He was probably first exposed to Christianity about age eight and was baptized two years later, in 1828. His Ojibwa name was Sowengisik, and he retained an English translation, "bird," as his middle name. He took the name Steinhauer after Methodist missionary WILLIAM CASE found him a benefactor. Adam Steinhauer of Philadelphia agreed to provide for the education of the Indian youth if the boy adopted the name of Steinhauer's deceased son, Henry. The investment was richly rewarded.

Henry Bird Steinhauer was an excellent student and was included in a fund-raising tour of the eastern states in 1829. In Philadelphia, artist John Neagle painted a portrait of the boy, which is now in Calgary's Glenbow Museum. Steinhauer excelled in languages and many years later— as a missionary to the Canadian west—actually prepared his sermons from the original Greek texts of the New Testament.

After attending Cazenovia Seminary in New York, Steinhauer returned to teach first at the Credit Mission on Lake Ontario and later at the Alderville Mission School in Northumberland County. At these and other Methodist mission schools, students were taught practical skills as well as religion.

In 1840, the Hudson's Bay Company asked the British Wesleyan Methodist Society to "minister to the religious and educational needs of the Indians in the Hudson Bay Territories." Steinhauer answered the call and travelled to the northern tip of Lake Winnipeg, arriving at Norway House in 1843 and taking charge of the school at nearby Rossville.

Because of his belief that students should be taught in their own language, Steinhauer's first goal was to learn the Swampy Cree language. Upon accomplishing this, he set out to translate major portions of the Scripture, from Psalms to the end of the Old Testament and from Romans to the end of the New Testament, into the Cree syllabic system developed by Methodist missionary James Evans. During this time, Steinhauer married Jessie Mamanuwartum, a Swampy Cree. Together, they tried to establish a new mission at Oxford House, but the winters were severe, and they nearly starved to death.

In 1852, Steinhauer was recommended for ordination. He postponed his ordination and chose instead to travel to England, where he undertook a fund-raising tour for Methodist work in Canada. He was finally ordained at the Canadian Methodist Conference of 1855.

After a brief stay at Lac La Biche, north of Fort Edmonton, Steinhauer moved his family and his Ojibwa band to Whitefish Lake to start a mission among the Cree. The location had land suitable for agriculture and a lake abounding with fish. In "Beginnings at Whitefish Lake," a reminiscence published in *Missionary Outlook* in 1880, Steinhauer wondered how he might achieve the difficult task before him: "What can an Indian do with Indians to make prayer men and women of them?" He underestimated himself.

He worked to make the Bible relevant to the Cree, comparing their way of life with that of the early Jews—wandering tribes who lived in tents. The Cree of the region had no agricultural experience, so Steinhauer taught them to break land, plant gardens, and build homes. While Jessie taught the women to knit, sew, and cook, just as she had learned at Norway House, Steinhauer also helped construct a church and a schoolhouse. Supplies arrived from Fort Garry only once a year. So, though they had the beginnings of an agricultural community, they continued for many summers to travel with the buffalo hunt.

Even on the hunt, and in spite of the threat of attack from other tribes, daily devotions were an integral part of life. On Sundays, there were four services and an adult Bible study. The celebrations of the "love-feast"—with the sacrament of communion— were emotional events in which individuals gave testimony of God's effect on their lives. Steinhauer further ensured the well-being of his mission by discouraging traders from establishing trading posts in the area to reduce the influx of alcohol.

Steinhauer's children shared his commitment of faith. His oldest daughter, Abigail, helped with the school. In 1863, she married John McDougall, the son of missionary George McDougall, and together the young couple set off to reestablish a mission at Pigeon Lake. With the help of teacher Elizabeth Barrett—who worked with Steinhauer from 1875 to 1877—Steinhauer's sons Robert and Egerton prepared for college in the east. Despite many financial hardships, both were eventually ordained.

In an unusually critical letter to the Missionary Society of the Wesleyan Methodist Church in Canada, published in 1875, Steinhauer articulated the need for indigenous missionaries. "A foreigner, either as a missionary or otherwise, will never take so well with the natives of this country … there is always a distrust on the part of a native to the foreigner, from that fact that the native has been so long down-trodden by the white man." He also criticized the missionary society for not heeding his pleas for essential materials.

Steinhauer played a significant role in political changes occurring in the west. Together with Barrett, he persuaded the territorial government to help fund their school, and it became the first Protestant Indian school in the west to receive such recognition. Throughout his life, Steinhauer faced many obstacles—starvation, the deaths of several children, tribal war, and smallpox epidemics—yet his faith never wavered. He died on December 29, 1884, but his influence lived on. When rebellion broke out the following year, an Indian chief who did not involve his tribe explained that he chose not to go to war as a tribute to his friend, the man of God who taught peace: "I owe a great debt to my old missionary who recently left us, Mr. Steinhauer."

Dora Holdaway (1922–)
Portrait of Joseph Medlicott Scriven, 1819–1886
conté, 40 x 50 cm

What a Friend We Have in Jesus
Joseph Scriven

1819–1886

*"I consecrated my heart, my life,
and my fortune to the service of Christ"*

Michael Clarke

Joseph Medlicott Scriven's legacy is a beautiful hymn that has been printed over one billion times. Scriven, a sad-hearted Irish immigrant to Canada, composed "What A Friend We Have in Jesus," never intending it for publication.

Scriven was born into an affluent family in Seapatrick, about seventy-five miles north of Dublin. In 1827, Scriven, aged eight, and his family became Christians through the influence of Plymouth Brethren. He later called the experience "everlasting, penetrating, and reassuring."

After earning his bachelor of arts from Dublin's Trinity College, Scriven worked as a tutor and pursued artistic interests, particularly poetry and sculpting. Tragedy struck, however, when, on the eve of his wedding, his fiancée drowned. Amid profound sorrow, Scriven later remarked, "true solace and support was only found in my dearest friend, Jesus Christ."

Eager to distance himself from daily reminders of what might have been, Scriven sailed for Canada in May 1845. After two months, he became ill, and by December he was back in Dublin, tutoring a wealthy physician's son.

Scriven travelled with the doctor and his family to the Middle East, including a visit to the city of Damascus, where Scriven began writing a poem called "Pray Without Ceasing." Its first line was "What a friend we have in Jesus." He sent a draft to his mother in Dublin.

In the 1840s, the Great Potato Famine killed more than a million people in Ireland. Scriven escaped by setting sail for Upper Canada (Ontario) again in 1847. He established a school in Brantford and later in Clinton, where he also did some preaching and often distributed religious tracts and at times a verse or two that he had composed. Scriven eventually settled near Peterborough in the Rice Lake area, where he tutored in the home of Robert Pengelly, a retired British Navy officer.

The Pengelly property included a small chapel for religious services. It was there that Scriven met Pengelly's niece, Catherine Roche. Deeply attracted, they began courting. Catherine even agreed to convert to the Plymouth Brethren faith, and a baptism in Rice Lake was held prior to their impending marriage.

Sadly, the icy April waters of Rice Lake proved fatal to Catherine, who developed pneumonia. She died in August 1850 and was buried in a private cemetery adjacent to the Pengelly chapel. Scriven later remarked that, looking upon the still face of "my sweet Catherine, I consecrated my heart, my life, and my fortune to the service of Christ."

Faced with the loss of a second fiancée, Scriven's thoughts turned to his mother in Ireland. She had been looking forward to his marriage and would be brokenhearted. To ease her grief, Scriven completed the first stanza of "Pray Without Ceasing":

What a Friend we have in Jesus,
All Our sins and grief to bear;
What a privilege to carry,
Everything to God in prayer.

In the late 1860s, Scriven left the Pengelly's for Port Hope, where he acted on his belief that "if the people will not go to church, then the church should go to the people." Bible in hand, he preached on street corners, to small gatherings in homes, and to crowds at fall fairs, calling sinners to repentance. He spoke with humility and modesty. His sermons were marked by frequent quotations from Scripture, and sometimes entire chapters recited from memory. In return, he was jeered, assailed with mud balls, and beaten. Once, he was even jailed by an overzealous constable for preaching on the streets of Port Hope, where many residents began referring to him as Lonely ol' Joe.

Abuse notwithstanding, Scriven continued to demonstrate his faith, in words and in deeds. He sawed wood for those who could not afford it. When he found a mother with small children and a dying husband, he paid their rent; secured for them a newer, better home; moved them; and provided them with a stove, wood, and other necessities. Above all, he introduced the dying husband to Jesus, the sinner's friend.

Scriven consistently gave away the regular remittances that he received from his family in Ireland. Frustrated, they sent clothing. That, too, he gave away. For Scriven, frugality was a necessity insofar as it could benefit the needy: "If I spend five cents on some unnecessary thing, it costs … money [that] would buy something for a needy person."

In 1869, Scriven published a booklet of hymns and verses. He explained in the foreword: "The first part contains [ninety-four] hymns … to be sung … [by] the children of God. The second part contains [twenty] verses intended … to express truth, as well as to convey comfort, instruction or reproof to our hearts." Scriven did not include "Pray Without Ceasing."

The hymn for which he is known was first published when an individual to whom Scriven had given a handwritten copy submitted it to the editor of the *Port Hope Guide* in 1850. A copy of that paper ended up in New York as a parcel wrapping. The recipient of the package saw the hymn and had it published in a local paper. It next appeared in 1865 in H. L. Hasting's *Social Hymns, Original and Selected*. In 1879, it was included in *Gospel Hymns by Sankey and Others* as "What a Friend We Have in Jesus," and Scriven's authorship was first officially recognized. Whenever he was asked about the hymn, Scriven would reply, "The Lord and I did it between us."

As Scriven's health began to fail, he was placed in the care of a fellow Plymouth Brethern, James Sackville. While Scriven was bedridden, Sackville heard him repeating, "I am the Lord, I will never leave thee or forsake thee." Later, on entering Scriven's room, Sackville found the bed empty. At noon the following day, Scriven's body was found in a creek a few yards from Sackville's home. It is believed that Scriven sought a drink from the cold waters and, in his weakened condition, fell into the water and drowned. Townspeople remarked that water had once again played a tragic role in Scriven's life. He was buried beside his Canadian sweetheart, Catherine Roche.

Following his death, Scriven gained growing recognition as the author of one of the most popular hymns in the world. In May 1920, a monument to Scriven was unveiled at the Pengelly cemetery by Premier E.C. Dury of Ontario. Patrons included Sir Robert Borden and Mackenzie King. The service included the reading of Psalm 112: Blessed is the man that fears the Lord. … Good will come to him who is generous and lends freely, who conducts his affairs with justice. For Scriven, the embodiment of Christian charity, it was a fitting epitaph.

Father Charles Pandosy, omi (1824–1891)
Colourization of black and white photograph
Courtesy: Archives Deschâtelets, Ottawa

inset: B.C. Archives / B-09611

A Missionary of the Northwest
Father Charles Pandosy

1824–1891

"I expend myself and over this is spent God's grace."

Ted Gerk

Old-timers in the Okanagan who knew him well remembered Father Pandosy as a huge, powerfully built man, capable of amazing feats of strength, with a big booming voice and a ready wit. Although a deeply religious Oblate missionary, Pandosy was also known to settle an argument by challenging his opponent to a fistfight. Today, Pandosy is best remembered as Canada's Johnny Appleseed.

Charles John Félix Adolph Pandosy was born in Marseilles, France, in 1824 to Marguerite Joséphine Marie Dallest and Étienne Charles Henry Pandosy. His father was a navy captain and a landowner and was thus able to provide comfortable living conditions and a good education for his family.

It was his father's navy career that drew Pandosy to the adventure of distant ports. As a step in this direction, while attending the Bourbon College at Arles, France, Pandosy decided to enter the Oblate Juniorate of Luminères, a seminary for men seeking ordination into the Oblate Order of priesthood in the Roman Catholic Church. He took his final religious vows in 1845.

Bishop de Mazenod, founder of the Missionary Oblates of Mary Immaculate, provided him with an inspiring admonition: "There are in this world but two loves, the love of God extending to the contempt of self and the love of self extending to the contempt of God. All other loves are but degrees between these two extremes. Do not fear, you obey the One who rules the world." This wisdom would guide Pandosy's missionary endeavours in the Pacific Northwest for over four decades.

In February 1847, the twenty-three-year-old Pandosy and four others were sent from France to the mission fields of the Oregon Territory. It was an arduous eight-month journey, culminating in their arrival at Fort Walla Walla. Here, the men began to fulfill the objective of their journey: the evangelization of the Yakima Indians.

Pandosy and the others quickly discovered the violence of the region. On November 29, 1847, the Marcus Whitman Massacre took place in which several Cayuse Indians killed thirteen people and took more than forty hostages. In February 1848, American troops were dispatched, and the Cayuse War began. The war was to last two-and a half years.

Motivated by these perilous events, Pandosy's superiors allowed for early ordination. Pandosy and a colleague officially entered the Oblate Order in early January 1848, the first priests ordained in what was to become Washington State. Pandosy altered his name at this point to Charles Marie Pandosy.

The missionaries not only cared for the spiritual needs of the natives, they also served as translators and as peacekeepers. Pandosy and his co-workers managed to keep the Yakimas from entering the war.

Pandosy became fluent in the Yakima language and eventually compiled its first dictionary. He later acted as a mediator and an interpreter between the Yakimas and the white man while continuing his missionary work among the Indians and serving as an army chaplain. In March 1859, war flared between the U.S. Army and the Spokane and Yakima Indians, and the Oblates made the difficult decision to close their missions among the Yakimas and the Cayuses.

In summer 1859, Pandosy was sent to the Okanagan Valley in British Columbia, where he established a mission known as L'Anse au Sable, the Cove of Sand, in an area that is now the City of Kelowna. Pandosy quickly recognized the agricultural potential of the Okanagan's temperate setting and planted its first apple trees, encouraging new settlers to do the same. A friend of Father Pandosy wrote: "The first trees planted by the missionary produced a beautiful apple, deep red, shaped like a Delicious—a good winter apple." Pandosy's orchards eventually established the Okanagan Valley as one of Canada's chief fruit-growing areas.

Pandosy was a devout pastor who also served his flock as doctor; teacher; lawyer; orator; botanist; agriculturist; musician (he played the French horn); voice instructor; and sports coach. He fast became known as a troubleshooter, a peacemaker, a defender of justice, a champion of the underdog, and, above all else, a great humanitarian.

But Pandosy was not your typical priest. Once, when his young Indian interpreter and guide gambled away Pandosy's brand new saddle, Pandosy immediately challenged him to a fight. Love and respect for his priest kept the native man's hands down by his side, causing Pandosy to grab the culprit by the scruff of the neck and demand that he put up his fists and defend himself. Pandosy, however, tripped on his cassock, allowing his opponent to jump on top of him. Those who observed the spectacle were surprised at Pandosy's unpriestly behaviour. Dusting himself off, Pandosy thundered, "I'm not mad at him, I'm mad about the *saddle*!"

Pandosy, who experienced other missions throughout British Columbia—Esquimalt, Fort Rupert, Fort St. James, the lower Fraser, Stuart Lake, Mission City, and New Westminster—was among those who believed that Indians and their culture should be respected and that the ways of the white man were largely responsible for the indifference that many Indians displayed toward Christianity. He wrote to a superior in the 1850s: "But, I shiver Reverend Father, when I think of the miserable state of the Savages, as I cannot delude myself, at least in the country where we live, the Savages around us are what the Whites have made them and what we have let them become instead of working hard and generously to make them otherwise with the help of the grace of God."

On February 6, 1891, Father Pandosy died near Penticton, B.C., after a pastoral visit during cold weather to Keremeos. His body was brought to the mission that he had founded on the site of present-day Kelowna and lovingly laid to rest.

Pandosy influenced whites and natives alike and saved the lives of thousands during the various wars between natives and settlers. He taught that two cultures and two worlds could live together peacefully based on mutual trust and respect.

Pandosy's life of faith and sacrifice are evidenced by the missions he founded and so diligently served. On his own behalf he said, "I expend myself and over this is spent God's grace."

HON. JOHN ROBSON.
PREMIER, 1889-DE.
1824--1892.

Honest John

John Robson

1824–1892

"Reforms for the moral and intellectual improvement of the people."

Bob Burkinshaw

John Robson served British Columbia as a journalist, reformer, legislator, cabinet minister, and premier. He is considered a father of Confederation because of his strong support for B.C. entering Canada.

Robson was born in 1824 in Perth, Upper Canada, and was raised in a Presbyterian home. Unlike his younger brother Ebenezer, who was influenced by Wesleyan revivalists and became an important Methodist missionary in B.C., John remained a Presbyterian all his life. Strongly committed to his church, he nonetheless loudly stressed the equality of all denominations in B.C.

The gold rush lured Robson west from his dry goods business in 1859. He had married Susan Longworth in 1854, but he left her and their child behind, and they did not join him for several years. Robson was unsuccessful at gold panning, so he worked at various labouring jobs, including helping his missionary brother Ebenezer build the first Methodist church in New Westminster, the capital of the mainland colony. In 1861, Robson began his rise in public affairs when he became the editor of the city's *British Columbian* newspaper. In 1869, he became the editor of the *Daily British Colonist* in Victoria. Robson's journalism made him a popular figure and earned him the nickname "Honest John" among his readers.

Robson quickly became known as a reformer and especially as an advocate of responsible government. James Douglas, the governor of the two colonies of Vancouver Island and British Columbia, had almost absolute power in the mainland colony, where a legislative body did not exist. Robson, an admirer of GEORGE BROWN in Ontario, demanded the establishment of an elected legislature to which the administration would be responsible. He argued: "The only effectual and satisfactory mode of redressing grievances is by representatives, chosen by the people ... to expect that Douglas, or, indeed any other autocrat, can much longer continue to govern the Colony, is to display an amount of verdancy it would be prudent to conceal." Robson was strongly supported by many, but his sharp attacks on the government earned him the opposition of powerful colonial figures, including Douglas and Judge MATTHEW BEGBIE.

Robson's support of responsible government was not based on political beliefs alone. It was typical of evangelicals throughout British North America, who believed that such government had biblical underpinnings—individuals were equal before God and all were responsible to Him for their actions. The stability of society rested on converted individuals, whose consciences served as moral rudders, steering them in a responsible direction in their personal and social lives. Likewise, government must be held accountable, and the best suited to do so were the peoples' elected representatives.

Robson also became a champion of public schools. He advocated the Ontario system of public education founded by EGERTON RYERSON and strongly resisted the practice of the government to favour a particular denomination by funding its schools. He believed that government must be involved in education to make it affordable for the people, but he feared the sectarian rivalry that developed when one or more denomination benefited from government. However, although he advocated nonsectarian education he did not favour strictly secular education, or "godless" schools. Specific denominational positions should not, he felt, be taught in public schools, but he believed that the Bible should be used in classes, the Lord's Prayer should be recited, and moral training based on general Christianity should be provided.

He described himself as a strong supporter of reforms "for the moral and intellectual improvement of the people," regardless of whether or not the reforms were popular causes. Not only did he campaign for responsible government and for educational improvements, he also provided steady support for the temperance and the sabbatarian causes, the Bible Society, and the Young Men's Christian Association and assisted in the establishment of Presbyterian churches throughout the province. He went against prevailing opinion when in 1885 he introduced a bill to grant the franchise to women because of their "support of morality." The legislature defeated his motion, but each year thereafter until his death he reintroduced it.

Robson did not, however, challenge the prevailing views of Chinese immigration and often joined in the calls for restrictions on the admission of Chinese into the province. His language, however, was often more moderate than that of many, and his rationale did not seem to be based on a hatred of other races, as was often the case. His fear was that the coolie system of labour, under which many Chinese entered B.C., was not only unfair to the Chinese but endangered the standard of living of white working men and their families. He, along with many, believed that workers in the province should become bona fide settlers, support families, and contribute to the local economy, rather than saving money for a return to their homeland.

In the late 1860s, the colony of B.C. was forced to decide its destiny. Robson had earlier stated his belief that all the colonies of British North America should federate, and he continued to advocate that position against those who desired to remain a colony of the British Empire and those who sought annexation by the United States. His editorials and eloquent speeches are credited as a major factor in the colony becoming part of the Dominion of Canada in 1871.

Robson's career in the provincial legislature began in 1866 and lasted, with two breaks totalling eight years, until his death in 1892. He served as the provincial secretary, which included education, and, successively, as the minister of finance, of agriculture, and of mines. He became premier in 1889 upon the death of Premier A. E. B. Davie and was serving in that post when he died. His administration is noted for good relations with the federal government, an unsuccessful attempt to establish a provincial university, the encouragement of railway development, and reforms in land and resource granting policies. Robson strongly opposed the prevailing practice of alienating vast tracts of provincial lands and resources by means of grants to speculators. His efforts in these regards led one writer to observe that he was "the single reformer in a dreary fifteen-year period of provincial politics."

Robson's accomplishments as a reformer and a politician are not as well known as they deserve to be, perhaps because of his untimely death in 1892 after only three years as premier. He died of blood poisoning following a minor injury to his hand while on business in London. According to one historian, he was "one of the most influential British Columbians of his time."

Sir Edmund Wyly Grier (1862–1957)
Portrait of William Holmes Howland
1900, oil on canvas, 162.5 x 112.0 cm
Courtesy: Collection of the City of Toronto

William Howland

1844–1893

"He chose the more lowly, and more Christ-like place."

Peter Bush

There are times when the inhabitants of a city decide to improve it. Such was the year 1886 in Toronto, when William Holmes Howland was elected mayor on a platform of righteousness. Throughout the campaign, Howland urged voters, "Let us keep the city, a God-fearing city, and I would rather see it thus than the greatest and richest city in the continent."

Howland was born in 1844 into a prosperous family; his father became the first lieutenant governor of Ontario in 1867. William was educated at Upper Canada College and entered the family business at age sixteen. By twenty-nine he was the youngest insurance company president in Canada. He was one of Toronto's leading young business executives and served as the president of the Toronto Board of Trade and later as a spokesperson for the Ontario Manufacturers' Association.

While in England in 1876 he was unsettled by a wall plaque that read, Fear not: for I have redeemed thee, thou art mine (Isaiah 43:1). The verse haunted him. Upon returning to Canada, Howland found Toronto amid a revival centered on the ministry of Anglican evangelist William Rainsford. Through Rainsford, Howland was converted from his nominal Anglicanism to a vibrant evangelical faith.

Howland began to channel the ability and energy that had led him to prominence in the business community into work among the needy. It is safe to say that Howland had a part in virtually every philanthropic and relief enterprise in the Toronto of that time. Howland worked hard on behalf of the poor—particularly children—in the lower St. John's ward of Toronto, the most impoverished part of town. His experiences there transformed his perceptions of humanity. He learned of the evils of alcohol abuse. He discovered that the underclasses of Toronto did not feel welcome in the city's fine churches.

Not one to just observe a problem, Howland was also a man of purpose. He founded the Toronto Mission Union, which ministered to the needs of the poor, the hungry, and the abused through its inner-city mission centres. He also founded the Christian Missionary Union, an evangelistic effort that sought to reach those Torontonians who would not normally attend the city's more traditional churches.

In late 1885, a group of reformers in Toronto, made up of prohibitionists, union leaders, and those concerned about the poor, urged Howland to run for mayor. Although winning seemed impossible, he ran as an independent against the Tory party machine. Helped by the vote of landowning women—voting for the first time in a municipal election—Howland won a surprisingly easy victory.

Once in office, however, he realized that it was not going to be as easy to achieve the desired reforms, as he did not have a reform majority among the city councillors. Undaunted, Howland put a twelve-foot banner on his office wall: Except the Lord keep the city, the watchman waketh but in vain (Psalm 127:1). This was to be his guiding light through the next two tumultuous years.

Howland left his mark on Toronto in many areas, particularly in environmental issues. He began by enforcing tough rules in the areas of sanitation and public health. He instituted regulations requiring the cleanup of lands used for slaughterhouses and factories. The Don River was cleaned up, and significant attempts were made to supply safe drinking water to a rapidly expanding city. He also encouraged the development of suburbs so that working-class people could get out of the squalor and pollution of the inner city.

In addition, Howland challenged the large monopolies and business cartels that dealt with the city, forcing them to become responsible in their business dealings. He supported the employees of the Toronto Street Railway when their unreasonable and powerful employer locked them out. And through a judicial commission Howland was able to end the monopoly that an elite group of Toronto coal merchants had enjoyed for years by prosecuting city employees and coal merchants for kickbacks and for the embezzlement of city funds.

Through Howland's reform in the area of public morality, Toronto received its well-known nickname, Toronto the Good. Staff Inspector David Archibald was appointed by Howland to head a special police squad whose task was to "combat cruelty to animals, women, and children, and to oppose gambling, prostitution, Sabbath-breaking, and unlicensed drinking." This unique squad initiated the closure of brothels, prosecuted the operators of illegal drinking establishments, and reduced by a third the number of licensed saloons. It also introduced programs to curb the abuse of women and children. These were tangible manifestations of Howland's desire to serve the people of Toronto.

Howland, though, did not stop here. He managed, against old-guard resistance, to launch public works for the unemployed and to interest investors in good working-class housing, and he personally spearheaded the drive to create the Mimico Reformatory for Boys, removing youngsters from the horrors of the Don Jail. He failed utterly, however, when he tried to create a hospital for dipsomaniacs; alcoholism—righteous citizens felt—was either a shame to be hidden or a crime to be punished.

Administratively, Howland implemented a new management system in the mayor's office. Until then, councillors had controlled the direction of the city with parochial ward interests, a situation that led to a fragmented approach to city government. With Howland's election, a new type of mayoralty was born, a mayoralty for the whole city. After Howland, the mayors of Toronto were expected to have a vision for the entire city.

Howland did not run for mayor in 1888. He choose instead to return to his involvement with charity work and the Christian Alliance (later the Christian and Missionary Alliance), of which he was Canadian president from 1889 until his death.

Howland died in 1893 of pneumonia. Toronto mourned, for it had lost one of its finest citizens. Poet Eliza Wills wrote a poem to express the sense of loss the city felt:

"In thousand hearts are planted deep,
Forget-me-nots of loving deeds,
Springing from broadcast scattered seeds,
To blossom while he rests in sleep."

Howland was further eulogized as someone who "chose the more lowly, and more Christ-like place of feeding the hungry, visiting the sick, going amongst the hospitals and the prisons, and following in the very steps of the Lord himself."

Jane Woodill Wilson
Colourization of black and white photograph
Courtesy: Betty Ward
Photographer: A. E. McCollun

inset: Courtesy of Betty Ward

Jane Wilson

1824–1893

"Full of the Holy Ghost and of faith."

Elizabeth Gillan Muir

Many young women in Methodist denominations became deeply involved in religion in their teens after a radical conversion. Jane Woodill Wilson was one of these. By the time she was eighteen years old she was preaching on the Etobicoke Circuit west of Toronto. Her denomination, the Primitive Methodists, was one of the few that permitted women to preach. As a single female itinerant, she would have been paid the equivalent of forty dollars a year, about half of what a male itinerant earned and approximately one-third of a farm labourer's wage at that time.

Jane was born on a pioneer farm north of Toronto in February 1824. Her parents, Robert Woodill and Mary Pickering, had only recently emigrated from England. Robert was a zealous Ranter, or Primitive Methodist, and served as a preacher and the local postmaster. He passed on his disciplined lifestyle and religious enthusiasm to Jane.

In December 1849, Jane married a first cousin, Isaac Wilson, who had settled in the area. He, too, had begun to preach soon after his conversion at age seventeen. Jane and Isaac were a popular ministerial couple. It is reported that churches and gatherings were always packed when they preached. Some even said that Jane was intellectually "superior" to her husband and that he did "half as much preaching" as she did.

They were supportive of each other's ministries. Often when Jane was away preaching, Isaac kept their youngest child in the Sunday school class that he taught. Jane and Isaac travelled long distances on circuits; Jane thought nothing of riding thirty miles and of preaching two or three times on Sunday. She rode a spotted Spanish horse called Toby that achieved certain notoriety. When Jane rode him, he was as gentle as a kitten. But every time Isaac tried to ride him, Toby ran away.

Jane's home was a haven for other ministers, and she became known in the community as Mother Wilson. She had a reputation as a good nurse and was often called on to care for the sick. Once, when a local family fell ill with scarlet fever, Jane was the only person who would help out. She changed her clothes in the woodshed after each visit to prevent the spread of germs. Some time later, a local Wesleyan Methodist Church asked to join with the Wilson's Primitive Methodist Church; Jane's care of this family when they were ill was said to have been partly responsible for that unusual union.

Much of Jane and Isaac's ministry was in the Salem Church north of Tullamore, near present-day Toronto. They began the first Methodist class in their kitchen, but such large revivals took place that a log church was built. By 1862, this had been replaced by a small but substantial stone church building. The stone came from their property.

In the 1840s and 1850s, the Bible Christian movement was at its height in the Cobourg-Peterborough area. New chapels were being built, and the churches were rapidly paying off their debts. Jane preached inaugural sermons; laid cornerstones; and conducted love feasts, prayer meetings, field meetings, ticket meetings, and services indoors and out. Camp meetings were popular.

Jane had four daughters and one son, but she managed to maintain a preaching career. She was financially more secure than some other Primitive Methodist workers: the Wilson's could afford to have a maid at home; they gave generous donations to the church, even offering money to a competing Methodist society for the repair of its church roof; and they increased the size of their farm. They were socially well connected and were related to "Squire" Woodill, a close friend and fishing and hunting companion of politician D'Arcy McGee and publisher GEORGE BROWN.

Yet, Jane retained a simple lifestyle and wore plain clothes. She dressed in grey, brown, or black and preached wearing a bonnet without decorative flowers. Plain dress was recommended for all Primitive Methodists, but required for preachers. Like the other early Methodist societies, the Primitive Methodists demanded a hardworking, sober existence and serious conversation. Attending worldly amusements and public houses was forbidden, as was dishonesty. Itinerants, such as the Wilsons, had to keep and submit journals regularly.

The Woodills and Wilsons refrained from drinking alcoholic beverages. There is a story that when Jane's father and her husband held a barn raising, Jane served only coffee and sandwiches, much to the amusement of some of the neighbours. Generally, more time was spent drinking at these bees than working. The Woodill's barn, however, went up in record time and earned the designation "the temperance barn."

By the 1860s, the Primitive Methodist societies were becoming institutionalized and hierarchical. Camp meetings gave way to regulated theological study. A book room and a newspaper were established. Lay workers became subordinate to ministerial personnel. What women could and could not do was hotly debated in the Primitive Methodist *Christian Journal*, and an exegesis of a biblical passage about women's relationship to men described the position of women as one of "curiously subordinated equality."

Some of the male preachers would not accept women in a preaching role. R. L. Tucker, a Primitive Methodist preacher and the son-in-law of a female minister, claimed that "female preachers" often lacked "meekness, charity and domestic qualities." He wrote that it could be useful for a woman to be "public" occasionally as long as she could "blend" this with a domestic life and a "meek and quiet spirit."

As this shift took place, there was a noticeable decrease in Jane's preaching appointments. She was more likely to be asked to be a guest preacher on special occasions than to be a regular preacher. However, she was remembered fondly in her denomination for her work and her spiritual depth.

After her death, a plaque was erected in the stone church on their farm. It bore the inscription: "Sacred to the memory of a beloved mother Jane Wilson who was for forty years teacher preacher and class leader in this church. Born in little York, now Toronto February 20, 1824. Fell asleep in Jesus July 17, 1893. She was truly a Mother in Israel being full of the Holy Ghost and of faith."

John Innes (1863–1941)
Detail of *Governor Douglas Takes Oath at Ft. Langley*
oil on canvas, 148.9 x 205.7 cm
Courtesy: Native Sons of B.C. and Simon Fraser University
Photographer: I. M. C. Simon Fraser University

inset: B.C. Archives / E-07841

Matthew Begbie

1819–1894

"God, be merciful to me a sinner."

David R. Williams

Sir Matthew Baillie Begbie was a tall, strong man with a restless streak. As a lawyer in London, he longed for a life of adventure. He was delighted when, in 1858, he became British Columbia's top jurist. Begbie was described by a miner as "the biggest man, the smartest man, the best-looking man, and the damnedest man that ever came over the Cariboo Road." Although he is often and undeservedly referred to as the hanging judge, Begbie strove to incorporate the sanctity of his legal decisions with biblical principles.

Begbie was of Scottish descent. He was born on a British ship at the Cape of Good Hope in 1819. He was educated in the Channel Islands and at Cambridge and practised law in London before his appointment as the first high court judge of the newly constituted colony of British Columbia. Begbie's assignment was a response to the discovery of gold on the Fraser River in 1857 and to the subsequent influx of tens of thousands of gold seekers.

Begbie arrived in British Columbia in November 1858, bringing with him the proclamation of his own position and another naming James Douglas as B.C.'s first governor. In 1866, British Columbia joined with the then separate colony of Vancouver Island, and in 1871, upon the united colony entering Confederation, Begbie became chief justice of the new province, a position that he held until his death in Victoria in 1894.

Begbie visited the most remote areas of the colony to hold court in mining camps and small settlements. He often travelled by horseback and lived under canvas, revelling in the outdoor life. By the force of his personality, he left no doubt in the minds of those whom he encountered in rough surroundings that the full majesty of British law had come among them. As a consequence, widespread frontier violence never occurred in the fledgling colony, and any thoughts that the colony might join the United States were banished.

As chief justice of the new province, Begbie shaped the development of its legal system, bringing to the task the resolute will exhibited in the colonial period. He was impelled by a strong sense of duty to do right and was determined to uphold the queen's law. Yet, he was also sympathetic to the native and Chinese minorities and frequently took the side of the little man in legal disputes. In 1872, he committed four Indians convicted of attempted murder (for which the death penalty could have been imposed) to the custody of the Indian mission at Metlakatla, operated by WILLIAM DUNCAN, whom Begbie much admired.

An establishment figure, Begbie did not fit the mould of relentless Victorian judicial figures—though he could be stern—who so often took no account of the frailties and weaknesses of human nature.

Begbie was a staunch churchman—a devoted member of the Church of England all his life. He was thoroughly familiar with the King James Bible and with the Book of Common Prayer, passages from which often appeared in his legal decisions. During his travels through colonial British Columbia, he attended services at frontier churches from Barkerville to Yale. When no church was available, he would often read the evening service to companions gathered around a campfire. In 1870, Begbie moved from New Westminster and took up a settled existence in Victoria. He became a parishioner of St. John the Evangelist, the old iron church of Victoria, where he sang in the choir for many years.

Begbie was resolute in his belief that Christianity was an essential element of English common law. In 1874, he heard a celebrated ecclesiastical case involving the Anglican bishop of British Columbia, George Hills, who went to court for an injunction to prevent his former dean, Reverend Edward Cridge, from conducting services. The conflict arose over the much-debated question of ritualism and liturgical services, which Hills favoured. Cridge contended that Hills was a heretic because of his high church, or ritualistic, views. Refusing to give up his ministry, Cridge would not even allow the bishop into the cathedral to conduct a service. Hills went to the law, and Begbie, in a masterly judgement, castigated the dean and vindicated the bishop.

In a passage typical of his judicial style, Begbie declared: "The plaintiff [Hills] has his spiritual authority derived from the imposition of hands, which, though vague … can never be treated by any churchman as less solemn on that account but rather as all the more impressive. He is sent out here by all the authority of the Crown and of the Church, not to be taught, but to teach Orthodoxy, not to be reviled, but to reprove error, and to receive all due obedience from the members of the Church of England here."

Contrary to folklore, Begbie never carried out, or assisted at, an execution—it would have been totally out of character for him to do so. Moreover, it is doubtful if he stood by or witnessed one, even though many criminals whom he had sentenced to be hanged were publicly executed. The only close friend of Begbie to have written on this aspect of his character, Canon Arthur Beanlands, recalled Begbie's revulsion at the taking of human life, even that of a murderer. The phrase "painful duty" aptly portrayed Begbie's feelings when sentencing unfortunate prisoners to death.

During the last two decades of his life, Begbie diligently presided over civil litigation and constitutional disputes between the province and Ottawa. He also became something of a social lion in Victoria, particularly after receiving his knighthood in 1875. He entertained and was entertained widely and pioneered the game of lawn tennis in Victoria on three fine grass courts surrounding his spacious home. He enjoyed good food and wines, he was gregarious and he sang Italian opera well and often gave concerts in Victoria.

In 1893, he fell ill with what proved to be incurable cancer. Refusing surgery and drugs that might have clouded his mind, he soldiered on until, too weak even to sit, he was confined to his bed. He was carried to his church for his last public Communion service early in June 1894 and took Communion for the final time, in his home, a week later, two days before his death. Begbie was accorded a public funeral with a large procession through the streets of Victoria. On his dignified tombstone is carved the inscription he chose: God, be Merciful to Me a Sinner (Luke 18:13).

Robert Harris (1849–1919)
Hon. Sir Samuel Leonard Tilley
oil on canvas, 167.2 x 142.3 cm
Courtesy: New Brunswick Legislative Assembly Collection with permission from the Hon. Danny Gay, Speaker
Photographer: Tom Kerr

inset: William James Topley / National Archives of Canada / PA-12632

He Shall Have Dominion
Leonard Tilley

1818–1896

"His memory will live, not only in the hearts of all his countrymen,
but enshrined in the history . . . of the great Dominion
which he did so much to create, and which he so fondly loved."

Michael Clarke

Leonard Tilley was an affluent New Brunswick apothecary and temperance advocate who became premier and led his province into Confederation. In fact, it was Tilley, inspired by reading Psalm 72, who suggested the title Dominion of Canada.

Tilley was born in 1818 in Gagetown, New Brunswick. He was the son of a storekeeper and one of eight children. At thirteen, he apprenticed as a druggist, becoming a certified pharmacist in 1838. Success in business made him one of Gagetown's wealthiest citizens by the time he entered politics.

At twenty-one, Tilley heard a sermon of the Reverend William Harrison that moved him to make what he described as a "new departure." He immersed himself in the Bible and committed himself to God. His evangelical beliefs emphasized biblical faith with a social conscience and provided the framework for his life. He became a devoted member of the Church of England, teaching Sunday school and becoming a churchwarden, and was also a member of the Saint John's Religious Tract Society and a life member of the British and Foreign Bible Society.

Tilley entered public life partly as an extension of his involvement with the temperance movement. The brutal murder of a local woman by her drunken husband haunted him. Hearing the couple's young daughter's cries, he had rushed to the scene. What he saw remained with him: "There lay the mother withering in her blood, her little children crying around her, and the husband and father under arrest for murder, and rum the cause of it all." When the first New Brunswick branch of the Sons of Temperance opened in 1847, Tilley was named to its executive council.

In 1848, Tilley's strong temperance advocacy led to his election to municipal government in St. John. Two years later, in 1850, he was elected to the provincial legislature as a Liberal.

In 1855, Tilley introduced the Prohibition Bill as a private member. It included "the arbitrary arrest, imprisonment and the incarceration of intoxicated people until they revealed their source supply." It also proved to be the most controversial legislation of his career. When it came into effect in 1856, Tilley found the act and himself under continuous assault. Burned in effigy, his house attacked, his life threatened, he never flinched in defense of the legislation.

In 1857, Tilley was appointed provincial secretary. Seven years later, he became the premier of New Brunswick. Tilley thus stood at the helm of the province's political destiny during those crucial years when Confederation moved from dream to reality.

The move to unite the Canadian provinces was the most notable change within the British Empire since the American Declaration of Independence. Tilley realized that the time had come for the British possessions of North America to either join forces politically or else fall, one by one, to the influence of the United States. In 1864, the political leaders of the four Maritime colonies arranged a meeting in Charlottetown. When the delegates from Upper and Lower Canada arrived—after having requested an invitation—the dimensions of the issues changed, and everyone agreed to continue discussions in Quebec later in the year. At the Quebec Conference, Newfoundland and Prince Edward Island opted out, but Tilley and Charles Tupper—who headed the Nova Scotia delegation—accepted Confederation. Together with the Canadian delegates, they worked out a formula for presentation to Britain.

Tilley's enthusiasm, however, was not shared by all his constituents. When he called an election in 1865 for a mandate to continue negotiations, his party was narrowly defeated. Confederation and Tilley's career were threatened. New Brunswick was an essential link in the union, and Tilley had staked everything on its joining. Fortunately, another election was called in 1866, and with the Fenian raids creating fear of a possible American invasion, Tilley and his Liberals were returned to power.

In December 1866, the Westminster Conference finalized the details of the British North America Act, which Tilley helped to write. Tilley's best-known contribution, though, came when discussing a name for the new union. A letter written by Tilley's son describes how the Dominion of Canada came into being:

> When the fathers of Confederation were assembled discussing the terms and conditions of Confederation and the drafting of the British North America Act there had been considerable discussion the day before and many suggestions as to what the new United Canada should be called, and no conclusion had been reached. The discussion on the name stood over until the next day. The next morning, as was Sir Leonard's custom, he read a chapter from the Bible, and that particular morning he read Psalm Seventy-two. When reading verse eight of the said Psalm—He shall have Dominion also from sea to sea—the thought occurred to him, what a splendid name to give Canada. When he went back to the sitting of the convention that morning he suggested the word "Dominion," which was agreed to, and Canada was called the "Dominion of Canada."

> A letter signed by John A. Macdonald explained to Queen Victoria that the name was "a tribute to the principles they earnestly desired to uphold."

> When the British North America Act came into force by royal proclamation on July 1, 1867, Macdonald was the first to lay his hand upon a Bible and be sworn in as a member of the Privy Council, followed by George-Étienne Cartier. Tilley was next, and he became the minister of customs in Canada's inaugural federal government.

> Tilley's impeccable character and reputation remained intact even when others around him fell. When charges of corruption were brought against Macdonald's government in connection with the Canadian Pacific Railway, Tilley was not among the guilty. Prior to that government's resignation in 1873, the fifty-five-year-old Tilley was thus appointed the lieutenant governor of New Brunswick.

In summer 1878, Tilley resigned his provincial post to reenter federal politics. When Macdonald defeated Alexander Mackenzie, Tilley was named the minister of finance.

Queen Victoria made Tilley a Knight Commander of the Order of St. Michael and St. George in 1879. In 1885, amid failing health, he received yet another honour by once again being appointed New Brunswick's lieutenant governor, a position that he filled for the next eight years.

Sir Leonard Tilley, aged seventy-eight, died in June 1896 from blood poisoning received through a minor cut. One of his last wishes was that a plain tombstone be erected to his memory with the inscription "His trust was in Jesus." Tilley hoped that "passers-by might be helped in their earthly pilgrimage."

Tilley's rector paid him homage at his funeral, saying, "His heart went out in sympathy and brotherly recognition to all who loved the Lord in sincerity. And the reason ... was in the reality of his Christianity. For him it was a real thing." Even the *Telegraph*, a St. John paper that had been politically opposed to Tilley for many years, stated: "His memory will live, not only in the hearts of all his countrymen, but enshrined in the history of this his native province, and of the great Dominion which he did so much to create, and which he so fondly loved."

G. M. Leskey (unknown)
Mrs. Letitia Youmans
pastel, 80 x 60 cm
Courtesy: The Woman's Christian Temperance Union, Archives
Photographer: Steve Boyko

inset: Courtesy of the Christian Temperance Union Archives

Temperance Crusader
Letitia Youmans

1827–1896

"Devoted to work, family, and religion."

Terry Crowley

Letitia (Creighton) Youmans emerged as one of Canada's foremost female reformers and advocates of temperance in the late nineteenth century. She was born in a log cabin in 1827 on a farm several kilometres from Cobourg in Upper Canada, and her early life was devoted to work, family, and religion. At the age of forty-seven, however, she assumed a prominent public role by advocating the prohibition of alcoholic beverages. Her leadership qualities and her ability to inspire were critical to the emergence of women as a collective social force through the Woman's Christian Temperance Union (WCTU).

Letitia was raised in the Methodist Church and acquired a love of learning and a devout adherence to evangelical Christianity from her Irish and American immigrant parents. She was schooled at the Cobourg Ladies Academy and, when it closed, at the Burlington Ladies Seminary, where she was involved in many extracurricular activities and was eventually hired to teach English after graduating. Letitia then moved on to become an assistant at the Picton Academy. During this time, she met Arthur Youmans, a farmer and miller and father of eight, whom she married in August 1850. She educated her eight stepchildren at home.

A bad business transaction forced the couple to sell their rural property and to move into Picton, where Letitia began teaching Sunday school at the local Methodist Church. There, she saw the afflictions families suffered as a result of cheap, tax-free alcohol. This caused her to organize the Band of Hope, which, following a British practice begun in 1847, educated children against drinking. When some Methodists raised objections to using their building for this purpose, she abandoned the church for a local hall, where over one hundred children attended.

In 1874, a visit to the newly established summer camp of Christian educationalists at Chautauqua, New York, changed Letitia's life. Americans were enthusiastic about the WCTU, established that year, so when she returned to Picton Letitia formed a union in the town's Methodist church. Restricting the sale of alcoholic beverages and ending retail liquor licensing through local option became the priorities of the Picton WCTU.

Female temperance advocates quickly advanced to centre stage, as their involvement in this contentious political issue challenged the prevailing view that restricted a woman's influence to home and family. Because the Liberal Party was more favourable to temperance than John A. Macdonald's Conservatives, women associated with the temperance movement were usually accused of being "Liberal dupes." Although a libel suit was brought against the ever-crusading Letitia in 1875, however, local option was secured in Prince Edward County by a majority of six hundred votes, and the court action was dropped.

Two years later, a second vote failed, and the retail sale of liquor resumed. The WCTU felt the need for larger organizational resources if it was to be effective. In 1877, the Ontario WCTU was formed, and Letitia emerged as a seasoned campaigner able to give inspirational speeches on behalf of women and children. She was elected the union's first president and adopted a white ribbon as the WCTU symbol.

Letitia excelled at the podium, where she provided long addresses typical of nineteenth-century oratory. She was an advocate of prohibition and of temperance, and as the WCTU leader she based her critique of alcoholic beverages on social reality and biblical themes. She believed that liquor devastated families, caused financial and moral bankruptcy, and at times produced the abuse of women and children.

Letitia's speeches intertwined temperance themes with the Old Testament books of Esther and Nehemiah and proved very popular; she put a new spin on the biblical account of a woman saving her people. She declared the Bible "a complete compendium of the temperance question" and believed that the Scriptures taught total abstinence. So convinced was she of the rightness of her cause that she was able to tell prison inmates that they were "privileged to be in an environment free from the temptation."

By 1880, with Letitia as its foremost spokesperson and official organizer, the Ontario WCTU began to expand rapidly. When her husband died in 1882, Letitia resigned the presidency of an organization that had grown to include 2,500 members in ninety-six societies. The following year, the Dominion WCTU was created, and when it held its first annual meeting in 1885 Letitia was elected its president, giving her international recognition. Earlier, while speaking in the United States in 1876, Letitia provided American temperance worker Frances Willard with her rallying slogan, "Home protection." She also appeared before the Maryland Senate in 1880 and represented Canada at the British Woman's Temperance Association in 1883. Letitia purposefully created the WCTU in Canada to be different from other international models. More decentralized in structure, more consciously evangelical in ethic, and less inclined to fight legislative battles was her Canadian way.

Making her mark as a campaigner and a speaker, Letitia was deeply involved in the drive to obtain local prohibition under the 1878 Canada Temperance Act. She took her message across Canada and formed the first WCTU in Quebec in 1883. In that same year, she also met Sir John A. Macdonald, who asked her to explain how it was that her home county had voted out local option. "Lack of enforcement by the government," she replied. Letitia then questioned the prime minister on when he was going to implement prohibition. "Just as soon as men are sent to Parliament who will pass the law," responded Macdonald shrewdly.

Letitia was not an advocate of women's suffrage, although many of the women schooled in the WCTU espoused that position. Single-minded in her fight against alcohol consumption, she did not want other issues to sidetrack it, though she did vote in 1885 when Ontario granted the franchise to property-owning women. While she was active, the WCTU moved along four lines to achieve its goals: political channels to influence legislation; educational activities in schools; religious activities, such as prayer days and temperance revivals; and social and philanthropic initiatives.

By the time Letitia was named honourary president of the Dominion WCTU in 1889, all of the counties that had previously approved prohibition had voted it out. The woman who had inspired others to carry on found herself increasingly debilitated by inflammatory rheumatism in her last years. Letitia died in penury in Toronto, but the WCTU continued to work for human betterment and eventually saw much greater success.

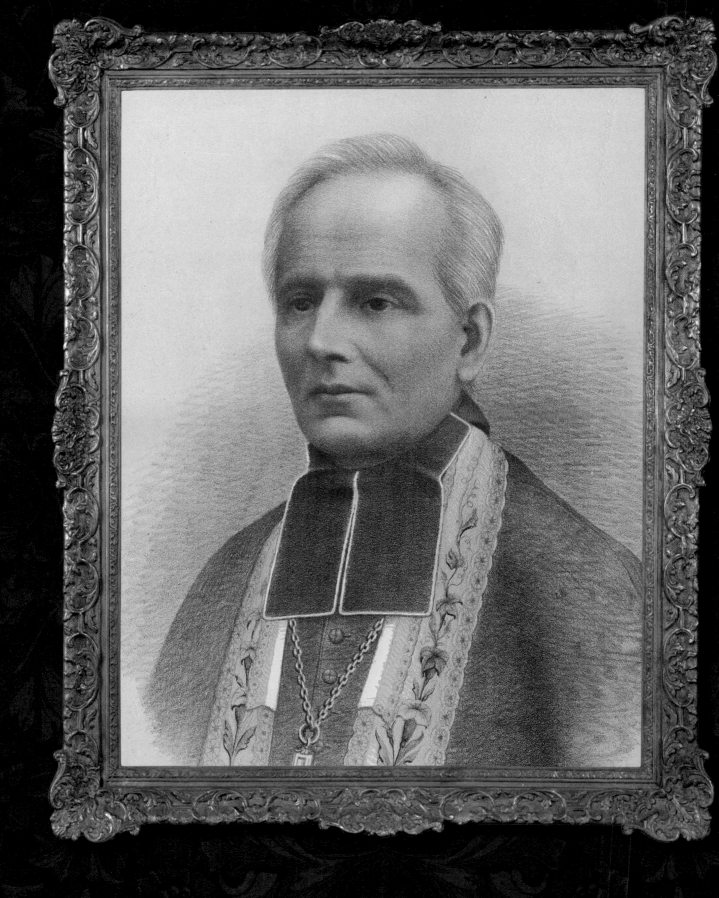

J.A. Rho (1835–1905)
Mgr. Louis–François Laflèche
Lithograph, 35.5 x 26.2 cm
Courtesy: l'Évêché de Trois-Rivières

inset: Fonds Thomas Chapais / Archives nationales du Québec à Québec / photographe: P.F. Pinsonneault

Louis-François Laflèche

1818–1898

"Saving our nation depends, no less than that of our souls, on our constant, unyielding adherence to Catholicism."

Preston Jones

During the eighty years from his birth in Lower Canada's Sainte-Anne-de-la-Pérade to his death in Trois-Rivières, Quebec, Louis-François Laflèche was, variously, a capable student, a Roman Catholic priest, a missionary, a political activist, an educator, an author, and the second bishop of Trois-Rivières. Best known as one of nineteenth-century Quebec's most combative proponents of ultramontanism (supremacy of papal over national or diocesan authority in the Roman Catholic church), Laflèche is also remembered as among the most eloquent proponents of what he termed "the providential mission of the French Canadians."

For Laflèche, and for other Québecois clergy and intellectuals until well into the twentieth century, the belief that God had assigned the French in Canada with a special, religious task was a truth at the core of life. The French-Canadian mission, they thought, was to preserve the Catholic faith, which many in France had abandoned in the late eighteenth century. Like the faithful on Noah's ark who were saved from a global deluge, Laflèche declared in 1866, true Roman Catholicism had been preserved in Canada. For Laflèche, guarding that faith was French Canada's first purpose.

Laflèche did not hesitate to state his views. During the federal election campaign of 1896, he publicly denounced Sir Wilfrid Laurier, just as he had denounced many other Liberals in earlier decades, for promoting ideas that in his view were born of revolution and the Enlightenment— ideas he thought to be at odds with traditional Catholic teaching.

Unlike some of the independently minded French-Canadian intellectuals of an earlier generation, including his grandfather, Laflèche was deeply conservative. In 1868, for example, he supported sending some 135 French-Canadian infantrymen to fight against Italian nationalists who wished to end the Pope's temporal control of pontifical states. He also took pleasure in the papal decree of infallibility at the first Vatican Council in 1870. And though he had spent many years as a missionary in the British North American northwest he emphatically discouraged French Canadians from seeking a better life in the west or in the United States. Laflèche urged Québecois to retain their God-given French-Canadian birthright. Knowing that many French Canadians who had left Quebec were being assimilated into English-speaking North America, in 1880 Laflèche counselled his compatriots to put the kingdom of God first and their material needs would be met. If French Canadians remained true to their providentially ordained calling to be a French-speaking Catholic light to the world, God would see to their earthly needs.

Laflèche was sure that the materialism he saw in English-speaking North America was a threat to Quebec's French-speaking Catholic population. So, too, was he certain of the threat from Protestantism, which he believed promoted individualism and, eventually, social disorder and anarchy. Not surprisingly, the Protestant Bible societies seeking to put the Scriptures into Québecois' hands were counted among Laflèche's many opponents.

Although Laflèche was opposed to allowing laymen to read the Bible unaided by trained teachers, he was biblically literate. He deepened his theological knowledge by reading Abbé René-François Rohrbacher's *L'histoire universelle de l'église catholique* (General History of the Catholic Church). Laflèche later quipped, "As for me, I have learned all my theology from *L'histoire*, and I am convinced that you will not learn anything more at the college in Rome."

Biblical texts informed Laflèche's public discourse. "[T]here is more than one point of resemblance between the ancient history of this people [the Hebrews] and our own," he wrote in his influential collection of essays *Quelques considérations sur les rapports de la société civile avec la religion et la famille* (Some Thoughts on Civil Society's Relationship with Religion and the Family) published in 1866. Comparing Jacques Cartier's claim on the New World to that of Abraham's on the Promised Land, he drew attention to the role of Providence. Like the Hebrews of old, Laflèche pointed out, French Canadians had a choice: either accept and remain faithful to their divine mission and form the center of Roman Catholicism in the New World, or squander their heritage. For Laflèche, there was no middle ground.

There is no doubt that Laflèche was a French-Canadian nationalist. He is reported to have said once that he hoped sections of New England, where large numbers of French Canadians resided, would one day annex themselves to Quebec. Yet he consistently preached loyalty to the British crown. French Canadians, he said, had enjoyed "deep peace ... under the shelter of the British flag while the violent storm of the French Revolution was raging." And his enthusiasm for Confederation in 1867, although based on a belief that it would afford French Canadians greater self-determination than previously, stands out in comparison with the reluctant acceptance of it by his ultramontane mentor, Bishop Ignace Bourget of Montreal.

Laflèche has been often scorned in recent decades for his admonitions to strict obedience to Roman Catholicism; for his political campaigns against liberal thinkers and the Liberal Party (he declared on more than one occasion that it was a sin to vote Liberal); and for his skirmishes with other conservative Catholics whom he perceived to be soft on modernism and its ills. But while the high-strung Laflèche surely went out of polite bounds on occasion, there can be no doubt that he was committed to his fellow French Canadians, his language, and his church.

During his twenty-seven years as bishop, Laflèche was devoted to his people, and they to him. His door was always open, especially to the poor, to whom he distributed the little money that came into his hands. A familiar figure in Trois-Rivières, he was equally well known to people throughout the diocese, whom he met on frequent visits and whose problems he knew and made his own.

Laflèche's vision for Quebec—informed by his sincere commitment to Roman Catholicism—provided generations of French-speaking Quebecers with a context for their lives. "Saving our nation depends, no less than that of our souls, on our constant, unyielding adherence to Catholicism," he said. Only since the 1960s, when Quebecers abandoned the Catholic Church en masse, has an alternate vision for Quebec been presented on a large scale. Time will tell which vision for French-Canadian nationalism will prove more lasting.

Robert Harris (1849–1919)
Sir William Dawson
1889, oil on canvas, 74.9 x 59.1 cm
Courtesy: Visual Arts Collection, McGill University, Montreal
Photographer: Robert Rohonczy

inset: National Archives of Canada / C-49822

A Defender of Creation
William Dawson
1820–1899

"O God, thou hast taught me from my youth:
and hitherto have I declared thy wondrous works."

Michael Clarke

Sir John William Dawson was a geologist of international acclaim who gained worldwide attention as one of the first opponents of Charles Darwin's evolutionary theories. Dawson's sense of religious and scientific calling produced a missionary zeal to conquer evolution, which he qualified as crass materialism and atheism. As an educator, he served as the superintendent of education in Nova Scotia and as McGill University's principal for almost forty years.

Dawson was born in 1820 in Pictou, Nova Scotia. His parents were Scottish Presbyterian immigrants who raised him in a devout Christian faith. At fifteen, Dawson enrolled in Pictou Academy, where, under the tutelage of the Reverend Dr. Thomas McCulloch—later to become the first principal of Dalhousie College in Halifax—his faith and his intellect were strengthened. At sixteen, Dawson delivered his first scientific lecture at the Pictou Natural History Society. Never short on ambition, he entitled it *On the Structure and History of the World*. He graduated with a solid foundation of Latin and Greek, a working knowledge of Hebrew, and a grounding in physics and biology. In 1840, Dawson travelled to the land of his forefathers and enrolled at the University of Edinburgh to study geology. After completing his studies, he returned to Nova Scotia, in 1847, as "the first trained geologist in British North America."

Joseph Howe—who later became Nova Scotia's premier in 1860—was impressed when he heard Dawson give a lecture series and asked him to become the colony's first superintendent of education. From 1850 to 1853, Dawson laid the foundation for education in Nova Scotia. He visited over five hundred schools at a time when there were no railways and authored *The Journal of Education for Nova Scotia*, a manual that standardized teaching methods. He initiated curricula development and the construction of new schools. Dawson also recommended that a teaching college be established to ensure that qualified instructors were teaching the province's children.

In 1855, Dawson received an offer from Montreal's McGill College to become its fifth principal. When Dawson began his tenure, McGill was on the verge of ruin—the college grounds were literally a cow pasture. Under Dawson's leadership, McGill would become a world-class university.

Dawson changed McGill's academic focus. He believed that the teaching of the natural and applied sciences—especially geology and paleontology—was foundational. In addition to his principalship, Dawson was a professor of chemistry; agriculture; and natural history, which included geology, zoology, and botany. He and his wife even planted trees and designed the grounds. Stephen Leacock, humourist and professor at McGill, recalled: "More than that of any one or group of men, McGill is *his* work."

Charles Darwin gave birth to evolutionary theory in 1859 when he published *On the Origin of Species*. A year later, Dawson reviewed that work in the *Canadian Naturalist and Geologist*, praising Darwin for his careful investigation of the nature and laws of variation within rock pigeons. However, Dawson was highly critical of Darwin's arguments concerning the fossil record. Unlike Darwin, Dawson believed steadfastly that nature was the result of a divine creator and that nature could not be mindless, random, and without plan. Dawson observed: "It [natural selection] proved insufficient to change one species into another." He argued that Darwin's belief in natural selection producing varieties and incipient species showed a "huge hiatus" in his reasoning. He argued that not only did Darwinism sweep away Christianity and natural religion, but that a populace imbued with "the doctrine of the struggle for existence" would cease to be human in any ethical sense, and must become brutes or devils or something between the two." In Dawson's opinion, Darwin had committed countless absurdities.

A voluminous writer, Dawson wrote more than four hundred books and articles, the majority focusing on origins. *The Story of the Earth and Man* (1872) went through eleven editions and stated unequivocally that humankind was created in the image of God.

Dawson placed Psalm 71:17 on the flyleaf of his autobiographical work, *Fifty Years of Work in Canada, Scientific and Educational*, (published posthumously), as a testimony of God's faithfulness in his life: O God, thou hast taught me from my youth: and hitherto have I declared thy wondrous works.

Even though those who shared his views were becoming fewer, he persisted in defending what for him was the pivotal issue: "the spiritual nature of man as the child of a divine creator."

In 1878, Dawson received a tempting invitation to become a professor of natural history at Princeton. Dawson declined the offer, citing his obligation to continue the battle for Protestant educational rights in Quebec. In return for staying at McGill, Dawson received an endowment from his friend Peter Redpath for the construction of a museum of natural history. Inaugurated in 1882, the Peter Redpath Museum dominates McGill's lower campus. Prominent in its entrance hall is an illuminated plaque citing Psalm 104:24: O Lord, how Manifold are Thy works! in wisdom hast thou made them all: the earth is full of thy riches.

While the principal of McGill, Dawson supported the higher education of women and instructed female students in their science classes. As a result of this pioneering effort, during the 1888 convocation eight young women received, for the first time at McGill, bachelor of arts degrees.

Dawson was knighted in 1884 and in the same year became the first president of the Royal Society of Canada. Dawson's highest tribute, however, came when peers within the scientific community chose him as the president of the American and the British Associations for the Advancement of Science. No one had ever served in this capacity on both sides of the Atlantic before.

Principal Dawson and his wife, Margaret, were devoted parents. Each morning, he read from the Bible and prayed with his wife and five children. He also served other children as a Sunday school teacher at Stanley Street Presbyterian Church in Montreal, of which he was a founding member. As a grandfather, he was fondly remembered offering coins to his grandchildren if they could quote scripture passages from memory.

Sir William Dawson died on November 19, 1899. The *Montreal Gazette* paid tribute to Dawson, reminding readers of his lifelong devotion to Jesus Christ and of his devotion to the Bible. He was laid to rest in the Mount Royal Cemetery. The epitaph on his tombstone reads: Blessed are the dead which die in the Lord that they may rest from their labours, and their works do follow them (Revelation 14:13).

Robert Harris (1849–1919)
Portrait of George Munro Grant
1889, oil on canvas, 75.6 x 61.0 cm
Courtesy: Queen's University, Kingston
Photographer: Bernard Clark

inset: National Archives of Canada / C-37819

A Principled Principal
George Monro Grant

1835–1902

*"Public policy should be honest, just, and in accordance
with the will and purpose of God."*

William Christian

George Monro Grant—Principal Grant of Queen's College as he universally came to be known—was a celebrated churchman and university administrator who is best remembered for his travel narrative *Ocean to Ocean*. Grant's father, James, left his home on the Scottish Highlands at age twenty-five and immigrated to Nova Scotia, where he became a local schoolmaster. George's mother, Mary Monro, was the daughter of a clergyman and "a woman who combined great practical sagacity with a deep Scottish piety." James expected that George, his eldest boy, would take over the family farm, but in 1843 young George seriously damaged his right hand, and it became apparent that he would be unable to engage in strenuous farm labour.

Thus, George attended Pictou Academy instead and was then sent to the University of Glasgow, where he graduated in theology in 1860. A clerical position in Glasgow was offered to him, but he felt the need to return to his native land. He was ordained and sent home as a missionary to Nova Scotia. Upon arriving, Grant found the local Presbyterians squabbling over sectarian and political matters, an experience that established religious unity as his lifelong goal. Just shortly before Confederation, he married Jessie Lawson, the eldest daughter of a prosperous Halifax family.

Grant soon demonstrated the organizational and fundraising skills for which he became legendary. By February 1862, he had already built St. Peter's Church just outside Charlottetown. Not only was it debt free, it was also able to pay the $750 minimum stipend for a minister. So obvious were Grant's talents that by the end of the year he received an unconditional and unanimous call from St. Matthew's Church in Halifax, the oldest and most distinguished dissenting church in the province.

The next year, he began an engagement with higher education that lasted the rest of his life. To counter the influence of King's College and the Anglican establishment, Nova Scotia's Presbyterians urged the colony's government to reorganize Dalhousie College into a non-denominational school. Grant promptly raised $4,000 to endow a chair of mathematics and was elected to the school's board of governors. Later, in 1877, he raised the enormous sum of $80,000 to endow Pine Hill Theological College.

Grant became increasingly active in public and denominational issues. From 1865 to 1867, he was—sometimes to the annoyance of his parishioners—an active advocate of the cause of Confederation. He even took on the celebrated journalist and politician Joseph Howe, whom he otherwise greatly admired and whose biography he was later to write. From 1868 to 1873, he was convenor of the home mission board and actively supported the union of the Church of Scotland in the maritime colonies. In 1875, he was one of the leaders of a national Presbyterian union, and he regularly defended liberal religious causes. Grant vigorously defended the Reverend D. J. Macdonell against attempts to drive him from the church on the grounds of an injudicious sermon he had preached in Toronto, even though Grant himself considered the sermon unwise.

In 1872, Grant was invited by Sandford Fleming to accompany him on a cross-Canada expedition to conduct the preliminary survey of the railroad that John A. Macdonald had agreed to build as the price of British Columbia's entry into Confederation. From this trip emerged Grant's best-known publication, his travel narrative *Ocean to Ocean*. He developed a strong admiration for many of the aboriginals he met along the route. "It is easy to understand how an Englishman, travelling for weeks together with an Indian guide, so often contracts a strong friendship for him; for the Indian qualities of patience, endurance, dignity and self-control, are the very ones to evoke friendship." Grant was one of the first Canadians to urge "liberal, and, if possible, permanent compensation" for native peoples.

On Sundays, Grant held a service. "We did not ask any of our men what denomination he was of, but took it for granted that he could join in common prayer, and hear with profit the simplest truths of Christianity." Once in British Columbia, he empathized with the plight of Chinese immigrants. Grant believed that it was unjust to allow the Chinese to work in unsafe conditions for poor wages, particularly as they were "repelled ... from us by systematic injustice and insult, and that when dead a Company may clear money by carrying their bodies back to their own land."

In 1877, Grant was invited to become the principal of a small Presbyterian college, known as Queen's, in Kingston, Ontario. Grant rose to the challenge and spent the next twenty-five years developing Queen's into a financially and academically sound institution. In 1883, Oliver Mowat, the premier of Ontario, asked Grant to become Ontario's minister of education. Grant declined, but he used his increasingly good political connections to press for greater governmental funding for Queen's.

Although a Conservative, Grant was not a great admirer of his local M.P., John A. Macdonald. He felt that the Scottish-born politician had introduced many corrupt practices into Canadian politics. Grant's political ideals lay along the lines of Imperial Federation, a movement in which his friend George Parkin would become a leading figure. Grant's son William would much later marry Parkin's daughter Maude, and they would become the parents of George Parkin Grant.

In 1893, two years after Macdonald's death, Grant abandoned the Conservative party in favour of Laurier's Liberals. Over the next three years, he fought vigorously against attempts to exclude the Chinese from Canada.

Grant also wrote numerous books, including *New Year Sermons* and *Our Five Foreign Missions*. In 1894, he travelled west and wrote a series of reports for the *Globe* on the Manitoba Schools question, an issue that was fiercely dividing Canadians along religious and linguistic lines. The same year saw the publication of his most important religious work, *The Religions of the World*. In 1898, he took a prominent role in the foundation of the Canadian Society of Christian Unity.

In 1901, Grant's wife died, and he sought relief in overwork—leading to his own physical collapse. By 1902, he was seriously ill. Grant was overheard uttering a whispered prayer from his deathbed: "Give me a chance; Oh my God, give me a chance." Four days later, Grant died.

He was buried in Catarqui Cemetery, Kingston, near the grave of Sir John A. Macdonald. Grant's beliefs were "held with a tenacity which he was willing to do and suffer everything." This was nowhere clearer than in the public realm in which he had lived so much of his life. There, his overriding desire was "that public policy should be honest, just, and in accordance with the will and purpose of God."

Robert Harris (1849–1919)
The Hon. Sir Oliver Mowat
1892, oil on canvas, 231.8 x 160.0 cm
Courtesy: Government of Ontario Art Collection, Toronto
Photographer: Tom Moore Photography, Toronto

inset: National Archives of Canada / PA-028631

Oliver Mowat

1820–1903

"A true renaissance Christian gentleman."

Dallas Miller

Oliver Mowat remained in office as premier of Ontario for twenty-four years, longer than any other first minister in a commonwealth parliament to that date. He is perhaps best known for his successful resistance to Sir John A. Macdonald's imposition of a strong centralist government, by advocating instead a strengthening of provincial rights.

Mowat was born in Kingston, Upper Canada, in July 1820. His father, John, was a former member of the British army who settled in Kingston with his wife, Helen. He went into business as a general merchant; and together they raised their children in the Presbyterian faith. As a youth, Oliver Mowat "studied the evidence of Christianity very earnestly … and came to the conclusion that Christianity was no cunningly devised fable, but was very truth." From his father, Mowat learned the value of good literature and became an avid reader. His tastes and studies in literature and poetry, history, biography, science, and theology earned him the reputation as a true renaissance Christian gentleman.

Before his sixteenth birthday, Mowat had completed his education and successfully passed the entrance exam for the Law Society of Upper Canada. In January 1836, he began his articles of clerkship with a Kingston lawyer who was to later reach fame as Canada's first prime minister, John A. Macdonald. Mowat enjoyed a successful legal career for almost twenty years, during which time he handled many cases ultimately decided by the Judicial Committee of the Privy Council in London, England, which then functioned as Canada's final court of appeal.

In standing for federal election in 1857, Mowat committed himself to the principle of representation by population and to law reform. He declared that if elected he would do his "duty in Parliament in the spirit and with the views which become a Christian politician." His first election saw him victorious over a seasoned political opponent by almost a two to one margin.

His duties as the postmaster general of Upper Canada prevented him from attending the Charlottetown Conference in September 1864, but he did attend the Quebec Conference a month later. There and thereafter, Mowat worked tirelessly to protect provincial rights and helped to create a truly federal system of government. He has been credited with putting the resolutions of the Quebec Conference, which eventually formed the British North America Act of 1867 and gave birth to a new nation, into "constitutional and legal shape."

Subsequently, Mowat took a position as a Chancery Court judge. Mowat's biographer notes that during his political career to that point "he had made many friends and few, if any, enemies; and when he left political life—forever as it seemed—it was with good wishes from both sides of the House and with many regrets from the Reformers."

A legal periodical of the day noted that as a judge "his reported decisions are clear and logical, and have always been held to be of high authority in our courts. He was an ideal Equity Judge—learned in jurisprudence, skilled in technique, familiar with precedents, but with all master of reason." In deciding cases, Mowat often cited principles of the law as enunciated by the Christian jurist William Blackstone. Mowat, however, also moved the law along when its archaic principles seemed unfair.

In 1872, Mowat was convinced to step down from the bench to take over the leadership of the Ontario Reform movement. He served as the premier and

the attorney general of Ontario from 1872 until 1895. His return to political life brought accolades from the press: "Mr. Mowat will no doubt prove acceptable to all parties. He stands very high as a Christian gentleman, and is moderate in his political views."

Mowat's goal was to create a strong administration that fought for provincial rights, opposing Macdonald's attempt to make the federal government constitutionally superior to the provinces. In this struggle, the knowledge of constitutional and legal procedures that Mowat had gained on the judge's bench stood him in good stead. Mowat's administration is remembered for constitutional litigation, much of it to the Judicial Committee of the Privy Council seeking to define provincial rights under the British North America Act—the very provisions that Mowat had helped draft at the Quebec Conference. In addition, Mowat was politically adept at balancing his pro-business policies with attention to the concerns of working people.

As shown by repeated electoral success, Mowat had the support of most Ontarians in his struggles against Ottawa. He also had the admiration of many Canadians in other provinces. During his long period in office, Mowat extended the provincial franchise, laid the foundations for orderly municipal government, and acquired the mineral-rich areas of the Canadian Shield when Ontario was extended northward to Hudson's Bay.

Throughout, Mowat displayed a sense of social justice that sprang from his Christian convictions, which, in turn, manifested themselves in his various affiliations. He became a director of the Upper Canada Bible Society and remained its vice president from 1859 to 1903, the year of his death. He remained a member of St. Andrew's Church of Toronto during his adult life and in 1851 became a director of the Anti-Slavery Society of Canada. For more than twenty years, Mowat served as the president of the Evangelical Alliance.

After careers in law, politics, and the judiciary, Oliver Mowat spent his concluding years, from 1897 until his death, as the lieutenant governor of Ontario. During this time, he studied theology and wrote apologetic works on the life and nature of Jesus Christ. His publications include *Christianity and Some of Its Evidences*, a compilation of statements concerning Christianity's validity and conclusions that can be drawn from the life and miracles of Christ, particularly His resurrection from the dead. Mowat also wrote *Christianity and Its Influence*, which began as a guest lecture to medical students. In his writings, he held to a solidly orthodox but not denominationally narrow creed.

Lieutenant Governor Mowat died in April 1903 at age eighty-two. Tributes portrayed him as the Christian politician and Canadian statesman that he was. Representative of the many tributes were the remarks of Dr. Armstrong Black: "May God still give us men who will sway the people with moderation, who will chasten and stay the sacred name of liberty by a cultured reverence for the past…. He owned himself a humble follower of Jesus Christ; enduring hardness for His sake as a good soldier, disciplining his moral nature, revering the Sabbath, haunting the sanctuary, studious of God's Word, observed of all as a man of faith and prayer, ever giving to Caesar the things that are Caesar's and to God the things that are God's."

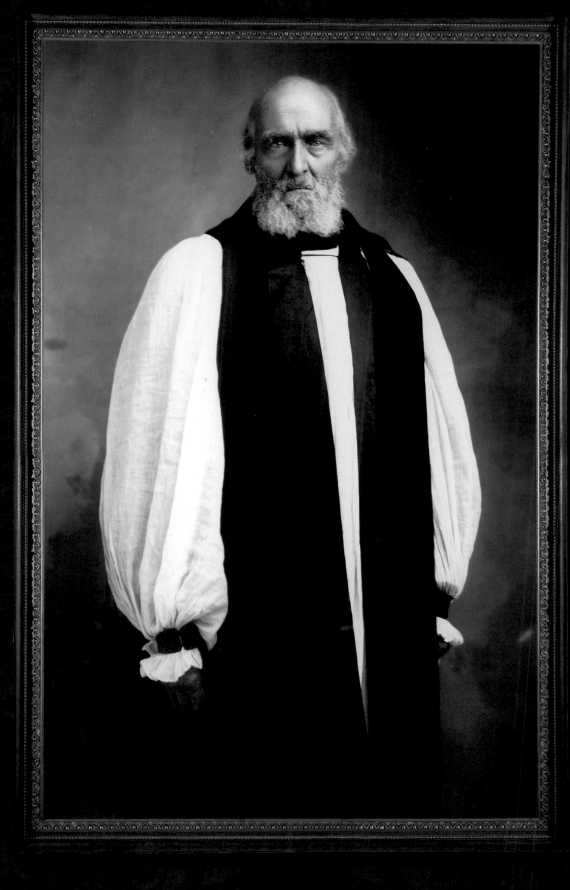

William Bompas
Colourization of black and white photograph
Courtesy: Provincial Archives of Alberta / A.3325

inset: Anglican Church of Canada / General Synod Archives, P7517-196

The Missionary Priest of the Canadian North
William Bompas
1834–1906

Kenneth Coates and William Morrison

"The belief that the work of God involved self-sacrifice in the interest of bringing the gospel to the non-Christian peoples of the world."

Photographs taken near the end of a life devoted to the Church of England show William Carpenter Bompas, the first bishop of Athabasca, of Mackenzie River, and of Selkirk (Yukon), to be an imposing figure. His flowing white beard and piercing eyes give him the appearance of an Old Testament prophet. A physically tough and spiritually determined man, Bompas was more comfortable with his native flock than with either the nonnative people of the north or with coreligionists in the south.

Bompas was born in London, England, the son of a prominent Baptist lawyer. Left fatherless at age ten, Bompas, too, tried a career in law, which he abandoned in his early twenties. In 1859, he was ordained a deacon in the Church of England. He spent the next few years as a curate in a number of English parishes, but like many young churchmen of his time he was attracted to foreign missions, particularly in Africa or China. The Church Missionary Society, however, refused to send him, convinced that he lacked spark and did not have the aptitude for language required for service in these high-profile mission fields.

It was in the less-desirable northern regions of North America that Bompas found his calling. In spring 1865, David Anderson, the former bishop of Rupert's Land, spoke in London of the urgent need for missionaries in northwest British North America because a shortage of Anglicans was leaving this fertile ground open to the Roman Catholics. Bompas heard the call and was ordained a priest in June 1865 and sent immediately to North America. Making a remarkable trek from the Red River to the Mackenzie valley, he arrived at Fort Simpson on Christmas Day 1865 and took up the work of itinerant preacher to the Dene of the Mackenzie and Yukon valleys and then to the Inuit of the Arctic coast.

He soon faced a crucial professional decision. In 1873, the diocese of Athabasca was created out of the huge diocese of Rupert's Land, and Bompas was asked to become its bishop. He balked at first; as a former Baptist he belonged to the Low Church wing of Anglicanism and shied away from ritualism and hierarchy. He enjoyed ministering to the indigenous people and was uncomfortable with the fundraising that was part of the work of a missionary-bishop. He returned to England in 1874 to refuse the promotion, but was convinced to change his mind. He was consecrated as the bishop of Athabasca in May 1874.

While in London, Bompas married his cousin, Charlotte Selina Cox. It was a match of practicality rather than romance—neither was young; he needed a wife to assist him; and Selina, who was to make her own mark in the north, had few prospects. Within weeks, they were in the north.

In 1883, the diocese of Athabasca was divided, with Bompas taking responsibility for the northern or MacKenzie River diocese. In 1891, this diocese was also divided, and Bompas became the bishop of Selkirk (later renamed Yukon). He did as little fund-raising and as few public relations exercises as possible, preferring instead to minister to the native people. Although highly sympathetic to these people, he was, in social matters, a Darwinist and was pessimistic about their short-term prospects of rising above what he considered to be their poverty and squalor.

In the 1890s, Bompas's world was disturbed by the arrival of miners looking for gold. These men gave alcohol to the natives and took advantage of native women. At the same time, whaling ships arrived at Herschel Island on the Yukon's Arctic coast, with a similar effect on the resident Inuit population. The abuse of the natives galvanized Bompas to action, and he bombarded the Canadian government with complaints. The chorus of complaints that Bompas started resulted in the establishment of Northwest Mounted Police posts in the northern Yukon in 1894 and 1895 and on Herschel Island in 1903. The presence of the police in the Klondike on the eve of the gold rush forestalled a potential American threat to Canadian sovereignty there and was perhaps Bompas's most useful service to this country.

Although an exemplary missionary, Bompas left the needs of nonnatives to others. In later years, he withdrew to Carcross in the southern Yukon, where he established a native residential school. He died at his desk in 1906 and was buried at Carcross. He was widely mourned, most of all by the native people with whom he had lived and worked for most of his adult life.

William Carpenter Bompas was not a self-promoter. He became widely known despite himself. His persistence set him apart from those around him, whether he was pushing through an Arctic winter to reach an isolated hunting camp or petitioning the government to protect more adequately the indigenous peoples of the far northwest. He was a man of conviction more than of vision, of faith rather than of innovation, of hard work instead of inspiration. He left a scholarly mark through his translations and his writings on matters spiritual and missionary.

But Bompas alienated many people in the church and in the north through what they perceived as either his self-centredness or his preoccupation with native people. His legacy nonetheless was of commitment and of tireless devotion to the Christian word and to the propagation of the gospel among the indigenous peoples of northern Canada. Paradoxically, in the end his legacy was more profound in the churches and Sunday schools of Canada and England, where his exploits were given as moral lessons, than among the natives, among whom, despite his sympathy for their cause, he enjoyed, at best, indifferent success in recruiting lasting converts to the Anglican Church.

It was in the Yukon and the Mackenzie River valleys, along the Arctic slope, and in the Athabasca district that Bompas discovered himself and founded a career that made him legendary in his lifetime. He was a man driven by God, pushed by his faith to reach beyond the bounds that others set for him. As a result, he ended his life not as a failed lawyer or a middling cleric in England, but as a symbol of the zeal of the nineteenth-century Christian church, of selfless devotion to faith, and of the belief that the work of God involved self-sacrifice in the interest of bringing the gospel to the non-Christian peoples of the world.

Shortly before his death, Bompas realized that his world had begun to change. In the north, a new order had emerged; there appeared to be little room for the solitary, itinerant preacher along the changing northern frontier. The missionaries who followed were different men and women, and the more successful for it. But they walked on ground that had been broken by the bold and confident strides of William Carpenter Bompas.

J. W. L. Forster (1850–1938)
Timothy Eaton
oil on canvas, 118 x 93 cm
Courtesy: Eaton's Canada
Photographer: Steve Boyko

inset: National Archives of Canada / C-14088

The Merchant Prince
Timothy Eaton
1834–1907

"To have the Sermon on the Mount wrought out in his daily life."

Michael Clarke

Timothy Eaton is known from coast to coast in Canada for revolutionary merchandising and for building a retail empire by supplying the needs of city dwellers and country folk alike. Despite his fame, Eaton preferred to remain largely in the background; he never became a public figure, and he refused to enter politics. He had three principal interests: his church, his family, and his store.

Eaton was born in Clogher, Ireland, in 1834. His parents were devout Presbyterians esteemed by their neighbours for their Christian character and ready generosity. Eaton's father was a farmer who named two of his sons, James and John, after his first and second favourite books of the Bible, respectively. He died before his last son was born, but his wife continued the tradition, naming Timothy after her husband's third favourite book of the Bible. She also ensured that her sons were familiar with the Presbyterian catechism through daily Bible readings.

Eaton left school at age eighteen and was apprenticed to a dry goods merchant. He slept under the store's counter—convenient for someone who had to work from early morning to late at night six days a week. During his apprenticeship, he learned much about the business of buying and selling and that the honesty taught him by his mother was the best policy for a merchant. In addition, he learned empathy for all who worked long hours for little reward. When his apprenticeship expired, he received only one hundred pounds sterling for five years' work.

Eaton immigrated to Upper Canada in 1857 to join his brother James, who had started a store in St. Mary's, near Stratford, Ontario. He remained there until 1868. During an open-air meeting, he heard a Methodist minister preaching the Gospel. When an opportunity was given for corporate prayer, Eaton withdrew to a barn to "debate with [himself] and seek the assistance of God in solitary prayer." On his return to the meeting, he made a confession of faith and soon joined the Methodist Church.

In 1861, Eaton met Margaret Beattie while attending St. Mary's Methodist Church. Within weeks, he had proposed, and the couple was soon married. In 1869, they and their three children moved to Toronto, where they purchased a dry goods business on the corner of Queen and Yonge Streets for $6,500. Thus was born the T. Eaton Co. of Toronto, launching a revolution in Canadian retailing.

Eaton's first newspaper advertisement shocked the competition. While other merchants perpetuated the long-standing practice of negotiable prices and the costly practice of extending credit to customers, Eaton had a better idea. He announced that his goods would be sold at one unalterable and fair price and that everything would be sold for cash. His timing was right. Shoppers were tired of never knowing the true price of anything they bought. Eaton's subsequent slogan, "Goods satisfactory or money refunded," would further rattle his competitors.

Eaton was revered for his inflexible integrity. He mandated that in all advertisements "the exact truth should be told with regard to the goods offered for sale." He decreed that if a customer was not satisfied, the price should be refunded. And he remained an unwavering Methodist who never sold tobacco, liquor, or playing cards in his store and did not allow them in his home.

Eaton's greatest initiative was the catalogue, first introduced in 1884. In such a vast country, where the rural population was spread out over enormous expanses and had no access to modern products, the catalogue soon became the way to shop. By the early 1900s, the Eaton's catalogue was an integral part of the culture. Settlers in the west relied so heavily upon it that they dubbed it the Prairie Bible. It was used not only to shop, but also to learn English. The catalogue's other uses—including hockey shin pads, building insulation, and outhouse toilet paper—are legendary.

During his career, Eaton never forgot the principles that had guided him since his youth. The passing years merely reinforced his reputation for fair dealing. He often urged his sales staff to "use no deception in the smallest degree—nothing you cannot defend before God or Man." And he always remembered the long hours of his apprenticeship in Ireland and decided that none of his staff would experience a similar fate. He led the country in introducing shorter working hours and paid welfare and pensions before most employers had even heard the terms. At a time when most Toronto stores remained open until 10:00 p.m., Eaton ran advertisements suggesting to his customers that they shop during the day to "Liberate Your Fellow-Beings."

Eaton's business boomed, and he moved into constantly larger buildings. By the 1880s, he was among Toronto's leading merchants. He demonstrated his largesse in 1889 as one of the chief founders of Trinity Methodist Church. The Methodist churches on Bloor Street and Robert Street were also built through Eaton's generosity, and he was an important benefactor to the denomination's Victoria College, endowing a chair in English Bible.

Eaton's only recreation was his horses; he kept a stable of ten fine carriage horses. When, late in life, he was thrown from his carriage and broke his hip, he refused to let his confinement to a wheelchair restrict his life.

Toward the century's end, however, Eaton's aggressive sales and advertising methods began angering smaller merchants. He endured protests, rallies, and political pressure for years. Problems notwithstanding, by the time he died of pneumonia in 1907, Timothy Eaton's retail empire had burgeoned to encompass nine thousand employees, or associates, as he preferred to call them.

At the funeral service in Eaton's home, the Reverend Joseph Odery mourned the loss of "one of the best friends I ever had," a man who in matters of faith had the "beautiful simplicity of a child" and who endeavoured "to have the Sermon on the Mount wrought out in his daily life." Dr. NATHANAEL BURWASH, the chancellor of Victoria College, further eulogized Eaton, saying that the "old-fashioned fear of God and faith in Divine Providence was deep-rooted within him."

In 1909, Eaton's wife learned that the Methodists were trying to raise money to build the first great Methodist church in the northern section of Toronto. She offered to donate all the money they needed to build one of the handsomest churches in the city and made only one request: that the church be named after her husband. The Timothy Eaton Memorial Church, on Toronto's St. Clair Avenue, was completed in 1914. It testifies to Eaton's steadfast faith.

J. W. L. Forster (1850–1938)
Nathanael Burwash
oil on canvas, 127 x 96 cm
Courtesy: Victoria University, Toronto
Photographer: Steve Boyko

inset: The United Church of Canada/Victoria University Archives, Toronto / 76.002 P / 2

Pastor, Educator, Chancellor, and Theologian

Nathanael Burwash

1839–1918

*"No man in Canadian Methodism has influenced and guided
the thinking of the ministry to so great an extent."*

Marguerite Van Die

Students spoke of him as an "evangelical mystic," but during his long tenure from 1887 to 1913 as the chancellor of Canadian Methodism's Victoria College Nathanael Burwash managed to balance an intense piety with renowned skills as a negotiator and administrator. He was one of the principal forces behind the Ontario university federation movement of the 1880s whereby Victoria College moved from Cobourg to become a federated college of the University of Toronto. Two decades later, in 1902, when negotiations for union began among the Presbyterians, Methodists, and Congregationalists. Burwash chaired the committee on doctrine that framed the statement of faith for the proposed United Church as his denomination's leading theologian. He then tirelessly defended church union until its acceptance in 1912. In keeping with an optimistic, postmillennial reading of history that saw Methodism at the vanguard of spiritual and moral progress, Burwash considered university federation and church union to be part of a wider goal—to permeate Canadian public life with the force of evangelical Christianity.

Burwash was a fourth-generation Canadian whose family had moved to Quebec shortly after the American Revolution. He traced his evangelicalism to his parents, Adam Burwash and Anne Taylor. As young people, they had converted to Methodism during the revivals that swept the St. Andrew's area northwest of Montreal in the 1820s and 1830s. His mother was raised in the Church of Scotland, and as a former school teacher she thoroughly instructed her six sons in the Christian faith, using the Shorter Catechism of the Westminster Assembly of Faith, supplemented by what she considered to be the essence of Methodism: the constant need to repent and to ask divine forgiveness. For Nathanael, the eldest, her emphasis would have significant results. Later, as a theologian, he would react strongly against the liberalization of North American Methodist thought, which began to replace the need for conversion with religious nurture. His adherence to evangelical theology would, in turn, favour theological rapprochement with the Presbyterians during the church union negotiations.

A second and equally important influence can be traced to his college education. In 1844, his family moved to a farm near Cobourg, Ontario, the home of Victoria College, where Burwash enrolled in 1852 to prepare for the ministry. Stretching over an eight-year period, first as a preparatory school student and then as an undergraduate—with a brief break at age sixteen for a year of school teaching to supplement the family income—Burwash's college education laid the groundwork for his spiritual and intellectual development. In 1853, he underwent conversion at a college revival, an experience that, thanks largely to the enlightened leadership of Samuel Nelles, Victoria's principal from 1850 to 1887, he was able to integrate into the broad Christian principles that shaped the college curriculum of the period. As a result, learning and piety were never compartmentalized, and in time both helped to inform Burwash's response to the evolutionary teaching of Charles Darwin, and to the new "higher criticism" of the Bible, two of the severe challenges to the Christian faith in the nineteenth century.

The unsettling impact of those challenges was already apparent in the 1860s during Burwash's brief pastorates in Newburgh, Belleville, Toronto, and Hamilton. These were unusually prestigious stations for a young minister and were indicative of the church's desire to place its college-educated ministers in Canada's growing urban centres. Burwash quickly became involved in educational efforts to reach Methodist young people and also forged valuable contacts with wealthy lay people, some of whom would become benefactors of Victoria College. His work convinced him of the need for Methodism to move from its practice of ministerial training on the circuit to a college-educated ministry capable of providing intellectual leadership in a more sophisticated age.

To this end, Burwash accepted an offer to fill a vacancy at Victoria College in natural science in 1866, hoping that this might lead to the establishment of a faculty of theology. When this did occur, in 1873, he was appointed the dean of theology, a position for which he had prepared himself by taking the exam for a bachelor of divinity degree at the Methodist Garrett Biblical Institute in Evanston, Illinois, later followed by a doctorate in sacred theology. Deeply concerned to ensure a balance between religious faith and scientific thought, he applied the inductive or Baconian method to the study of Scripture and to the nurture and analysis of the spiritual life of the theological student in practical theology with the help of John Wesley's sermons. His commentary on Wesley's sermons was published in 1881, followed in 1887 by his *Handbook of the Epistle of Paul to the Romans* and in 1900 by a two-volume *Manual of Christian Theology on the Inductive Method.* Although the latter was studiously nonsectarian in language, it was unmistakably Wesleyan in its theological emphasis.

The central role of Wesleyan spirituality in Burwash's teaching and scholarship enabled him to take a more receptive attitude to the new biblical criticism. Because of its emphasis on religious experience, Methodism was less prone to the extremes of fundamentalism and modernism than those branches of Protestantism for which Christianity hinged on the infallibility of the Bible. Not without controversy, but largely because of Burwash's insistence that doctrine was derived not just from Scripture but from four coordinate authorities: the Bible, reason, tradition, and "the inner light which is given to every true Christian," Methodists voted in 1910 to accept the teaching of the new biblical criticism in their theological institutions.

Shortly thereafter, in 1913, Burwash resigned as the chancellor of Victoria College. He nonetheless continued to teach church history there and devoted himself to chronicling the history of Methodist higher education in *A History of Victoria College,* published posthumously. Burwash died in 1918 after a brief illness, increasingly disillusioned by perceived social and moral decline in Canada and by the First World War. One of the most apt evaluations of his long career appeared in the *Globe* the day after his death: "No man in Canadian Methodism has influenced and guided the thinking of the ministry to so great an extent."

E. McGillivray-Knowles (1866–1928)
Mrs. Burwash
oil on canvas, 91.4 x 71.1 cm
Courtesy: Victoria University, Toronto
Photographer: Steve Boyko

A Faith-Filled Partnership
Margaret Burwash
1842–1923

"A faith formed, tested, and strengthened by family tragedy."

Marguerite Van Die

Margaret Proctor Burwash had a keen interest in the welfare of female students at the University of Toronto's Victoria College, and believed that their education should be largely in the hands of women. To this end, she wrote in 1895, "I believe in men and women standing together in intellectual work, but there is a side of our nature which is exclusively feminine, which cannot be developed or moulded by men. It is a great misfortune for any young woman to be dwarfed … in this 'quality.' " Although in time she hoped to see women instructors in university work, to achieve the more immediate goal of creating a space for women, she drew on her educational background and her friendship with well-to-do Methodist women to lead the fundraising and furnishing of Annesley Hall, a Victoria College women's residence completed in 1902. Her efforts were formally acknowledged in 1912 when grateful supporters presented her with a portrait by McGillivray-Knowles (*see opposite page*) to be hung permanently in the residence. In a warm tribute, reference was made not only to her generous and loving character but also, discretely, to its source, a "heroic fortitude when the crushing storms of life fell heavily on her."

Like many women of her time, this reserved and dignified woman had experienced the loss of a child; in her case, not once, but eight times. Of the twelve children born to Margaret and her husband, NATHANAEL BURWASH (the chancellor of Victoria College), only four sons reached adulthood. And once, in less than a week in June 1889, the couple was confronted with the deaths—from black diphtheria—of four children, including their youngest: twin sons aged four. The losses marked her for life, causing her to transfer some of her interest, in the words of her eldest son, to a "higher and more spiritual vision of the life beyond." These tragedies also stimulated her to work with her professor husband in advancing student concerns at Victoria College once her domestic life became less demanding.

From childhood, Margaret had seen, as had her husband, that Methodism and education were natural partners. Margaret was born on a farm in Lambton County, near Sarnia, Canada West (Ontario), in 1842, to Edward Moore Proctor and Janet Burns, both recent English immigrants. She grew up surrounded by a large extended family. Her grandfather, Samuel Proctor, who lived nearby, had converted to Methodism as a young man in Lincolnshire. By refusing to pay the church tithe, he had more than once seen the seizure of items of furniture as a bailiff tried to enforce payment. Although Margaret's father was not known to be particularly religious, he shared his father's political convictions and agitated on behalf of free public schooling in Ontario. His daughter was among the first to reap the benefits of the new common school system in 1850.

At age five, Margaret began attending a nearby school privately conducted by a Scottish Baptist lay preacher. Relying heavily on the New Testament for reading material at the primary level, he also ensured that by the time she was eight she had read *Pilgrim's Progress*. In 1851, her family sold their farm and moved to Sarnia, where she received a grammar school education and secured a first-class teacher's certificate. After several years as a teacher in sur-

rounding country schools, she enrolled in 1863 in the Wesleyan Female College in Hamilton, Methodism's recently opened institution of higher education for women.

When two years later she graduated with the diploma Mistress of Liberal Arts, she had reached the highest educational achievement open at the time to women and, in her own words, "the fulfillment of my most earnest hopes." These hopes soon took a turn to domesticity, however. Among the Methodist dignitaries who attended the graduation ceremony, where she gave the valedictory address, was Nathanael Burwash, who soon began to court her. Asked to join the Wesleyan staff because of her previous teaching experience and high academic standing, she remained at the college until August 1867, when she was offered the position of preceptress of the Mount Allison Ladies' Academy in Sackville, New Brunswick. By then engaged to Burwash, she resigned her new post at the end of the first session, and on Christmas day 1867 the two were married at her parents' home. Shortly thereafter, on a professor's modest annual salary of $1,000 (with $150 in arrears, and another $400 committed to the college endowment fund-raising drive), the two established a home on the ground floor of Victoria College's academic building.

By all accounts and as evident in their correspondence, the marriage became a strong partnership where each was able to drop the reserve assumed in public life and share fully feelings and concerns on a wide range of issues. From the beginning, they established the habit of Scripture reading and prayer in the morning and evening. Although Margaret's religious expression was more practical and less theologically informed than that of her husband, their faith formed a common bond, tested and strengthened by family tragedy. In addition, both were raised on farms; were successful teachers, and shared a love of music, literature, and nature, the latter enjoyed especially in later years at their summer cottage at Go Home Bay in the Muskokas, a resort area for a number of University of Toronto faculty. There, they often entertained members of nearby Indian tribes and hosted visiting students from Japan. Such contact arose from their interest in home and foreign missions, and in 1913, at the request of Victoria graduates serving in Japan, the Burwashes made an extended visit to Methodist and other educational centres in that country.

Although grueling for a couple in their seventies, the visit served to cast in a more positive light the end of Nathanael's long tenure as the chancellor of Victoria College. It was at Margaret's instigation, but with her husband's support, that complaints were lodged in 1912 against perceived curfew infractions by women students at Annesley Hall. The dispute culminated in her husband's resignation shortly before the trip to Japan. By the time of Margaret's death in 1923, all grievances were reconciled, thanks to the leadership of Margaret Addison, the dean of women.

Often lonely after the death of her husband in 1918 and at times uncertain about the whereabouts of her four adult sons, two of whom served overseas during the First World War, Margaret did not cling to this life in old age. Her last recorded words were of longing "to pass over to my Father's house."

William Duncan
Colourization of black and white photograph
Courtesy: B.C. Archives / A–08354

inset: B.C. Archives / A-01175

William Duncan

1832–1918

"What good is wealth … if I can go and do good?"

Peter Murray

Of all the European missionaries who came to Canada in the nineteenth century to convert the aboriginal population, few had more impact than William Duncan. For sixty years Duncan was the controversial leader in a movement that would bring far-reaching cultural and economic change to the Indians.

Born in 1832 in the rural Yorkshire hamlet of Bishop Burton, Duncan's background was humble. His mother was a servant girl and his father unknown. His grandparents brought him up in nearby Beverley, where—after winning acclaim as a boy soprano in the cathedral choir—he came under the influence of Reverend Anthony Carr. Carr recruited Duncan to teach Sunday school and became the missing father figure in young William's life. From Carr, he absorbed the evangelical views that he held all his life.

Duncan became successful as a wholesale leather merchant. However, Duncan's life irrevocably changed when he went to a church meeting and heard a speaker urging young men to join the ranks of the Anglicans' Church Missionary Society (CMS). "Well, that *is* a new idea," Duncan later recalled thinking at the time. "Before I left the room I felt very inclined to it. And I woke up that night and thought … what good is wealth … but if I can go and do good somewhere, that will be something worthwhile."

Duncan trained for two and a half years at the CMS school at Highbury College in north London. He studied school organization and teaching and some theology and medicine. Upon graduating, Duncan boarded a Royal Navy ship bound for Victoria, British Columbia.

He arrived October 1, 1857, at Fort Simpson, a Hudson's Bay Company (HBC) trading post between the mouths of the Skeena and Nass Rivers, just north of present-day Prince Rupert. Duncan set to work immediately with the energy and diligence that became the hallmarks of his career. He visited all the Indian houses surrounding the fort stockade, where the twenty-nine Tsimshian tribes had gathered to trade with the HBC and to carry on their traditional trading with each other. Duncan next undertook the difficult task of learning their language, a step urged by Henry Venn, the secretary of the CMS, who set the society's policy from 1841 until his death in 1873. Duncan also enlisted the natives' help in building a schoolhouse for adults and children adjacent to their village.

Although Duncan attempted to follow most of Venn's instructions, in some ways he went against Venn's wishes. He argued, with some justification, that by being on the scene he could judge how to adapt Indian ways better than anyone like Venn in faraway London could.

Venn wanted the missionaries to work with native chiefs, but Duncan met considerable opposition from tribal leaders, who considered him a threat to their power and prestige as he gained converts to Christianity. This conflict was one of the reasons that he, along with seventy supporters, established a new community away from the fort. The site chosen was Metlakatla, the former winter home of the Tsimshians who had moved to Fort Simpson. It offered more room and better land, including spacious beaches for pulling up canoes. There would also be relief from the drunkenness and violence surrounding the fort. And so, in spring 1862 the move was made.

After drawing up a list of rules to govern Metlakatla, Duncan set to work with prodigious effort to turn it into a model Indian community. He did his best to turn his followers into good Victorian workingmen, dressing them in English clothes, putting them in houses resembling English cottages, and creating a native police force. He set up a store, bought a trading schooner, established a sawmill, and held workshops to make rope and nets.

The population of the new townsite increased rapidly as other natives fled Fort Simpson because of a major smallpox epidemic that had spread up the coast from Victoria. Duncan was able to save many lives with his rudimentary medical training and a supply of vaccine, thus weakening the power of the tribal medicine men and gaining a credibility that attracted new converts.

Duncan supervised the construction of a 1,200-seat church, the largest on the coast north of San Francisco. He also taught the Tsimshians such trades as weaving, coopering (barrel making), and printing. They were also encouraged to continue their traditional occupations of hunting and fishing; the latter assisted by Duncan building a large salmon cannery.

By the mid-1870s, the fame of Metlakatla had spread widely, and it was used in England to gain support for the missionary cause. Both the provincial and Dominion governments sought Duncan's advice on matters affecting the Indians, especially land title issues. Over the next decade, however, the little community's population had increased to one thousand, and it was wracked by discord. Most was the result of Duncan's feud with Anglican Church officials and with Henry Venn's successors in London, who were taking the CMS away from Venn's pragmatic policies.

Despite constant CMS and church pressure, Duncan declined ordination and so was unable to administer some church functions, which were left to visiting clergy or other ordained missionaries. Duncan, however, blocked even them from administering Communion, as he was well aware of Indian cannibalism rituals and feared that the ceremony would be misunderstood. Unlike other missionaries who measured their success by their number of baptisms, Duncan withheld baptism until he was convinced that the applicants were ready to receive it.

In 1887, Duncan departed Metlakatla to set up a new mission on Annette Island in Alaska. Most of the Indians sided with Duncan, and eight hundred—the majority of the Metlakatla community—accompanied him to create yet another successful industrial mission village, New Metlakatla, where he died in 1918.

Duncan's critics point to his almost dictatorial control over the Tsimshians and his emphasis on business and secular affairs. Nonetheless, his compassion for the natives—whose lives had been upturned by cultural change—is unquestioned, as is the love and respect the majority accorded him. He had begun his ministry among the natives critical of their ways, but over time he took a more positive and enlightened attitude toward their culture and most of it artifacts. One modern scholar described Duncan as "a daring, determined social reformer who was a century ahead of his time."

Artist unknown
John Hunter
oil on canvas, 124 x 96 cm
Courtesy: The United Church of Canada / Victoria University Archives, Toronto
Photographer: Steve Boyko

inset: The United Church of Canada / Victoria University Archives, Toronto / 76.002 P / 2927

John Hunter

1856–1919

*"A man who was single-minded in his determination
to transport his listeners to the gates of heaven."*

Kevin Kee

As one-half of Canada's most famous evangelistic duo, John Hunter's mesmerizing preaching and dramatic delivery attracted the attention of hundreds of thousands of Canadians—including the nation's first prime minister, Sir John A. Macdonald. Hunter's forte was Bible exposition, using extemporaneous preaching with theatrical overtones. With an actor's sense of informed improvisation, he drew on his surroundings to enliven and enrich his message. In this way, he tried to make religion a vital and attractive force capable of changing lives.

John Edwin Hunter was born in Durham County, Ontario. Fifteen years later, he was born again. Hunter's conversion during a backwoods Methodist revival meeting marked a new life in Christ and the beginning of a lifelong passion. Hearing God's call to preach the gospel, he responded immediately.

Hunter returned home and began to witness to his family. In a short time, his father, mother, four sisters, and two brothers followed his lead to conversion and joined the Methodist Church. This initial success was a sign of things to come.

At Victoria College in Cobourg, Hunter's zeal for evangelism burned bright. No opportunity was wasted; even train trips to and from Cobourg were used to attempt the conversion of his fellow passengers. At college, the exuberant young preacher met another budding evangelist, HUGH CROSSLEY, and the two quickly became friends. Together, they organized meetings for their fellow students and were soon fanning the flames of revival in Cobourg.

Ordained as a Methodist minister, Hunter subsequently served in several churches. However, at the first opportunity he requested the position of full-time evangelist. The church agreed, and in 1884 he and Crossley were reunited in a joint evangelistic mission. In the years that followed, Crossley and Hunter would become—in terms of the number of converts—the most successful Canadian evangelistic team ever.

Their early successes were remarkable. During the course of a month-long campaign in Toronto, it was estimated that the duo held fifty-five meetings and spoke to between seventy-five thousand and one hundred thousand people. A revival in Ottawa in 1888, however, would dwarf even these early successes.

That winter, Canadian prime minister Sir John A. Macdonald attended the Crossley-Hunter services along with several senators and members of parliament. Macdonald, in fact, celebrated his seventy-third birthday at a service. On the final night of the six-week revival, it was requested that Crossley and Hunter remain for one more week, and Macdonald asked if he could second the motion. That same evening, a significant event occurred in the life of the hard-drinking prime minister, who during the election of 1878 had joked that Canadians preferred him drunk to his opponent—the pious Alexander Mackenzie—sober. As a newspaper reported: "When in answer to an appeal by Mr. Hunter, that all who wished to become Christians and desired the prayers of the audience would stand up, the premier of the Dominion ... arose with his wife." According to another journalist, "When the well-known form of the Honourable Premier arose in the centre of the church many strong men bowed their heads and wept for joy. The right honourable gentleman himself was deeply affected." After dining at the prime minister's home several days later, Hunter confirmed that "Sir John is a changed man."

The message that drew the prime minister appealed to Canadians from all walks of life. Listeners were encouraged to turn from their sinful ways, to commit their lives to Christ, and to help make Canada a Christian nation, a land that could truly call itself God's dominion. The support of mayors, members of parliament, and especially the prime minister was central to realizing that goal.

Hunter's mission was to share the gospel with as many people as possible. He used a variety of mediums of expression, including several pamphlets of his own authorship. He was, however, most at home behind the pulpit. While his partner took a calm, quiet approach to preaching, Hunter was constantly on the move. In the words of one reporter, he "was a hotbed of enthusiasm, active on his feet and ready with his tongue, a restless spirit who does two hours work in one." As far as Hunter was concerned, not a second should be wasted when ushering souls into the kingdom.

He was neither a theologian nor an intellectual, but he was a genius in his ability to read human nature and to adjust to the conditions of each meeting. His remarks were often sprinkled with jokes and funny stories. Hunter improvised as he preached and, in so doing, displayed astonishing theatrical instincts. Often, he would elaborate on a passage of Scripture or read a suitable story. "The Heavenly Railroad" was among his favourite stories. Purported to be true, it related a conversation between a young girl and a conductor. The child had boarded a train convinced that she was bound for heaven to visit her dead mother, who had sung to her of the railroad to heaven. When she learned that the conductor had a daughter who had recently died, the child asked, "What shall I tell your little girl when I see her? Shall I say to her that I saw her pa on Jesus' railroad? Shall I?" In an era when death was ever present, this testimony to a child's innocence and faith prompted mothers and fathers to examine their hearts and to consider their example to their children.

Hunter conducted a gospel train of his own, carrying his listeners from the heights of joy to the depths of grief. The thoughts of the audience were directed by its engineer, a man who was single-minded in his determination to transport his listeners to the gates of heaven.

His zeal for evangelism brought new life in Christ to thousands. But it took its toll. Hunter's hectic schedule shattered his fragile health, and as a result in 1910 the Crossley-Hunter revival team disbanded. Only fifty-four years of age, the esteemed revivalist quietly retired to his home in St. Thomas, Ontario. He died nine years later.

In eulogizing Hunter, the Reverend S. D. Chown spoke for the Methodist denomination, observing that the "Reverend J. E. Hunter was a man possessed of a consuming passion for the saving of souls, a passion which wore out his nervous and physical constitution long before his sun ordinarily should have set."

Rev. Hugh Thomas Crossley
Colourization of black and white photograph
Courtesy: The United Church of Canada / Victoria University Archives, Toronto / 77.002 P / 1302

inset: Archives of the United Church of Canada Victoria University (Toronto) / 76.002 P / 1294

The Singing Evangelist
Hugh Crossley

1850–1934

"Crossley brought more converts to the penitent form than any other single individual of his generation."

Kevin Kee

Hugh Thomas Crossley, partner in the well-known Methodist revival team of Crossley and Hunter, was born on an isolated homestead in King Township in present-day Ontario. When he was seventeen, a visit to a Methodist camp meeting changed his life. After several days of attending the revival, Crossley dedicated his life to Christ.

He spent several years teaching, then moved to Cobourg, Ontario, to attend Victoria College. There, he met JOHN HUNTER, who would become Crossley's lifelong friend and evangelistic partner. Hunter's passion for saving souls was infectious, and soon the two were preaching together in Cobourg. Their partnership was interrupted upon graduation, as Crossley, who was ordained in 1880, began a pastoral ministry.

Although Crossley enjoyed his work, he longed to conduct revivals more frequently than a single church could support. One evening in 1883, he penned a letter to Hunter. It had been nine years since they had conducted revivals as a team. Crossley felt that it was time for them to reunite and to enter full-time evangelistic work. Unaware of Crossley's intentions, Hunter wrote a similar note the same evening. The letters crossed in the mail, and the friends took the remarkable coincidence to be a sign of God's calling to conduct revivals together. They met one evening at Hunter's home in Essex Centre and began their work there that night.

The partnership bore fruit immediately. During their first year together, over 2,500 people professed conversion. In a short period of time, their contemporaries came to view Crossley and Hunter as the greatest evangelistic team of its day. Requests for their services poured in, and soon engagements for their revivals were booked three years in advance.

Crossley and Hunter conducted meetings throughout the United States and Canada, focusing most of their attention on smaller communities. They were the talk of the town in these centres, where town councils would frequently proclaim a holiday to allow those in the vicinity to attend church en masse. The meetings were almost always interdenominational, and the ministers of each participating church played a role in the services. All were united in a community drive for evangelism.

Within this whirlwind of activity, Crossley was the essence of calm. He almost always wore a smile, causing one observer to remark that Crossley's face "oft-times is radiant with an almost supernatural light." His musical talents especially elicited favourable comments. Known as the singing evangelist, he frequently delivered his thoughts in the form of a song sermon, underlining the important themes of his message with relevant hymns intoned in his mellow baritone voice. Many of the crowd favourites were his compositions.

Whatever the format of his presentation, the message was always the same. Drawing on passages of the Bible, Crossley would seek to convince his listeners of the need of repentance for sin, the possibility of redemption in Christ, and the opportunity for regeneration with the help of the Holy Spirit. His sermons inevitably concluded with an earnest appeal to "accept Christ at once."

But Crossley's influence did not end there. He was convinced that Christianity should be applied to all aspects of a believer's life. In sermon and song he encouraged his listeners to consider God's place in all things. As far as Crossley was concerned, a conversion to Christianity involved a conversion to a whole new way of living. Furthermore, individual reform was to express itself in a changed society, and Crossley worked with Canadians in all Protestant denominations to try to create a country devoted to the principles of evangelical Christianity.

As a result of Crossley and Hunter's efforts, the character of many towns changed visibly during a revival. Drinking establishments were frequently emptied and on several occasions theatres closed for lack of business. Local newspapers often noted the widespread changes. A report regarding a series of services in Calgary was typical. "Many non-church-goers have been brought in; a prize fighter, and at least one saloon-keeper being among the number."

Crossley and Hunter's legacy remained long after they left town. In the homes of many of their converts, the evangelists' portraits graced parlour walls, and Crossley's hymnbook, *Songs of Salvation*, sat ready on the parlour organ to be opened to a revival favourite. His book, *Practical Talks on Important Themes* (1895), which guided converts as they applied their faith to all aspects of life, might be found resting beside a chair.

In this book, Crossley attempts to articulate a faith that is intellectually sound. "God does not stifle reason and enquiry about religion," he counsels, "but says, 'come now, and let us reason together.' " At the same time, Crossley reminds his readers, some realities lie beyond human understanding. "Faith," Crossley notes, "is not contrary to reason. The mystery of the telephone I cannot reason out, but I believe in the telephone and telegraph."

The influence of Crossley and Hunter was evident in the lives of several Canadian leaders. In addition to their impact on Sir John A. Macdonald [see JOHN HUNTER], their preaching brought conversion to the lives of Sir William Hearst, the premier of Ontario, and the Reverend William Henniwell, who later became an associate of evangelist Billy Sunday.

After Hunter's retirement in 1910, Crossley continued to evangelize before retiring in 1926. In his final years, he received a doctor of divinity degree from Wesley College—the first Canadian evangelist to be so honoured. A lifelong bachelor, he spent his last years in the home of the Reverend Ernest Crossley Hunter, the son of John Hunter.

Hailed as "the last of the great Canadian evangelists" of his era, Hugh Crossley died in 1934. Together with Hunter, he had conducted approximately four hundred revivals in twenty-six years. According to one obituary, "over 200,000 publicly accepted Christ following their numerous campaigns." In the words of a Toronto *Daily Mail and Empire* writer, "their fame was as great as that of [Americans] Sankey and Moody, or Torrey and Alexander and some old-timers declare even greater." Summarizing a lengthy evangelistic career, the writer concluded that "the late Mr. Crossley brought more converts to the penitent form than any other single individual of his generation."

Mrs. Nell Gillis (1918–1991)
Dr. A. B. Simpson, Founder (1843–1919)
oil on canvas, 100.0 x 66.7 cm
Courtesy: The Christian and Missionary Alliance in Canada
Photographer: Steve Boyko

inset: Lafayette Ltd. / Courtesy of The Christian and Missionary Alliance Archives, Colorado Springs

Self-Denying Service
Albert B. Simpson

1843–1919

"Jesus Christ, Saviour, Sanctifier, Healer and Coming King"

Darrel Reid

When A. B. Simpson died, a *Christian Herald* writer wrote: "His epitaph is written in the hearts of countless multitudes at home and abroad … no one in this age had done more effectual, self-denying service for Christ and His Gospel than [Simpson]. Of the denomination Simpson founded, the *Globe* observed that "the Christian and Missionary Alliance stands as a monument of his devotion to God's purpose for him…. Eternity alone will show the full results of his earthly ministry."

Albert Benjamin Simpson was born in Bayview, Prince Edward Island, in 1843 to pious Presbyterian parents who made their living provisioning and building ships. When he was four years of age, an empirewide depression forced Simpson's family to leave Prince Edward Island for the frontier farming area of Chatham, Ontario.

Simpson was a sensitive, frail, and deeply impressionable youth. He later said that his religious upbringing made him deeply aware of the demands of a stern and distant God. At age fifteen, he underwent a crisis characterized by months of mental and spiritual turmoil. It culminated in his rebirth. He felt the call of God and in 1861 entered Knox College, Toronto, to study for the Presbyterian ministry.

Intellectually and spiritually, Knox College was an exciting place to be, and Simpson drank deeply of the spirit of faith and activism that permeated the institution. He was an exceptional student and a gifted speaker. His rising profile within Canada's Presbyterian Church was confirmed when in 1865, at age twenty-two, he was called to the pastorate of one of the denomination's leading churches in Hamilton.

Simpson ministered successfully for seven years in Hamilton. Yet, for all his success as an urban pastor he was growing increasingly dissatisfied with the traditional ministry. His restlessness was heightened when he came into contact with the innovative urban evangelism of Dwight L. Moody, with the YMCA movement, and with the worldwide evangelical ecumenism of the Evangelical Alliance.

In 1874, sensing God's call to a broader ministry, Simpson left Hamilton to take up the pastorate of Chestnut St. Presbyterian Church in Louisville, Kentucky. Over the next five years, his conception of ministry changed dramatically in the face of late nineteenth century evangelicalism. Increasingly dissatisfied with his spiritual life, Simpson was drawn to the teachings of the Holiness movement. His reading of William Boardman's *The Higher Christian Life*, produced a powerful sanctification experience to which he attributed the tremendous power and success of his subsequent ministry. Soon after, Simpson played a major role in a series of revival meetings that shook Louisville in 1875. Through these meetings, Simpson saw for himself the limitless power of the Holy Spirit to change lives.

Simpson felt drawn to overseas missions. Although he never became a missionary, he did become one of the most successful missions administrators of his time. He credited much of his rising passion for evangelism and missions to his adoption of premillennial and prophetic doctrines that emphasized the imminent return of the Lord and the extreme peril of those not ready to meet him.

In late 1879, Simpson moved to New York, where he spent a short, dissatisfying stint as the minister of New York's prestigious Thirteenth St. Presbyterian Church. Once in the teeming metropolis, he felt an irresistible call from God to begin a new ministry that would reach out to the unchurched masses in unconventional and innovative ways. He resigned from the Presbyterian ministry and began an independent fellowship. It was during this time of spiritual ferment that Simpson experienced divine healing of his frail constitution. He soon became one of the leading exponents of the Divine Healing movement. After this experience, Simpson felt "wholly dependent upon a vital and continuous connection with the Lord for his life."

Between 1881 and 1887, Simpson's church grew rapidly. In his pulpit ministry, he was known as a spellbinding preacher with a deep knowledge of the Scriptures and a passionate love of God. He and his congregation provided social welfare to New York's untouchables, cared for orphans, educated the laity for ministry and missions, conducted high-profile evangelistic and healing campaigns, published a highly regarded missions periodical entitled *The Gospel in All Lands*, and generally promoted foreign missions.

Of these activities, missions quickly predominated. In 1887, Simpson founded two fellowships that would eventually merge to become the Christian and Missionary Alliance, an ecumenical and evangelical fellowship dedicated to promoting the deeper Christian life and to reaching the world for Christ. This burgeoning denomination spread rapidly to Canada, where, under the Reverend John Salmon, it formed its own Dominion Auxiliary in 1889 and counted among its numbers such prominent members as WILLIAM HOWLAND, the crusading mayor of Toronto; Dr. Jenny Trout, a pioneering woman doctor; and William Christie, the biscuit maker. By 1897, Simpson's organization was a leading missionary agency, supporting more than three hundred missionaries overseas.

The Christian and Missionary Alliance's motto "Jesus Christ, Saviour, Sanctifier, Healer and Coming King"—known as the fourfold gospel—became the rallying cry for a new generation of evangelicals dissatisfied with traditional forms of piety and drawn to preach Christ's word worldwide. Simpson's hymns such as "Jesus Only" and "Himself" set this evangelistic passion to music.

With notoriety, however, came controversy. Simpson was criticized for his promotion of Divine Healing, a doctrine that most of his evangelical counterparts did not endorse. The first missionary expedition he sent to the Congo, moreover, ended in disaster and brought criticism from other missions organizations. In the first decade of the twentieth century, Simpson found himself under attack from Pentecostals who insisted, as Simpson did not, that speaking in tongues was a necessary evidence of being filled with the Holy Spirit. Many prominent members of the Christian and Missionary Alliance broke with Simpson and went on to provide crucial early leadership for the emerging Pentecostal movement.

A. B. Simpson nonetheless had a profound influence upon North American evangelical spirituality. In his teachings many recognized their own struggles, failings, and ultimate victory in Christ. By the time Simpson died in 1919, the Christian and Missionary Alliance circled the globe, carrying Simpson's passion to proclaim "Jesus Only" to the world.

Alphonse Jongers (1872–1945)
Portrait of the First Lord Tweedsmuir
1940, oil on canvas, 90 x 70 cm
Courtesy: National Capital Commission's Crown Collection
Photographer: Marc Fowler, with the kind permission of Rideau Hall, Ottawa

inset: Yousuf Karsh / National Archives of Canada / PA-165803

A Pilgrim's Progress

John Buchan,
Lord Tweedsmuir of Elsfield

1875–1940

George Grant

"He was the Christian statesman extraordinaire."

Like one of his best-selling novels, the life of John Buchan was full of adventure and achievement. He was one of the most accomplished men of the twentieth century: a successful barrister, a respected scholar, a popular journalist, a trusted diplomat, a prolific author, an efficient colonial administrator, an innovative publisher, a progressive politician, a relentless reformer, an active churchman, and Canada's governor-general from 1935 to 1940. Best known for his historical romances and thrilling spy novels—he practically invented the genre—he was also the author of more than a hundred nonfiction works, including an authoritative multivolume history of the First World War and biographies of Oliver Cromwell, Caesar Augustus, Lord Montrose, and Walter Scott.

Buchan was born in Scotland in 1875, the eldest son of a minister in the Presbyterian Free Church. His early years in the strict Calvinistic manse would shape his worldview and stimulate his imagination for the rest of his life. Following a brilliant academic career at Glasgow and Oxford—during which he wrote prolifically—he went to work as a lawyer in London. He nonetheless maintained his journalistic and literary interests, writing for *Blackwood's* magazine and the *Spectator*.

Always interested in politics, Buchan later accepted an invitation to join the staff of Lord Milner, the high commissioner of South Africa following the Boer War. Buchan's efficient administrative reforms earned him a trusted place in His Majesty's court, and his foreign dispatches earned him renown as one of the British Empire's finest correspondents.

Following his tenure in the foreign service, Buchan was offered lucrative posts as a director of the Edinburgh publishing firm Thomas Nelson and of the international news service Reuters. He published several highly acclaimed novels and historical studies. When war broke out in Europe in 1914, however, he set aside his wide-ranging pursuits and joined the British Intelligence Corps as a department director.

After the First World War, Buchan was elected to Parliament as a representative of the Scottish universities, a position he held until 1935. Meanwhile, he had resumed his flourishing literary career—between 1922 and 1936 he averaged five books a year. For much of that time, he was ranked among the world's best-selling authors, alongside his close friends Rudyard Kipling, Virginia Wolfe, G. K. Chesterton, Hilaire Belloc, and Hugh Walpole. Several of his books, including *The Thirty-Nine Steps*, *Prester John*, *Huntingtower*, and *John McNab*, were even made into full-length motion pictures by the likes of Alfred Hitchcock and Arthur Lammis. Although his work was popular, it often explored serious theological themes and profound human dilemmas. Indeed, according to T. E. Lawrence, Buchan was "the greatest romancer of our blind and undeserving generation."

Throughout the crowded hours of his career, Buchan maintained a vital interest in his family and in his faith. He was married in 1907 to Susan Grosvenor, and together they had a daughter and three sons. He always made certain that his children remained a priority in their lives. Likewise, he was a faithful member of the Presbyterian Church, serving his congregation as a Bible study leader and elder for most of his adult life.

His political, cultural, and spiritual prominence made him an appropriate choice as the king's lord high commissioner to the General Assembly of the Church of Scotland for several years beginning in 1933. The post enabled him to promote the vital relationship between the dynamics of the Christian life and the preservation of Western civilization—a relationship that he believed was threatened by the hubris of modern secularism. This was a theme that resonated throughout his work. "Our enemies are attacking more than our system of Christian morals on which our civilization is founded," he lamented. "They are attacking Christianity itself, and they are succeeding. Our great achievement in perfecting the scientific apparatus of life have tended to produce a mood of self-confidence and pride. We have too often become gross materialists in our outlook on life."

Despite this obvious twentieth-century cultural retrogression, Buchan remained confident. "I believe that the challenge with which we are faced may restore us to that manly humility in the presence of the Unseen which alone gives power," he said. "It may bring us back to God. In that case our victory is assured. The church of Christ is an anvil which has worn out many hammers. Our opponents may boast of their strength, but they do not realize what they have challenged."

His tireless activities on behalf of Christ and crown brought him greater and greater prominence. Despite deteriorating health, he served as the curator of Oxford University Chest, the trustee of the National Library of Scotland, the president of the Scottish Historical Society, and the chancellor of Edinburgh University.

In 1935, King George V ennobled Buchan as the First Lord Tweedsmuir of Elsfield and—at the request of Canadian prime minister Mackenzie King—appointed Buchan the fifteenth governor-general of Canada. Despite recurring illness, Buchan threw himself into these new proconsular duties with especial fervour. He moved to Ottawa and quickly fell in love with the great beauty and diversity of Canada—a land he called "God's manifestation of grace among the nations."

Serving as governor-general allowed Buchan to make full use of his diverse talents. An avid outdoorsman, he toured every province and explored every aspect of Canadian life and culture. He lectured widely across the land, making strong pleas for vigilant national unity, keen historical awareness, and unflinching spiritual integrity. He constantly promoted Canadian arts and sciences—acting as an advocate for the nation's universities and establishing the Governor-General's Literary Awards. In the tumultuous days during the advent of the Second World War, he became a beloved symbol of faith, stability, and constancy in the face of great evil.

Buchan's sudden death on February 12, 1940, was caused by a freak injury sustained in a fall in his official Ottawa residence, Rideau Hall. The sad news made front-page headlines around the world, from South Africa and Australia to Britain and the United States, but nowhere was he mourned as sincerely as in his adopted home. As the British historian G. M. Trevelyan commented in the *Globe and Mail*, "I don't think I remember anyone who has died during my lifetime whose death ever had a more enviable outburst of sorrow and love and admiration, public and private. He was the Christian statesman extraordinaire."

Bernard Gribble (1873–unknown)
Sir Wilfred Grenfell on board "Strathcona"
oil on canvas, 16 x 20.5
Courtesy: Sir Wilfred Thomason Grenfell Historical Society, Grenfell House Museum, St. Anthony

inset: courtesy of Sir Wilfred Thomason Grenfell Historical Society

The Good Samaritan of Labrador
Wilfred Grenfell

1865–1940

"Life is a field of honour."

John G. Stackhouse, Jr.

Evangelical Christianity in the late nineteenth century generated a number of missionaries of "muscular Christianity," which championed body and spirit. None was more typical and more well-known in his day than Wilfred Grenfell, missionary doctor to Labrador.

Grenfell was born in Parkgate, Cheshire, in southwestern England and raised in the upper middle class values that equated Church of England membership with being an English gentleman. He trained as a physician at London Hospital and London University and was mentored by the eminent Christian surgeon Sir Frederick Treves. Toward the end of his studies, Grenfell happened upon a tent meeting in London conducted by American evangelist D. L. Moody. He was struck by Moody's good humour and even more by his challenge to follow Christ in active, courageous service: "I seemed to have suddenly waked up and to be viewing from outside the life which before I just took for granted as it came."

Grenfell was not quite ready to accept the challenge, but soon after the tent meeting he attended a public meeting featuring the testimonies of the Cambridge Seven—famous student athletes who had become missionaries to China. These were muscular Christians indeed, men of deeds and not just words and of the same class and talent as Grenfell himself. At the close of the meeting, when the speakers called upon those who had made a decision for Christ to stand, Grenfell stood. His practical attitude to the event is evident: "This step I have ever since been thankful for…. The decision to fairly try out that faith, which has challenged and stirred the ages, in the laboratory of one's own life, is, I am convinced, the only way to ever obtain a fixed heart on the matter. The prize is to be won, not swallowed." Grenfell was much encouraged as he saw his medical colleagues get over their initial sneering at his new enthusiasm. They did so, he wrote, "when they realized that religion made one do things."

Grenfell's mentor, Sir Frederick Treves, helped him turn his practical attitude into a needed, albeit unusual, ministry on the Atlantic. Treves, a expert mariner, suggested to Grenfell—the descendant of navy men in Devon and Cornwall and himself a skilled sailor—that he serve on the Atlantic with the Royal National Mission to Deep Sea Fishermen. Soon, Grenfell's medical services complemented the floating libraries, clothing stores, and chapels sent out on mission ships to compete with the brothels and saloons located at fishermen's ports of call and on other vessels known as "hells."

In 1892, after five years with the mission, Grenfell visited Labrador and resolved to devote his life to alleviating the misery of the poor folk he found in wretched shanties up and down the rugged coast. Food was scarce much of the time, loneliness endemic, and hygiene at a very low level. Grenfell realized that a broad program of relief was necessary to respond to such a wide range of problems.

Grenfell was a natural speaker and always ready to testify to the gospel, whether before a large audience or a single, troubled fisherman. Early in his medical work in Labrador, he held simple services during which he would rely on remembered scripture passages and sermons that he had heard from his father. Numerous persons were converted or strengthened in faith through his counsel.

But Grenfell's faith was more a matter of practice than of doctrine or spiritual experience. Late in life, he wrote that "Christ's religion to me is primarily for this world, and the New Jerusalem is to come down from Heaven onto this earth and we are to be the Washingtons and Nelsons. We are to save that city—and we are to have all the fun of really creating it." Although his trust in the atonement of Christ was basic, his evangelicalism was not the doctrinal precisionism of fundamentalism or the emotionalism of revivalism. Instead, it was the practical reformism of a social gospel anchored in orthodoxy.

Grenfell recognized especially people's physical and social needs, and he inspired other Christians to support his work. Many came out to join him, short and long term, in serving the desperate and the poor of Newfoundland and Labrador. His over forty years of labour helped produce six hospitals, seven nursing stations, four hospital ships, four boarding schools, twelve clothing distribution centres, about a dozen cooperative stores, a cooperative lumber mill, a dry dock, and a YM/YWCA. He developed cottage industries to broaden the economic base of the fisherfolk and to give them useful work year-round. He also broke the stranglehold of traders who controlled all the goods coming into Newfoundland and who extorted inflated prices for them from the inhabitants. Beyond this, Grenfell's practical vision extended also to directing the first mapping of the treacherous and beautiful Newfoundland coast.

D. L. Moody had convinced Grenfell that "loyalty to a living leader was religion, and that knightly service in the humblest life was the expression of it." Christ, Grenfell was fond of saying, was not a theological subject to be understood, but an admirable champion to be followed. With his unswerving confidence in God, Christianity, and Victorian civilization, Wilfred Grenfell put that lesson into decades of dramatic action.

With the help of his American wife, Anne MacClanahan (whom he married in 1909), he authored more than thirty books and devoted many of his later years to fund-raising tours of Britain, Canada, and the United States. Bluff, confident, passionate, and impressive, Grenfell left a lasting mark on his audiences, and his work brought him international acclaim. Among other honours, he was made Oxford University's first honorary doctor of medicine in 1907 and was knighted in 1927. The International Grenfell Association continues his work to this day.

Grenfell died in Vermont, but his ashes were deposited near the site of the first hospital that he helped found, in St. Anthony, Newfoundland. A brass tablet, without any conventional Christian symbolism, is inscribed simply with his name, a date, and a summation of his view of Christianity: "Life is a Field of Honour."

Nicholas de Grandmaison (1892–1978)
Hon. William Aberhardt
1943, oil on canvas, 137.5 x 99.0 cm
Courtesy: Collection of the Government of Alberta
Photographer: K. J. Clark

inset: Glenbow Archives, Calgary / NA-2771-2

Bible Bill
William Aberhart

1878–1943

"A Canadian original."

John G. Stackhouse, Jr.

William Aberhart founded the Social Credit Party during the Depression and led it to dominance in Alberta. But before he was a politician, and even after he had become one, Aberhart was a preacher—popular and notorious.

Aberhart was born in December 1878 in southwestern Ontario to a German father and an English mother. He studied to become a school teacher and principal, graduating from programs in several schools in geometry, drawing, and business. He then pursued with difficulty a correspondence degree from Queen's University in Kingston, Ontario, graduating in 1911 after he had moved to Alberta. As a child, he had attended a Presbyterian Sunday school near his home. As a school principal, he became active in the Presbyterian Church.

Like many educated Christians of his time, Aberhart was challenged by the new higher criticism of the Bible—the critical application of historical and literary interpretative techniques to the study of Scripture. Unlike most Presbyterians, however, he rejoiced to find answers in dispensationalism, the doctrine that human history is divided into various epochs, or dispensations, that will culminate in the millennial reign of Christ on earth. He began to teach that the true church could not produce a Christian society, but could only add converts and await the Second Coming.

Aberhart moved to Calgary in 1910 and by 1915 was teaching at Crescent Heights High School and preaching at Westbourne Baptist Church—a poor, struggling mission that, under Aberhart, retired its debt a year and a half later. Aberhart held a Bible class on Sunday afternoons at Westbourne. He attracted people by preaching dispensationalism and especially with his explanations of the end times or last days before the Second Coming of Christ, which Aberhart thought to be quite near. Eventually, the class moved to Calgary's Grand Theatre to accommodate the crowd.

Aberhart adopted other media as well. October 1924 saw the first issue of his *Prophetic Voice* magazine, and in 1925 he began the Calgary Prophetic Bible Institute. In 1926, Aberhart inaugurated the Radio Sunday School correspondence course, in whose peak year, 1938–39, enrolment topped nine thousand students. By 1935, Aberhart was broadcasting five hours every Sunday over several Alberta stations to a radio audience estimated at 350,000 people.

The 1920s, which saw so much apparent success for Aberhart, also saw him alienated, however, from the general evangelical community. He made friends with a Jesus Only Pentecostal pastor and began to teach that baptism not only declared one's faith in Christ and introduced one formally into the church but also marked the reception of the Holy Spirit. Moreover, Aberhart taught that baptism should be performed in the name of Jesus only, with no mention of God the Father or the Holy Spirit. Evangelicals and most Pentecostals saw this as a step removed from even the Jesus Only unitarian tendencies current on the periphery of the Pentecostal movement.

Aberhart went further, assuming the title apostle and pushing his followers into a more radical sectarianism. He originally had intended his Prophetic Bible Conference to bring Christians of many denominations together, but in 1922 he forced members of other churches to break either with him or with their own groups. At mid-decade, Aberhart began to denounce other Canadian denominations, referring to the Baptists as Ephesus and to the newly formed United Church as Sardis of the second and third chapters of Revelation. In 1927, he pulled Westbourne out of the Baptist Union of Western Canada and declared it an independent church.

By the early 1930s, Aberhart had lost much of his support among evangelicals because of his unusual doctrine, his sectarianism, and his arrogance. His subsequent foray into politics would cost him most of the rest, as many evangelicals came to believe that he had improperly given up his earlier emphasis on evangelism and unwisely embraced politics as his new crusade. Other Christians and Albertans of various religious backgrounds, however, were to rally around Aberhart as never before.

It is hard for those born since the Great Depression to grasp the plight of whole provinces of destitute farmers. William Aberhart had a pastor's concern for people, and he was thrilled to come across the monetary reform doctrines of a British engineer Major C. H. Douglas, who believed that conventional capitalism would flounder because the private control of credit would lead to a chronic insufficiency of mass purchasing power. In 1933, Aberhart wrote an outline that he titled *The Douglas System of Economics*. He used his religious radio broadcast to teach fledgling Social Credit ideas—that a few financial powers in the big cities were squeezing the farmers, and that the government's supervision of the credit system and its payment of a monthly dividend to each citizen would improve things dramatically.

Alberta's governing party, the United Farmers of Alberta, refused to listen to Aberhart's ideas. So, as sexual scandals emerged involving government leaders, and as the socialist Cooperative Commonwealth Federation appeared on the political horizon, Aberhart formed a new party to contest the 1935 election. His party sang "O God, Our Help in Ages Past" as its anthem and declared Social Credit "an economic movement from God himself."

Aberhart's party won the election with fifty-seven of sixty-three seats and with fifty-four percent of the popular vote, making Aberhart premier. It won again in 1940, although by a much smaller margin. Over the years, the Supreme Court of Canada declared most of Aberhart's distinctive Social Credit legislation to be beyond the scope of the government's legal authority, but Aberhart did reform Alberta's educational system and protect at least some farms from foreclosure through debt legislation. Aberhart died in office in 1943, but his Social Credit Party, under his protégé ERNEST MANNING, went on to dominate Alberta politics for a generation.

The career of William Aberhart, known to many as Bible Bill, fascinates Canadians. Aberhart's experiment with Social Credit was unique in the Western world in the political success of its combination of unusual ideas with evangelical fervour. His pioneering of religious broadcasting set the pace for many Canadians to follow. He articulated an alternative to the social gospel and United Church ecumenism prominent in his region of Canada. The irony of William Aberhart is that he became a popular figure politically just as he was becoming a marginal figure religiously. As Apostle and Premier Aberhart grew in prominence, Bible Bill lost his influence in Canadian popular religion.

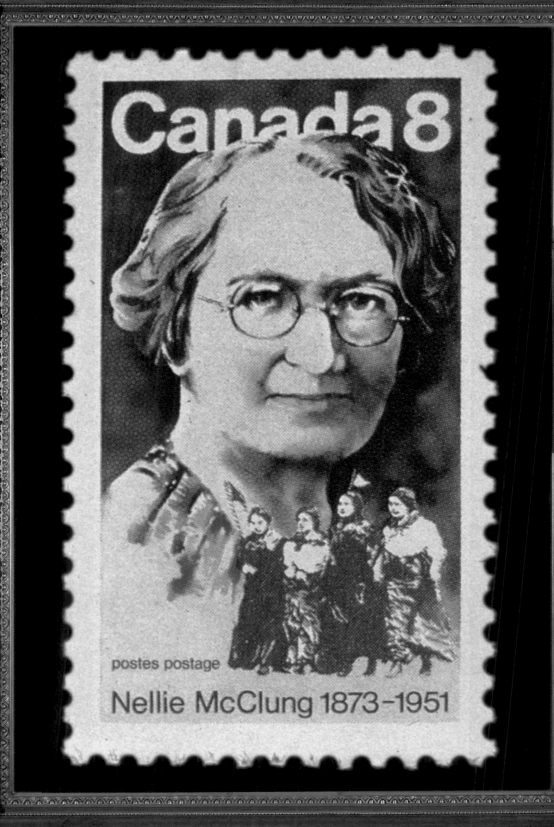

Canada 8

postes postage

Nellie McClung 1873-1951

Using Literature as a Pulpit
Nellie McClung
1873–1951

"Loving service, freely given."

Randi Warne

Nellie McClung had a vision for Canada and for western Canada in particular. Calling it the Land of the Second Chance and the Land of the Fair Deal, McClung believed that the western prairie was a perfect place to build a new civilization based on her understanding of God's intention for creation. As she firmly claimed in 1915, "To bring this about—the even chance for everyone—is the plain and simple meaning of life."

McClung was born on a small farm near Owen Sound, Ontario, in October 1873. Her father, John Mooney, emigrated from Ireland in 1832 to work as a logger in Bytown (Ottawa) then began farming the stony soil of the Bruce Peninsula. Eventually, he married Letitia McCurdy, an emigrant from Scotland several decades his junior. Her Methodist father's jaunty good humour and her Presbyterian mother's dour dedication to duty marked McClung's imagination, and the twin qualities of optimism and determination feature in the fiction that she later wrote as essential elements for prairie life.

The Mooney family moved west to Manitoba in 1880, travelling by steamship, foot, and oxcart to a homestead southwest of Brandon. Nellie, the youngest of six, gloried in the prairies and worked on the farm until she began school at age nine. By fifteen, she was a country schoolteacher. It was at this time that she met Annie McClung, the wife of a Methodist minister and the person who would change her life. Part of Annie's evangelical passion was a dedication to the causes of temperance and women's suffrage. Nellie had found her mentor. She had also found, as she remarked, "the only woman I have ever seen whom I should like to have for a mother-in-law." Nellie married Annie's son, Wes McClung, in 1898, and bore five children over a long and happy marriage.

Annie McClung was instrumental in starting Nellie's writing career. Insisting that McClung enter a short story contest, Annie cared for the children and household while Nellie wrote. The story did not win the contest, but it did become the opening chapter of McClung's first novel, *Sowing Seeds in Danny*, the Canadian best-seller of 1908 and the best-selling Canadian novel to that date. Annie also initiated McClung's career as a public speaker, arranging an event for the Woman's Christian Temperance Union in which Nellie read from her recent novel. As it was for many reformers of the period, male and female, prohibition was an issue of lifelong concern for McClung.

McClung also worked for women's rights. When she and her husband moved to Winnipeg, she joined the Political Equality League. In these two causes she developed into a witty and persuasive orator whose pragmatic approach to politics was captured in the motto: "Never retract, never explain, never apologize." Political activism in the service of social transformation and religious commitment were thus entwined for McClung from the beginning. Indeed, her social gospel novel about the suffrage battle in Manitoba, *Purple Springs*, underscores her understanding that social activism was mandated by God.

Denied ordination by virtue of her sex, McClung used her literature as a pulpit to preach her gospel of feminist activism and social transformation. Her homely tales of rural Manitoba life came on the scene at precisely the time that the country was looking for a national literature to define its character. Through her humourous, semi-didactic stories, McClung shaped her audiences' imaginations about the nation's future, seeing here, too, a religious duty. Her "Writer's Creed," a speech given to the Canadian Authors' Association, clearly outlines her view of the writer's responsibility in this regard.

Her fame as a novelist and skill as a public orator made her a potent political force when the battle to grant women the vote escalated. By 1914, McClung was giving speeches around the country in support of suffrage and temperance, to the dismay of her political opponents. Her efforts were catalytic; the right person at the right time, she galvanized support for women's political enfranchisement. It was no surprise that Manitoba women were the first in Canada to receive the vote, on January 28, 1916. Indeed, McClung's platform skills were such that she received numerous requests from international audiences. She accepted extensive speaking tours in the United States in 1916 and 1917, raising Canada's national profile in the process.

McClung moved with her family to Alberta in December 1914. There, she became part of a network of activist women, including Judge Emily Murphy, the first woman magistrate in the British Empire. With Murphy, Henrietta Muir Edwards, Irene Parlby, and Louise McKinney, McClung became one of the Famous Five who brought the Persons Case to the British Privy Council in 1929 in which women were declared legally persons in Canada. In addition, McClung ran successfully for the Alberta legislature in 1921 as a Liberal, serving until 1926. In 1921, she was the only female Canadian delegate to the Fifth Ecumenical Methodist Conference, held in London. She was also the first female member of the CBC Board of Governors, in 1936, and in 1938 she was appointed to the Canadian delegation to the League of Nations, where she served briefly on the League's committee for social legislation.

Throughout this period, McClung continued to be active as a writer, publishing novels and numerous short stories and speeches. She later undertook a weekly newspaper column, but poor health eventually forced her to give it up. McClung also actively lobbied for the ordination of women in the United Church of Canada, believing that "Christ was a true democrat. He made no discrimination between men and women. They were all human beings to Him, with souls to save and lives to live, and He applied to men and women the same rule of conduct."

Nellie McClung's life reflects a passion for a cooperative community of equals, a vision grounded in the belief that God wishes our "loving service, freely given." In *My Religion*, she lays this out clearly: "It is not, 'Chant my praises'; 'Defend my theories'; 'Kill my enemies.' No, no—but a greater, better, lovelier task: 'Feed my lambs.'"

McClung was a best-selling author, a political and social activist, and a forthright Christian whose liberal theology was grounded in a confidence that "no one has a corner on light or grace." She believed that faith should be professed in action and made her own life an example, struggling to overcome the prejudices of her culture in herself and in others. Nellie McClung—celebrated throughout Canada as Our Nell—died in Victoria, British Columbia, in September 1951.

Vézina (unknown)
Portait d'Henri Bourassa
ca. 1920, oil on canvas, 19 x 14 cm
Courtesy: Collection Musée Régional de Vaudreuil-Soulanges
Photographer: Pierre Lépine

inset: Centre de recherche Lionel-Groulx / P1 / T1, 30.23

A Prophet Crying in the Wilderness
Henri Bourassa

1868–1952

"Preserve in Canada … this home of social Catholicism."

Preston Jones

On September 2, 1952, three days after Henri Bourassa died at the age of eighty-four, the Quebec newspaper he founded—*Le Devoir*—remembered him fondly as "prophetic." It was a sentiment echoed in *Saturday Night*: "Bourassa was the prophet crying in the wilderness."

Whether or not he was a prophet, Bourassa was unwavering in his political and religious beliefs, and he forthrightly proclaimed them. He was the son of painter and architect Napoléon Bourassa, from whom he inherited his freedom of expression. More relevant, however, to the traditions that he absorbed is the fact that his maternal grandfather was the patriote rebel Louis-Joseph Papineau.

In 1896, as a young man, Bourassa was elected to Canada's Parliament, where he attracted the attention of Wilfrid Laurier. He was regarded as one of the most promising young Liberals, destined for a cabinet post, perhaps for the party leadership. But very soon—in 1899—he quarrelled with Laurier's decision to send a volunteer Canadian force to the Boer War, an act that seemed to him an acceptance of imperial domination. For the rest of his life, Bourassa remained outside the major parties.

Bourassa resigned his seat in Parliament in 1899 and was reelected as an independent. In 1903, he helped to found the Ligue Nationaliste. Four years later, despairing of achieving anything through federal politics, he resigned from the House of Commons and entered the Quebec National Assembly. In 1910, he founded *Le Devoir*, which became one of the best Canadian newspapers, always anti-imperialist, always loyal to the French language and tradition in Canada, but never willing to accept without criticism the possibility of separatism.

From the federal Parliament to the National Assembly, Bourassa fought Laurier's naval and trade policies and is best remembered for his vigorous struggle against corruption and what he saw as Canada's over involvement in the First World War. "We are trying to convince our compatriots that Canadians should put their duty to Canada first," he wrote in *Le Devoir* in 1915, "before their responsibilities to England or France." Although he no longer held a political post at this time, his influence in Quebec was considerable and helped to solidify French-Canadian resistance to participation in the war.

Unlike such Quebec nationalists as the fiery American expatriate Jules-Paul Tardivel and, later, LIONEL GROULX, who entertained the idea of secession, Bourassa was committed to Canada. His differences with Quebec's hard-line separatists were signaled in 1932 by his resignation from the editorship of *Le Devoir*.

Bourassa believed that the Canada founded in 1867 was a nation of two equal races and that religious and linguistic minorities should be protected throughout Canada. When French language education was curtailed in western Canada, he spoke out forcefully on behalf of francophone minorities outside Quebec. So, too, he defended the rights of minorities within Quebec. During his tenure as the mayor of Montebello, Quebec, in the early 1890s, he ensured that a school was established to accommodate Protestant families. There was never a time that he felt either of the two Canadian nations could exist alone; the price of their survival, he always argued, was a mutual recognition of their separate and complete identities.

Although Bourassa believed that English and French should be preserved in Canada, he did not think highly of bilingualism among the French-speaking masses. He feared that if his French-speaking compatriots learned English they would become like the Irish and the Scots who had lost their Gaelic. Only Quebec's elite, he thought, should learn English.

At the heart of this idea was the belief that Quebec's French language and Roman Catholicism were inextricably linked. In his view, if Quebecers lost their language they would lose their faith and culture. "Our language received no divine promise of preservation," he argued in 1912, "except the one that God made to all the peoples and men who have enough heart and energy to defend their soul, their body, and their national and family heritage; but this promise holds nothing for those whose hearts are so base that they would swap their birthright for a mess of pottage." In Bourassa's view, English was the "language of materialism, and especially in the United States the language of the most enthusiastic worshippers of the golden calf."

Bourassa believed that French Canadians had a religious duty to maintain their language. Yet, he also recognized that the Catholic Church was greater than any national or linguistic particularity. "The Catholic Church, precisely because it is Catholic, is not and will never be the Church of an epoch, of a country or a nation," he wrote in *Le Devoir* in 1910. Nevertheless, he believed that God had called French Canadians to a special task that they must fulfill.

Bourassa hoped that Quebec would serve as the heartland of Roman Catholicism in North America. "It seems to me desirable," he continued in *Le Devoir*, "to preserve in Canada and America this home of social Catholicism, which casts its rays from the banks of the Gulf of Saint Lawrence to the summits of the Rockies, which shines its light on all Catholic groups of New England, New York, Michigan, up to the borders of Oregon."

If Bourassa thought that Quebec could be a Catholic light in North America, he believed that the Vatican was a light to the world. Bourassa did not believe that the Pope should dictate to secular politicians, but he did believe that a nation's political and social life should be guided by Catholic teaching. At the end of the First World War, he wrote that when Europe had been brought to its knees its leaders should heed the Pope—who had "never led them astray" and who in his wartime proclamations had "pointed to the path of justice and salvation."

Following the end of the war, in 1918, and the death of his wife the following year, Bourassa devoted himself to his writing. He returned to the federal Parliament in 1925 as an independent and faithfully criticized the Liberals and the Conservatives until 1935, when he lost his seat in the riding of Labelle.

Throughout his life, Bourassa held to the faith that he had been taught as a child, first among the Sulpicians in Montreal and then among the Jesuits. He attended mass faithfully. And he passed that faith on to his children. The Catholic priest who administered absolution to him minutes before his death was his son.

Robert E. McAlister
Colourization of black and white photo, ca. 1950
Courtesy: Pentecostal Assemblies of Canada Archives

inset: Pentecostal Assemblies of Canada Archives

A Father of Canadian Pentecostalism
Robert McAlister

1880–1953

"Lifelong desire to bring people into a personal relationship with Christ."

James Craig

Robert Edward McAlister played a foundational role in the early growth of the Pentecostal Assemblies of Canada (PAOC), the nation's largest Pentecostal denomination. His labours as an evangelist, pastor, organizer, teacher, writer, and missions promoter helped the PAOC grow from twenty-seven churches in 1919 to over one thousand today.

McAlister was born in the Ottawa Valley near Cobden, Ontario, one of thirteen children born to James and Margaret McAlister, who were Presbyterians of Scottish descent. Robert left school after the third grade to help on the family farm. Aided by a photographic memory, he educated himself, so well that he later became renowned for extensive doctrinal writings. He would strap his Bible to the plough and memorize long passages while he worked the fields. In later years, he became known as the Walking Bible, often reciting lengthy passages of Scripture as he preached.

In the late 1880s, the Ottawa Valley came under the influence of Ralph C. Horner, a fiery Methodist evangelist. Horner's brand of holiness religion was welcomed by the Methodist church in Cobden, and when he was expelled from the denomination in 1895 that church became a branch of his Holiness Movement Church. It was in that church that McAlister converted to Christ around 1900. Sensing a call to the ministry in 1901, he entered God's Bible School, a small Holiness college in Cincinnati. Poor health during his second year of studies forced his return home. After his recovery he began preaching for the Holiness Movement Church instead of returning to school.

In 1906, McAlister learned of the events taking place at a small mission on Azusa Street in Los Angeles. People were experiencing spiritual phenomena similar to those on the day of Pentecost as recorded in the second chapter of Acts. They were speaking in unknown languages and witnessing miracles of healing. McAlister travelled by train to Los Angeles and went to the warehouse where the continuous services were in progress. He experienced what Pentecostals call the Baptism with the Holy Spirit, the hallmark of the Pentecostal movement. This definitive receiving and releasing of the power of the Holy Spirit includes speaking in tongues and imparts a dynamic ability and fervent desire to share the gospel with others. McAlister was among the first Canadians to receive the Pentecostal experience. The remainder of his life provided ample demonstration of the effects of his encounter with the Holy Spirit at Azusa Street. He passionately devoted his energies to bringing people into a joyous personal relationship with Jesus Christ.

Back in Canada, McAlister shared his new blessing. From his base in the Ottawa Valley, he travelled extensively in the United States and Canada, holding evangelistic meetings and teaching at Pentecostal conventions. Soon, churches were established in Ottawa and a number of other communities.

In 1911, McAlister began his career as a religious writer and publisher. He started a small paper, the *Good Report*, that contained accounts of Pentecostal conventions, testimonies of physical healings, conversion stories, and articles on the teachings of the Pentecostal movement. In the first issue, McAlister articulated the central characteristics of the movement. He stated that the Pentecostal movement was a restoration of the teachings and practices of the New Testament Apostles and was a "soul-saving agency in the hands of God." McAlister further claimed that it was a missionary movement intent on evangelizing the world, with no human founder, and completely centered upon Jesus Christ.

By 1917, the need for a formal structure to unite Pentecostal churches across Canada had become evident. Discussions among key leaders led to McAlister and six others ministers being granted a federal charter incorporating the Pentecostal Assemblies of Canada in 1919. McAlister's prominent role in forming the new organization is reflected in his serving as its first general secretary (1919–1932), and, at the same time, as its first missions secretary and in the dozens of resolutions that bear his name in the organization's official minutes. All of this was in addition to his pastoral duties.

In 1920, McAlister also founded the *Pentecostal Testimony*, a publication that still serves as the official organ of the PAOC. During his fifteen years as its editor, McAlister wrote expositions of Christian doctrine, warned of the dangers that threatened the fledgling movement, and promoted the cause of missions.

Two years later, he accepted an invitation to become the pastor of a thriving Pentecostal assembly in London, Ontario. Within three years, a larger church was built only to be expanded two years later.

McAlister was a caring shepherd and powerful Bible teacher. He demonstrated his emphasis on evangelism by beginning a daily radio broadcast in 1934 that aired for fifteen years. His program was instrumental in starting new churches in several Ontario towns, including Chatham, Blenheim, Dresden, and Ridgetown. Under McAlister's teaching and with his personal encouragement, dozens of young men and women entered the ministry as evangelists, pastors, and missionaries, influencing communities worldwide.

In October 1940, after nineteen years of fruitful ministry in London, McAlister resigned his pastorate and moved to Toronto. His remaining years were spent in itinerant teaching and preaching, including an extensive campaign from 1948 to 1952 to combat doctrinal controversies that threatened to divide the PAOC. This latter role further enhanced his reputation as a Pentecostal theologian.

McAlister's lifelong desire was to bring people into a personal relationship with Christ. His nephew Eric McLean recalls that while visiting McAlister, who had been admitted to hospital with heart problems in late September 1953, he learned his uncle had just shared the gospel with his roommate, leading the man to Christ. By the time Eric returned home from the hospital, McAlister had died.

The Pentecostal movement in Canada is the work of many dedicated pioneers, such as Andrew H. Argue, George A. Chambers, and Alfred G. Ward. But no one is better qualified to be called the father of Canadian Pentecostalism than Robert Edward McAlister.

39

Member of
Parliament
Députée

1890–1954

Agnes Macphail

Canada

39¢ Agnes Macphail
Postage stamp, issued October 9, 1990
Courtesy: Canada Post Corporation

inset: National Archives of Canada / PA-127295

Canada's First Female Member of Parliament
Agnes Macphail
1890–1954

"Her life might have been much easier.
But this was the path she chose—the craggy course."

Terry Crowley

Following the 1921 federal election, Agnes Macphail became the country's best-known woman as Canada's first female member of Parliament. But Agnes was not celebrated primarily as a fighter for women's suffrage; her campaigns were mainly for cooperation and against war, for a better deal for the farmers, and against the existing Canadian penal system. In fact, though she fought to better the conditions of women, she walked into politics as if sexual differences did not exist. She fought as an equal with men for the issues that moved her.

Agnes was born in 1890 in a three-room log house on a farm in Ontario. After completing elementary school, she remained at home to help her mother with two younger sisters. Her family eventually saved money for her board so that she could attend the nearest high school in Owen Sound. She graduated in 1908 to the new teacher's college in Stratford, where she lived with her uncle and aunt. Agnes was so impressed with their religious faith and social conscience that she joined the Reorganized Church of Jesus Christ of the Latter Day Saints. When her aunt presented her with a Bible, she read it diligently, noting passages in both the Old and the New Testaments that she found particularly significant.

Between 1910 and 1921, Agnes taught in rural schools in southern Ontario and Alberta. Her contact with the United Farmers and Farm Women of Ontario afforded her opportunities for political involvement. Although this agrarian movement for rural social and economic betterment had only begun in 1914, a grassroots upheaval during the 1919 Ontario election led to the formation of the Farmer-Labour government of E. C. Drury. While helping to organize local groups, Agnes gained recognition as a forceful speaker, leading to her 1921 federal candidacy on the Farmer-Labour ticket and to her becoming the first woman member of the House of Commons. In Parliament, she soon joined other Progressives led by T. A. Crerar. Despite the affiliation, her position as the only woman in the House of Commons until 1935 attracted significant attention. But the media spotlight intensified as a result of her unconventional ideas. She likened the agrarian revolt to a righteous uprising against corruption in government and the subordination of the needs of ordinary people to the special interests dominating the two old-line parties. Although she found the prophecies of Isaiah to be a source of personal inspiration in advocating ways to change Canadian life for the better, she was outspoken in support of religious and ethnic tolerance. Politics were a sufficient source of division; religion should not have to be as well.

Agnes believed in thinking anew about collective problems rather than reverting to outmoded prescriptions. Considered a radical, she found much of the establishment in Toronto and Vancouver closed to her. Despite her attacks on big business, the media, and her feminist ideology, her rural constituents continued to reelect her to Parliament—four times. She emerged as one of the best orators in the House of Commons, but often found herself praying silently for guidance about how to vote. Agnes supported the Progressives' anti-imperialism and their quest for Canadian autonomy, but it was her championing of the advancement of women, peace, and prison reform that really set her apart.

By working to remove laws that treated women differently from men in such matters as citizenship and divorce, Agnes strove to enhance the position of her gender. "I desire that women have equal rights," she said. As a regular on the Canadian Chautauqua circuit in the 1920s, she once was confronted by a male heckler who yelled, "Don't you wish you were a man?" She retorted, "Yes, don't you?"

In 1929, her activity in the Women's International League for Peace and Freedom along with Lucy Woodsworth led to her being appointed as Canada's first woman delegate to the League of Nations in Geneva. With the onset of the Great Depression she became increasingly critical of capitalism, an economic system that she likened to an elephant dancing among the chickens while crying "every man for himself." In 1932, she led the United Farmers of Ontario into affiliation with the new Co-operative Commonwealth Federation (CCF) headed by J. S. Woodsworth.

As prison populations burgeoned, Agnes intensified her efforts to end the inhumane treatment of criminals and the inordinately high recidivism rates that made beggars of inmates' wives and children. She was especially concerned that young offenders be treated apart from the adult population. Her courageous and well-orchestrated campaign led to a 1938 royal commission that revealed gross defects in the country's penitentiaries, resulting in prison reform after World War II.

In 1940, Agnes lost her seat in the House of Commons after nineteen years of membership. Following a family tragedy in which a niece shot an uncle, Agnes whisked her nieces and nephews off to Toronto, rented a large house, and began taking in boarders to pay the rent, all the while serving on the executives of the Canadian Civil Liberties Union and the Canadian Association for Adult Education. In 1943, she ran for the CCF in the Ontario election. She was elected for York East, becoming the first woman seated in the provincial assembly. She was defeated in 1945 and reelected in 1948. By advocating improved provincial correctional facilities for young women, Agnes inspired the founding of the Elizabeth Fry Society of Toronto. Genuine pay equity for women was another concern, but in the end the province legislated only equal pay for equal work before Agnes retired from public life in 1951.

Agnes lived in Leaside and attended Don Mills United Church, where she also taught Sunday school. No explanation is offered as to why she left her former church for a mainline Protestant denomination, but it is understood that faith played a meaningful role in her life. "No one person built the church," she reflected, "but each had its part in something which by its very age and continuity became something more than the sum of them all." She believed that to "be happy we all need to lose our little spirits in the Great Spirit which is called God. A person who has no bigger idea of himself is almost certain to be a deeply unhappy person."

After suffering various ailments throughout her life, including a thyroid imbalance, Agnes Macphail died of a heart attack in Toronto in 1954 at the age of sixty-three. At her funeral, her minister eulogized: "Her life might have been much easier. But this was the path she chose—the craggy course."

Alphonse Lesperance (1914–)
Lionel Groulx
1965, oil on canvas, 75.5 x 60.0 cm
Courtesy: Alphonse Lesperance et le Centre de recherche Lionel-Groulx
Photographer: James Gauthier

inset: National Archives of Canada / C-16657

Lionel Groulx

1878–1967

*"The essence of our being can be expressed
in two words, French and Catholic."*

Preston Jones

Lionel-Adolphe Groulx did not only write history, he made it, stoking the flame of Quebec nationalism. Groulx was a historian who believed that pride in the past would give French Canadians confidence in their future. Despite thirty-four years as a professor at the University of Montreal, Groulx was no ivory-tower academic. He engaged in popular journalism, wrote novels, advocated schemes designed to increase Quebec's economic independence, and initiated a Catholic students' organization in the province.

Groulx was born in Vaudreuil, Quebec, to a habitant family. His academic commitment was evident early in life. In 1898, he was awarded the Médaille Chapleau, which distinguished him as the best student of French, Latin, Greek, English, and modern history at the Séminaire de Sainte-Thérèse-de-Blainville. The following year, Groulx was awarded the Governor-General's Medal, again in recognition of his academic excellence. From 1918 to 1952, Groulx served as a fellow of the Royal Society of Canada. Prizes, honourary doctorates, and similar awards continued to be conferred on Groulx to the end of his life.

Abbé Groulx—as he became generally known—attended seminary in Montreal and was ordained as a priest in 1903. Groulx never became a parish priest; he taught at the Collège de Valleyfield in his home province; he studied in Rome, Fribourg, and Montreal; and in 1915, he became a professor of Canadian history at the University of Montreal. In his lifetime, Groulx wrote some thirty books, over twenty pamphlets, and hundreds of newspaper and journal articles. From 1920 to 1928, he edited the nationalist review *L'Action française*. He founded the Institut d'histoire de l'Amérique française in 1946 and launched its academic publication, *Revue d'histoire de l'Amérique française*, the following year.

Groulx never failed to speak and write his mind, for which he earned a reputation for controversy. In the mid-1930s, for instance, he publicly assailed HENRI BOURASSA, who had warned Groulx against excessive nationalism and racial pride. Bourassa's Canadianism, Groulx said, was a thing of the past. Groulx's heart and mind were with Quebec.

A major reason for Groulx's combativeness and fervent nationalism was that he came of age in a period of crisis in Canadian French-English relations. In 1890, separate French language schools were abolished in Manitoba, even as the memory of the hanged Louis Riel, whom many French Canadians considered a martyr, was still sharp. The conscription crisis during the First World War further revealed the chasm separating French- and English-speaking Canadians. From his youth, Groulx was a committed French-Canadian nationalist, and although he did not advocate outright secession from Canada he did entertain separatism as a political possibility.

What mattered most to Groulx was that Quebec should preserve its French language, its French culture, and its Roman Catholic faith. Like most French-Canadian clerics, he regretted the French Revolution, French anticlericalism, and modern French unbelief, but he consistently maintained that the French people were a chosen race. In his view, the French Canadians were the heirs of a special divine mission. "The little [French-speaking] Canadian people of 1760 possessed all the elements of nationhood," Groulx wrote in his *La Naissance d'une race* (The Birth of a People), published in 1919. "It had a land of its own, it had ethnic unity, linguistic unity, it had a history and traditions. But above all it had religious unity, the unity of the true faith." The French Quebecer's task,

he consistently maintained, was to preserve in North America the French, Catholic, and agricultural way of life that had been threatened by the British conquest in 1759.

Groulx's political pilgrimage extended along the verges of the ultraright. Not content with supporting Charles Maurras in the 1920s, in the following decade he at times praised figures like Mussolini, Salazar, and Dollfuss. But in spite of this ultraconservative orientation, Groulx's major historical works proved an inspiration to Quebec nationalists of all complexions, conservative or socialist, separatist or merely autonomist. Groulx enshrined his vision for Quebec nationalism in his massive *Histoire du Canada Français depuis la Découverte* (The History of French Canada Since Discovery), which appeared in several volumes between 1950 and 1952. That vision was given practical manifestation when combined with the political talents of men like René Lévesque.

Groulx maintained that if a Catholic, French-speaking community could be safely preserved within Confederation, then Quebec should stay in Confederation. But if Confederation imperilled French-Canadian culture, then Quebec should go its own way. Whatever the case, Quebec came first. Yet, Groulx did not believe that Quebecers should only turn inward. Indeed, their faith obligated them to be a witness to the world. In 1953, Groulx declared that he loved French Quebec for "the ties of blood and history" that bonded him to it, but that he loved it primarily because of the thousands of Catholic missionaries that it had sent all over the globe. If nothing else saved Quebec from being eventually set aside by Providence, the work of its missionaries would. "It's because of them that I hope," Groulx wrote.

Although Groulx's staunch nationalism paved the way for Québecois separatism, he did not approve of the secularism that he saw prevailing in Quebec, particularly after 1960. Against secularist nationalists, Groulx argued that Quebecers should not speak of their French language as if it could be separated from their Catholic faith. "In place of speaking of language and faith, I prefer to speak of the soul and faith," he had written earlier, in 1935.

In a 1949 speech delivered in Ottawa, he summarized: "The essence of our being can be expressed in two words, French and Catholic. French and Catholic we have been, not merely since our arrival in America, but for the past thousand years." Groulx believed that it was God's will for French civilization to survive in North America. For if it was true to its task, he wrote, "a small people united by the true faith" could surely radiate "the living splendour of a Christian civilization."

In his final years, Groulx saw the gradual rejection of many of his earlier ideas, and he knew that his legacy would be debated after his death. In his last will and testament, he wrote, "I think it will not be difficult to make sense of everything I said, wrote, or did, or even to understand the passion with which I did it." Nonetheless, his views on race have been a source of debate for decades, as has his anti-Semitism. What is clear, however, is that he loved Quebec, its people, and its traditional Catholic faith. Groulx never ceased to be in attitude completely a priest and in feeling completely a peasant. "In view of these motives and this inspiration for my actions," he wrote just before his death in 1967, "may God forgive me and grant me mercy."

A. Rosenthal
SE. Governor General Georges P. Vanier
oil on canvas, 70 x 57 cm
Courtesy: La Régie du Royal 22nd Régiment. En démonstration en Mess des Officiers de la Citadelle
Photographer: Andre Kedl

inset: National Archives of Canada / C-063531

A Man Who Walked with God
Georges Vanier

1888–1967

"May almighty God in His infinite wisdom and mercy bless the sacred mission which has been entrusted to me… and help me to fulfil it in all humility."

George Cowley

The announcement that General Georges Vanier had been appointed the governor-general of Canada came at a meeting of the Canadian cabinet in Halifax at which Her Majesty Queen Elizabeth II presided. Nationwide, cheers erupted as the former soldier and statesman was appointed the personal representative of the sovereign in Canada. As he took the oath of office in 1959, Vanier said to Parliament, "My first words are a prayer. May almighty God in His infinite wisdom and mercy bless the sacred mission which has been entrusted to me by Her Majesty the Queen and help me to fulfil it in all humility. In exchange for His strength, I offer Him my weakness. May He give peace to this beloved land of ours and … the grace of mutual understanding, respect and love."

Georges Phileas Vanier was born in Montreal in 1888, the son of a French Norman father and an Irish mother. He grew up bilingual, earning a degree in English and a degree in French law. As a student, he was deeply religious, led a church devotional fellowship, and began a lifelong habit of daily communion. He contemplated entering the priesthood, but when the First World War broke out he felt that his immediate duty was to his country. He took a leading role in recruiting and organizing the first battalion to be raised by and of French Canadians: the Royal 22nd Regiment, or Van Doos.

Vanier was twice decorated for bravery. "I sleep as ever on the fresh earth," he wrote to his parents, "one day we shall all go back to her." Shortly after, he lost his right leg to a German shell. After convalescing, he refused evacuation. "I simply cannot go back to Canada," he insisted, "while my comrades are still in the trenches in France."

At war's end, Vanier returned to Canada and was made the commanding officer and later the colonel of the Van Doos. He also met and married Pauline Archer (see PAULINE VANIER), a vivacious young woman who shared his religious faith. In 1927, Vanier held the rank of lieutenant colonel and was sent to Geneva as a Canadian military advisor to the League of Nations disarmament conference. He surprised the conference with moving calls for world disarmament: "I ask you to open your eyes to human suffering, to direct your hearts to those who have not the strength to ask for help. Let us go to them. They have already been waiting too long." His appeal fell on deaf, militarist ears, but his diplomatic skills won him a posting in 1931 to the Canadian High Commission in London, where he remained until 1938. In 1939, he was named minister at the Canadian Embassy in Paris.

Vanier's warnings of imminent war soon came true. Only after arranging the evacuation of Canadian nationals, and of many other imperilled refugees, did he leave Paris in a dramatic escape by car. He reached Bordeaux just ahead of the Germans and from there hitched rides on Allied naval vessels to England.

With the fall of France, the Germans set up a puppet regime known as the Vichy government. The Allied governments initially supported this nominally independent regime, rejecting Vanier's warnings of its inevitable treachery. Vanier called in vain for the recognition of French general Charles de Gaulle, who, from London, proposed to recruit a free French army to continue the war against the Germans.

Vanier's warnings were resented, and he was banished to Canada to an insignificant job—until his forecasts of Vichy treachery proved accurate. He was then returned to London as the minister to the Allied governments in exile, rallying support for de Gaulle. In 1944, he became Canada's ambassador to France, the first ambassador to enter the newly liberated country.

The war in Europe dragged on for another six months. The Vaniers were consumed by the many issues resulting from five years of war and dislocation. While Pauline helped settle the thousands of returning deportees, Georges worked with the French government on international agreements aimed at healing the wounds and the bitterness of war. He was particularly moved by the plight of Jewish survivors, orphaned children, and the elderly.

"It was on the road from Jerusalem to Jericho," Vanier declared, "that robbers stripped and wounded and left for dead the poor traveller of the gospel. We seem hardly to have advanced since those days: today millions have been stripped, wounded and left for dead on the bloodstained roads of Europe. Is not each one of these our brother or our sister?"

The Vaniers attended mass every morning. In the bitterness of 1940's and 1950's Paris, they felt the need to add a daily half hour of prayer and meditation together. Inner prayer, Vanier believed, was a necessary wellspring for sensitivity to the needs of others. Indeed, he rarely made any major decision without first considering its implications in prayer. His biographer, Robert Speaight, noted that "he was a man who walked with God."

Vanier retired from diplomatic service in 1954, hoping to continue serving Canada in "some modest capacity." The capacity offered him in 1959—at age seventy-one—was to become Canada's governor-general, the first Quebec native so honoured. His first initiative was to convert one of the state residence's small upstairs bedrooms into a simple chapel.

Friends were concerned for Vanier's health, but he thrived. He set out to rediscover his country and visited every corner of it. Wherever he spoke, he made stirring appeals to people's hearts and consciences.

In early 1967, Vanier's heart showed signs of weakening. His last official engagement was to address, from his wheelchair, a delegation of students from the University of Montreal on the favourite theme of his latter years: the importance of Canadian unity. Few figures in Canadian history have better demonstrated, by words and deeds, the urgency and sacredness of this cause. "The measure of Canadian unity has been the measure of our success…. If we imagine we can go our separate ways within our country, if we exaggerate our differences or revel in contentions … we will promote our own destruction. Canada owes it to the world to remain united, for no lesson is more badly needed than the one our unity can supply: the lesson that diversity need not be the cause for conflict, but, on the contrary, may lead to richer and nobler living. I pray to God that we may go forward hand in hand."

Shortly afterwards, on March 4, 1967, George Vanier's gallant heart, pressed to its limits for so long, quietly surrendered.

Philip de Laszlo (1869–1937)
Portrait of Madame Vanier
1929, oil on canvas, 162.3 x 100.6 cm
Courtesy: National Gallery of Canada, Ottawa. Gift of His Excellency Georges P. Vanier, Governor General of Canada, 1962
Photographer: Marc Fowler

inset: Cavouk / National Archives of Canada / C-8015

A Realm of Justice and Gentleness
Pauline Vanier

1898–1991

*"Faith, far from being outmoded or old-fashioned, imparts a beauty,
a richness, and a radiance that can be found in no other source."*

Deborah Cowley

Pauline Vanier was born in Montreal in 1898. She was the only child of Charles Archer, a Quebec Superior Court judge, and his wife, Thérèse de Salaberry, whose seigneurial ancestors had come to Canada in 1730.

Pauline's early studies in Montreal's Sacred Heart Convent gave her a strong religious foundation, and her subsequent readings with a worldly-wise tutor of English and French literature developed her lively mind and insatiable curiosity. She early contemplated becoming a nun, but when the First World War broke out she immediately applied to join the army, as a foot soldier. Unsuccessful, she secretly enrolled in a nursing course and to her parents' dismay accepted a job at a military convalescent hospital, where she laboured long hours until the war's end.

She was in her early twenties when she was introduced to Georges Vanier, a dashing and much-decorated war hero of the Royal 22nd Regiment. She was immediately attracted to him, chiefly because his spiritual sensitivities were so closely tuned to hers. Pauline and Georges were married in 1921 and moved to the Canadian army staff college in Kingston shortly before Viscount Byng, Canada's newly appointed governor-general, invited Georges to join his staff at Government House as an aide-de-camp.

Pauline was the perfect helpmate as they moved to postings in Geneva, London, and Paris. In every new location, she set up a warm and comfortable home, entertained with grace and dignity, and channelled her enthusiasm and compassion to dozens of social causes.

It was her escape in 1940 from wartime Paris to London with their four children, however, that gave Pauline a chance to show her courage and complete trust in God. With the Germans rapidly overrunning France, Georges insisted that she and the children leave Paris in the Vanier automobile. Every road south was jammed with refugees, who were being repeatedly machine-gunned by German fighter aircraft. Suddenly, an enemy airplane crashed beside the road just ahead of Pauline's car. Her reaction to her would-be assassin's plight was typical. She leapt from her car and ran to the smoking wreck hoping to drag the pilot to safety. Alas, he had died in the crash.

When Pauline and the children finally reached Bordeaux, they boarded an aging tramp steamer for a harrowing five-day journey to Britain. There, they were reunited with Georges just in time to endure some of the most devastating bombing of the blitzkrieg.

When Paris was liberated in August 1944, Georges, now confirmed as Canada's ambassador to France, was the first accredited diplomat to arrive in the city. But the French capital was still considered too dangerous for women civilians. Undaunted, Pauline persuaded Canadian Red Cross officials to allow her to be their representative in France. She then borrowed an ill-fitting uniform and hitched a ride to France on a military plane departing from London, becoming the first diplomat's wife to reach Paris.

Once there, she set to work to help handle the daily flood of returning refugees. She organized the wives of the diplomatic community to set up welcoming centres at the main railway station, she established an information network to reunite refugees with their families, and she helped French priest Abbé Pierre set up housing and workshops for the homeless. It was sixteen months of consuming, exhausting work before she could return to the normal life of ambassador's wife. A grateful French government awarded her the Légion d'Honneur for her Herculean efforts.

When Georges was named governor-general in 1959, Pauline, a tall, striking figure with snow-white hair, would become one of the most memorable First Ladies this country has ever known. She jumped into her new role with energy and fervour as the vice-regal couple crisscrossed the land visiting hospitals and schools, factories and prisons. "She was," noted Prime Minister Lester Pearson "one-half of a perfect partnership in the service of Canada."

Of all the causes she espoused, none was more important to her than the welfare of the family. So, in 1964 she and her husband convened the first Canadian Conference of the Family. The opening ceremony was unique in Canadian history: on the Vaniers' initiative, the leaders of seventeen different religious communities were asked to draft a benediction that they could all endorse. Out of this conference sprang the Vanier Institute of the Family, whose research work continues today.

After her husband's death in 1967, Pauline moved back to Montreal. In addition, she served as the chancellor of the University of Ottawa, in whose affairs she showed a keen interest. At her investiture, she shared her idealistic and ecumenical hopes for the university's future. "The realm of justice and gentleness should prevail," she said. "The true Christian spirit looks upon all spiritual values, of whatever source, as part of the divine treasure entrusted to mankind by the Creator.... Faith, far from being outmoded or old-fashioned, imparts a beauty, a richness, and a radiance that can be found in no other source."

In spite of such challenging commitments, Pauline felt emptiness in her life. After a two-week retreat with "my dear little sisters" at a Carmelite convent, she made a decision that startled many of her friends: though already seventy-three, she would move to France to join her son Jean, who had founded l'Arche, a community north of Paris for mentally handicapped adults. It was here that she found the perfect outlet for her warmth and compassion. Surrounded by some two hundred mentally handicapped men and women and as many young assistants from around the world, she quickly became a beloved grandmother to the whole community.

Pauline made many contributions to l'Arche. When she recognized that English-speaking assistants missed worshipping in their own language, she transformed her sitting room into a small chapel. There, she placed on a table a Bible, a silver cross, and a tiny candle and every week for almost four years welcomed several dozen assistants of all faiths to informal prayer meetings. "She offered a special moment of being home, a respite from a different culture, a quiet reassurance," recalled Sister Sue Mosteller, a longtime member of l'Arche. "Above all, she offered spiritual safety to so many people. You felt refreshed by having been there. Indeed, many people's lives were transformed by those meetings."

Pauline Vanier lived a full and fulfilled nineteen years in the l'Arche community, where she was active until the last day of her life. She died in 1991, a few days short of her ninety-third birthday. As *Globe and Mail* writer Michael Valpy observed: "Pauline Vanier invested her entire life with love, humour, service, compassion, and spiritual questing."

York Wilson (1907–1984)
Marshall McLuhan
1978, acrylic on canvas, 71.8 x 51.3 cm
Courtesy: Mrs. York Wilson
Photographer: Tom Moore

inset: reprinted with permission from *Letters of Marshall McLuhan* (Toronto: Oxford University Press, 1987)

The Medium is the Message
Marshall McLuhan
1911–1980

*"The incarnation was the ultimate extension of man,
the ultimate technology."*

Philip Marchand

At the height of his celebrity in the 1960s, Marshall McLuhan—Canada's best-known writer on communications—was often referred to as a prophet of the media. McLuhan never accepted the label in its popular sense, as someone who makes predictions about the future. In his witty fashion, he always said that he only made predictions about the present. Since most people were fixated on the past, it seemed as if he was talking about the future.

But neither was McLuhan's role that of a prophet in the biblical sense: as an individual chosen by God to warn a nation and call its people to repentance. He was not a Jeremiah. Indeed, as he surveyed the culture around him and its transformations because of technology, he almost went out of his way to avoid sounding a moral note. His task, he believed, was that of a scientist. It was to observe and to understand what was happening. He did not want to condemn television, for example—he wanted to discover what effects it had on our sensibilities and social habits. Once we understood these things, he felt, we could better decide what to do with it.

Yet, his studies of the media and communications were always implicitly grounded in a profound Christian faith, gained early in life. Marshall McLuhan was born in 1911 in Edmonton, Alberta, to Herbert, a Presbyterian, and Elsie McLuhan, a Baptist. Five years later, the family settled in Winnipeg, where Herbert McLuhan worked as an insurance agent and where Marshall and his younger brother, Maurice, spent the rest of their childhoods and youth. Both parents were of staunch Protestant heritage, and Herbert McLuhan, in particular, was deeply attached to the Bible his mother had taught him. Marshall McLuhan never lost the sense of high moral purpose that he absorbed in his parents' home.

Intellectually, Marshall's first love was literature, and he studied English at the University of Manitoba and at Cambridge University in England. In 1936, on his return from Cambridge, he took a job as a teaching assistant at the University of Wisconsin. It was during the year that he spent at Wisconsin that McLuhan, partly under the influence of the writer Gilbert Keith Chesterton, whom he greatly admired, converted to Catholicism, a faith he professed to the end of his life.

McLuhan found congenial the teachings of St. Thomas Aquinas, the great Catholic philosopher who—in the tradition of Aristotle—maintained that man could trust the evidence of his senses and the workings of his reason, when properly informed by Scripture. What McLuhan feared and detested, above all, was the ancient heresy of Gnosticism, which denied the goodness and reality of the created universe, including the human body, and promoted the idea of a special, mystical realm open to a favoured few. McLuhan was most truly prophetic, in all senses of the word, when he stated that the great threat to Christianity in our time would come not from scientific rationalism but from various forms of Gnosticism.

McLuhan was also concerned throughout his career with the ways in which our sensory lives are enhanced and distorted by technology, particularly the media of communications. He believed that our perceptions are powerfully shaped by such inventions as the printing press and television, in ways we usually don't recognize. And yet he never doubted, in keeping with his Thomistic leanings, that God had created a deeply coherent and ordered universe, capable of being understood by human beings.

Initially, McLuhan emphasized the power of literature, ranging from Chaucer and Shakespeare to T. S. Eliot, to help us understand our environment and ourselves. Indeed, he remained first and foremost an English professor. From 1937 to 1944, he taught English at the University of St. Louis, where, in 1939, he married Corinne Lewis, an actress and teacher from Fort Worth, Texas. His next posts were Assumption College in Windsor, Ontario, where he stayed from 1944 to 1946, and then the University of Toronto, which was his home until he was forced to abandon teaching after suffering a stroke in 1979.

While never losing his love for literature, McLuhan became increasingly interested in the media of communications during the 1950s. It was during this decade that he coined some of the phrases that made him famous. He hit upon the term global village, for example, to describe the way in which modern means of communication give us a jarring intimacy with the world's population. He proclaimed that, "the medium is the message" to convey his insight that our means of communication—such as radio and television—had profound effects on the way we view reality quite independent of the actual content of those media.

In books such as *The Mechanical Bride* (1951), *The Gutenberg Galaxy* (1962), and *Understanding Media* (1964), McLuhan elaborated his basic thesis. He maintained that the printing press, with its uniform and repeatable type, had fostered mental characteristics such as the Western emphasis on strict definition, linear thought, and precise classification. Television, on the other hand, lessened rationality and detachment and heightened a sense of visceral, holistic involvement in one's surroundings.

The prose with which McLuhan stated his arguments was extremely dense—he was famous for being incomprehensible—and his thesis remains controversial in many respects today. Before his death in 1980, he provoked heated debate, and his work continues to stimulate widespread discussion. *Wired* magazine lists McLuhan as its patron saint on its masthead. And many students of technology still take their inspiration from McLuhan as they try to understand the effects of the Internet and other aspects of computer technology.

For some of these students, the connection between McLuhan's Christian orientation and his work on media remains unknown. It is interesting, however, to note that McLuhan applied his pronouncement of "the medium is the message" to Christ. It is not only the sayings of Christ that are important, he maintained, but His very person. Echoing the subtitle of his book *Understanding Media: The Extensions of Man*, McLuhan wrote to a friend in 1968, "The incarnation was the ultimate extension of man, the ultimate technology." For him, all human technologies were negligible compared with the coming of Christ. In fact, McLuhan, who attended Mass and read the Bible daily, was fond of pointing out, especially in his later years when the television generation seemed intent on abandoning traditional morality, that "Satan is a great electrical engineer."

Lilias Torrance Newton (1896–1980)
Hon. Thomas Clement Douglas
ca.1964, oil on canvas, 127.0 x 101.5 cm
Courtesy: Legislative Building Art Collection, Government of Saskatchewan, Regina
Photographer: Paul Austring

inset: Duncan Cameron Photographs / National Archives of Canada / C-36219

The Conscience of Canada
Tommy Douglas
1904–1986

"He embodied the social democratic movement."

Ian McLeod

The political left in Canada has drawn an astonishing number of leaders from the ranks of clergy. The first leader of a socialist (CCF) government in Canada was the former Baptist minister Tommy Douglas in Saskatchewan, and the first leader of the federal CCF party was the former Methodist minister James Shaver Woodsworth. Both men arrived at a Canadian socialism with roots in an awakening social consciousness that permeated a number of Canadian churches at the beginning of this century.

Thomas Clement Douglas was born in Falkirk, Scotland. His father, an ironworker and Labour Party supporter, brought the family to Winnipeg in 1911, the commercial and industrial capital of western Canada. It was likewise a centre for the Social Gospel movement, also known as practical Christianity, or the application of the gospel to social conditions.

Tommy's father was a religious freethinker; his mother, along with Tommy and his younger sister, attended the evangelical Beulah Baptist Church in Winnipeg. In addition, the family developed ties with the All People's Mission, a social welfare and educational centre for immigrants run by J. S. Woodsworth. An eminent writer, lecturer, and social researcher, Woodsworth was a lobbyist for social measures such as workers' compensation and allowances for single mothers. Over the years, he became a role model for Douglas.

Douglas left school at the age of fourteen and became a printer's apprentice. In 1924, determined to further his education, he entered Brandon College, where he completed high school and received degrees in arts and theology. (He later earned a master of arts degree from McMaster University.) The Baptist Church operated Brandon College, but the college was regarded by many as an outpost of modernist thought and teachings, and tensions ran high between many congregations in the Baptist Union in western Canada. Douglas left the college with an almost agnostic view of Christian doctrines, regarding freedom of thought as part of his Baptist heritage. He rejected fundamentalism as "fairy stories" and regarded Christ as the greatest of moral teachers, one who recognized that "the great motivating force in society is love for your fellow man."

In 1930, Douglas became the pastor at Calvary Baptist Church in Weyburn, Saskatchewan. Here, he would be transformed into a social activist, a member of Parliament, and a provincial premier. Weyburn was an agricultural town, and Saskatchewan was entering a prolonged drought and economic depression. Farm families faced bankruptcy, even starvation, and hospital beds lay empty because of high health care costs. Douglas worked with local ministers to organize relief shipments from other parts of Canada. The basement at Calvary Baptist became "the distributing centre for the unemployed."

In 1932, Douglas wrote to Woodsworth for advice on political action, and the older man urged Douglas to join the Saskatchewan Farmer Labour Party, which soon federated with its counterparts in other provinces to form the Cooperative Commonwealth Federation (CCF). It pledged to work in Parliament for government medical, hospital, and unemployment insurance; for a national pension plan; for federal control of interest rates; and for other reforms. Douglas ran as the party's federal candidate in Weyburn in 1935 and joined Woodsworth and four others in the first CCF caucus in Ottawa.

The CCF's image as a party of extremists limited its success federally. In Saskatchewan, however, it attracted much of the rising talent in the farm cooperatives, town councils, and trade unions. Douglas assumed the leadership of the growing provincial CCF in 1942. Through brilliant internal reforms, he pulled factions into a campaign team and swept to power with forty-seven of fifty-three seats in June 1944.

Douglas was Saskatchewan's premier for seventeen years, winning five successive elections. His early years oversaw rapid change: the extension of state-operated electric power and telephone service to rural areas, the launch of a government automobile insurance corporation, and the introduction of free hospital care. Through the 1950s, his government diversified the economy and paid off the provincial debt, which had been the highest in Canada.

From the time he entered politics, Douglas had urged the federal government to introduce state-run health insurance. In 1959, he announced that Saskatchewan would go it alone. The legislation that he introduced in 1960 would continue to define Canada's Medicare system into the 1990s. Douglas and his successor, Woodrow Lloyd, faced demonstrations and a doctors' strike that attracted international attention, but the Saskatchewan CCF's universal Medicare system worked. Within a few years, Ottawa would extend that system to everyone in Canada. It was Douglas' greatest achievement as a public servant.

While premier, Douglas continued his church membership and Sunday school teaching. Although he shifted from the Christian language of the Social Gospel, he maintained an evangelistic tone, with frequent appeals to brotherhood and a sense of "a higher destiny" for humanity. His inspiring oratory and political record won him recognition across Canada. When a national party was formed in 1961 to succeed the CCF, Douglas agreed to become its first leader.

He had high hopes for the New Democratic Party, but in his ten years as its federal leader it never won more than twenty-three seats. Douglas, however, remained a prominent public figure, speaking at universities, conventions, churches, and synagogues and attracting large crowds to his political rallies even when votes went elsewhere. When he retired from Parliament in 1979, he embodied the social democratic movement; his speech to a dispirited NDP convention in 1983 is regarded as a moment of renewal for the party.

Douglas lived a quiet life, taking pride in his wife and two daughters. His hallmark was a cheerfulness that spilled over into his meetings with strangers and friends and that did not diminish during his battle with cancer, which ended his life in 1986.

The Social Gospel movement of Douglas' boyhood set out to build the kingdom of God on earth. Douglas had to accept more modest achievements and numerous political failures. "You're never going to step out of the front door into the kingdom of God," he said before he died. "What you're going to do is slowly and painfully change society until it has more of the values that emanate from the teachings of Jesus or from the other great religious leaders."

Charles MacGregor (1893–unknown)
Dr. Oswald J. Smith (1889–1986)
oil on canvas, 101 x 75 cm
Courtesy: The Peoples Church
Photographer: Steve Boyko

inset: Courtesy of The Peoples Church, Toronto

A Prophet to the Nations
Oswald J. Smith
1889–1986

*"The greatest combination pastor, hymn writer,
missionary statesman and evangelist of our time."*

John D. Hull

Oswald J. Smith was born in November 1889. He spent part of his childhood assisting his father at the Embro Station train depot near London, Ontario. His most sobering responsibility was to light the semaphore signal lamps about a half mile east and west of the train station. Using coal oil lamps, he lit the signals and hoisted them by pulley to the top of their poles. This frail, unassuming, often sickly youngster would eventually carry the light of the gospel to the world and inspire generations in the cause of global missions.

In 1906, at sixteen years of age, Smith was converted in a service conducted by R. A. Torrey at Toronto's Massey Hall. Torrey would become the successor to evangelist Dwight L. Moody, and Smith would stand in Massey Hall twenty-two years later and launch The Peoples Church. Smith had heard of Torrey's services from the conversations of travellers at Embro Station. A Toronto newspaper printed Torrey's sermons, and Smith read them and convinced his father to allow him to miss a day of school to attend services with his brother, Ernie.

Smith and his brother arrived at a special "men and boys only" session on the final day of the meetings. Torrey spoke from Isaiah 53, reading it with a personal emphasis: He was wounded for [my] transgressions, he was bruised for [my] iniquities, the chastisement of [my] peace was upon him; and with his stripes [I am] healed. Then the revivalist began his appeal to the audience: "All those men over twenty, who want to be saved, come forward." When next he called for "all those between sixteen and twenty," Smith and his brother went forward, shook hands with Torrey, and entered an Inquiry Room. Smith later related, "As I opened my heart to the Saviour, asking Him to be my sin-bearer, my substitute, I felt no great change, no wonderful experience, but I trusted Christ Jesus and from then on I experienced sweet peace."

Over the ensuing years, Smith pursued a career in overseas missions. Several mission boards turned him down because they were concerned about his health and questioned his ability to handle the strenuous labour associated with missionary life. Smith was disappointed but not distracted from his vision of reaching people for Jesus Christ. Failing to obtain a field posting, he received ministerial training at London Bible College, now Ontario Bible College in London, Ontario, and at the Presbyterian McCormick Theological Seminary in Chicago. A broken marriage engagement in 1914 was perhaps the most emotionally devastating event Smith faced as a ministerial student. However, amid despair he wrote some of his most memorable poetry, focusing explicitly on the need for intimacy with God.

Following his theological studies, Smith met and later married Daisy Billings, who, like Smith, was a serious-minded Christian. In the early to mid-1920s, Smith pastored several local churches in the Toronto area and briefly pastored a Christian and Missionary Alliance Church in Los Angeles in 1927

In 1928, Smith returned to Toronto with a desire to start a church that would reach people for Christ and collect funds to support missionaries. In September 1928, he stepped on stage at Massey Hall before two thousand people who had gathered with him to start The Peoples Church. A few months earlier Smith had articulated his vision: "I carry the burden of a Missionary-Evangelist. I must have a headquarters. I want to travel to foreign fields to get the vision firsthand and then return to broadcast the need and stir hearts all over the country on behalf of missionary projects. Only this will bring into use every talent and gift God has given me."

From its beginning, Peoples was big. Smith drew impressive crowds to morning and evening services. He captivated audiences with messages on evangelism, missions, and the deeper life. He also invited some of the world's most distinguished evangelical preachers to Toronto to speak at Peoples. This caused attendance to swell and compelled Smith to find a larger location. In 1934, Peoples purchased a large Methodist church at 100 Bloor Street in downtown Toronto. Through the years, thousands professed their faith at the Bloor Street location.

Smith, meanwhile, wrote profusely, eventually authoring thirty-five books, which would be translated into 125 languages and sell over six million copies worldwide. He composed over one thousand hymns and poems, including "The Song of the Soul Set Free" and "Alone with Thee." He also spoke in seventy countries. In addition, he developed and refined the "faith promise" offering—an approach to raising money for missions that involves trusting God for a certain amount of money each month that is, in turn, given to the church missionary fund—not only giving it its name but also witnessing its use in thousands of churches around the world.

Smith became a respected missionary statesman. He was in great demand and would spend months away from The Peoples Church travelling to mission fields to preach and motivate. When he returned, he would tell his church of his adventures, acquainting it with needs globally and raising millions of dollars for missionary causes. He was known for such memorable quotations as, "You must go, or send a substitute; No attack, no defense"; and "Why should anyone hear the gospel twice before everyone has heard it once?"

Oswald J. Smith died in January 1986. Just prior to his death, he said, "there is something within me calling, ever calling. I am restless, like a hunter's dog on the leash, straining to get away. It is that irresistible 'must go.' The divine fire burns within my heart."

Dr. Billy Graham conducted Smith's memorial service before an overflow audience in The Peoples Church auditorium. Graham eulogized his friend: "The name, Oswald J. Smith, symbolizes worldwide evangelism. Some men are called to minister the gospel in a city, others to a nation; and a few in each century to the whole world. Oswald J. Smith was a prophet to the nations of the world. He will go down in history as the greatest combination pastor, hymn writer, missionary statesman and evangelist of our time. He was the most remarkable man I have ever met."

Barbara Christian (1943–)
Detail of *George Grant and the Farther Shore*
1992, oil on canvas, 76 x 61 cm
Courtesy: Barbara Christian

inset: courtesy of Barbara Christian

Authoritative Christianity
George Parkin Grant

1918–1988

"Determined to understand the meaning of truth."

William Christian

When George Grant arrived at Oxford in October 1939 as the Rhodes Scholar from Queen's University in Kingston, it was his plan to study law and to then return to Canada to work as a constitutional lawyer. Such a career would have coincided perfectly with his mother's ambitions for him. His two grandfathers, Principal GEORGE MONRO GRANT of Queen's and Sir George Parkin, had both risen far in the world. And his father was the principal of Upper Canada College, a prestigious private boys school in Toronto, where, indeed, young George was born in 1918 and where he attended as a student.

At Oxford, Grant encountered a group of pacifists, with whom he trained for a volunteer ambulance unit. He then served as an Air Raid Precautions warden in Bermondsey, a heavily bombed, working-class district in London. The experience tore at his soul. Although he was already showing great physical and moral courage in the face of German bombing, his family was urging him to do his duty for king and country by joining the armed forces.

In 1941, Grant joined the merchant marine. However, when the medical examination revealed a tubercular lesion, he panicked and fled to the countryside outside Oxford, where he worked as a farm labourer. A few days after the Japanese attack on Pearl Harbor, Grant was riding his bicycle down a country lane. Dawn was breaking when he dismounted to open a gate across the road. By the time he had passed through the gate, he understood, then and forever, that God *was*. As he explained to his mother: "It is not a journey that one could call up or down; it is merely to a different plane of existence. Spiritually, it has been so far that it is as if it wasn't the same person who started out. Just recently," he wrote, "I feel as if I had been born again."

Emotionally and physically exhausted, Grant returned to Toronto, where he worked for the Canadian Association for Adult Education. After the war, he returned to Oxford and studied theology. He was determined to understand the meaning of the truth that he had experienced on that early December morning.

In 1947, Grant accepted a position at Dalhousie University to teach philosophy, and by 1951 he was discovering just how difficult it was to be a Christian in the increasingly secular atmosphere of Canadian universities. He began a report on the state of philosophy in the country's English-speaking universities with the provocative claim that "the study of philosophy is the analysis of the traditions of our society and the judgement of those traditions against our varying intuitions of the Perfection of God." Grant's article offended many of the most powerful academic philosophers in central Canada, and he feared that he had irreparably harmed his chances of ever teaching at an Ontario university.

However, in 1960 he was offered the chance to become the chairman of the philosophy department at Toronto's York University. But when he discovered that he was required to use a particular textbook in the first-year course, he resigned: "I could hardly be expected to use a textbook which misrepresents the religion of my allegiance." It was a brave act for a middle-aged Anglican with six children and no immediate job prospects.

The next year, he secured a place in the newly founded Department of Religion at McMaster University in Hamilton, and it was there that he taught during his years of increasing fame. Although his first important book, *Philosophy in the Mass Age* (1959), had brought him national attention, it was his brilliant philosophic and political polemic *Lament for a Nation* (1965) that made him one of the leading intellectual figures of the 1960s and 1970s. The work predicted the eventual disappearance of Canada as a sovereign nation, but he was nonetheless acknowledged by Canadian nationalists of both the left and the right as a major influence in their fight against American control over Canadian industry, culture, and politics.

For Grant, however, the political aspect of *Lament* was secondary to its spiritual message. "Beyond courage, it is also possible to live in the ancient faith, which asserts that changes in the world, even if they are recognized more as a loss than a gain, take place within an eternal order that is not affected by their taking place.'

In works such as *Technology and Empire* (1969) and *English-Speaking Justice* (1974), Grant sought to understand the forces at work in the world. Technology, he increasingly came to understand, had transformed nature. "My particular function in the midst of what seems to me the evident fall of western Christianity is to try to understand just a small amount of what was at fault in this particular manifestation of Christianity, so that one plays a minute part in something that will take centuries—namely the rediscovery of authoritative Christianity ... it has been given the truth in a way no other religion has."

Grant's last collection of essays, *Technology and Justice* (1986), showed the influence of the French philosopher and mystic Simone Weil. Grant considered Weil a saint and a philosopher of the highest order. Grant concluded that "faith is the experience that the intellect is enlightened by love."

After his retirement in 1984, Grant often wrote—with his wife, Sheila—on behalf of the Right-to-Life movement. "If tyranny is to come in North America, it will come easily and on cat's feet. It will come with the denial of the rights of the unborn and the aged. In fact, it will come to all those who cannot defend themselves." After Canada's highest court struck down criminal code restrictions limiting abortion, Grant denounced the decision on the CBC: "The Supreme Court decision on abortion fills me with terrible sadness at what lies ahead for our country—an increase in the mass killing of the weakest members of our species."

When Grant passed away in 1988, he had just begun an attempt to refute German philosopher Martin Heidegger's attack on Christianity and Platonism. Grant is buried in the simple churchyard of Terence Bay, Nova Scotia. His headstone reads: "George Parkin Grant, 1918–1988, Out of the Shadows and Imaginings into the Truth."

Doug Martin (1948–)
Northrop Frye Portrait
oil on canvas, 213.4 x 121.9 cm
Courtesy: Victoria University Library, Toronto. © Doug Martin
Photographer: Steve Boyko

inset: F. Roy Kemp / Victoria University Library, Toronto

The Order of Words
Northrop Frye
1912–1991

"Now religion and art are the two most important phenomena in the world....
They constitute, in fact, the only reality of existence."

Joseph Adamson

Northrop Frye, one of the country's most eminent thinkers, devoted his life to a study of literature and culture that was deeply rooted in the Bible. He was born in Sherbrooke, Quebec, in 1912, the son of devout Methodists. Frye's maternal grandfather was a preacher who moved from parish to parish in eastern Ontario and the eastern townships of Quebec. The family's religious background encouraged an attitude that Frye later defined as "Protestant, radical, and romantic." In particular, his mother's inculcation of Methodist views, combined with her liberal encouragement of artistic pursuits, did much to sow the seeds of the progressive social vision so essential to Frye's understanding of literature. "In Methodism," he would write at the end of his life, "there was an emphasis on religious experience as distinct from doctrine and on very early exposure to the story element in the Bible. Such a conditioning may have helped to propel me in the direction of a literary criticism that has kept revolving around the Bible, not as a source of doctrine but as a source of story and vision."

On graduation from high school in Moncton, where the family had settled, Frye won a scholarship to a local business college. However, in 1929, at the age of seventeen, he took advantage of a typing contest that included a free trip to Toronto and while there entered Victoria College, the United Church college at the University of Toronto.

After completing his bachelor of arts in 1933, Frye remained in Toronto to study theology at Emmanuel College. His growing interest in literature, however, drew him away from a calling as a parish minister. Moreover, his experience as a student minister in summer 1934, when for five months he served on the Saskatchewan prairie, made it painfully clear to him how unsuited he was to be a clergyman, although he would proceed to ordination and preach upon occasion.

The most important factor in Frye's shift to literature was William Blake. "I date everything," he said in an interview at the end of his life, "from my discovery of Blake as an undergraduate and graduate student." He described a moment of insight that he had while writing a paper on Blake's *Milton*, when "suddenly the universe just broke open, and I've never been, as they say, the same man since." At the centre of Blake's vision, as Frye saw it, was the expansive energy and consciousness belonging to an imaginative vision of reality, a faith in the power of the arts to "show us the human world that man is trying to build out of nature."

After his ordination as a minister in the United Church of Canada in 1936, Frye travelled to England to study English literature at Oxford University. In summer 1937, back in Canada, he married Helen Kemp, an art student whom he had met in his second year at Victoria College. Frye then taught for a year at Victoria College before completing his degree at Oxford. He returned to Toronto in fall 1939 to begin teaching as a member of the permanent staff at Victoria College. Princeton University Press published his first book, *Fearful Symmetry*, a study of Blake, in 1947. The success of the book established Frye as a major scholar and consolidated his growing reputation at the University of Toronto. Frye was to become the chairman of the Department of English (1952), the principal (1959), and finally the chancellor (1978) of Victoria College.

By the time Frye had finished his book on Blake, he was well on his way to outlining a global framework for understanding "the whole of literature as an order of words, as a potentially unified imaginative experience." This became the vast subject of his *Anatomy of Criticism*. That book's four essays appeared ten years after *Fearful Symmetry* and set out the framework of the interpenetrating contexts in which literature might be understood. One hundred thousand copies of *Anatomy* would be sold over the next twenty-five years—an astonishing number for a work of scholarship. The book made Frye the most important literary critic of his generation. In following years, Frye was to write more than twenty books on subjects from Western literature and culture to social thought.

In the mid- to late 1960s, Frye shifted his focus to the theory of culture and society. He began to articulate what he called the myth of concern, the idea that "myths are expressions of concern, of man's care for his own destiny and heritage." Frye believed that the human identity we should be concerned about "is the one that we have failed to achieve," that "is expressed in our culture, but not attained in our life." He identified culture with the creative works of the human imagination, found in poetry, literature, film, and art.

Frye's pursuit of the myth of concern culminated in his two books on the Bible. In 1981, his long-heralded *The Great Code* appeared. A decade later, in fall 1990, *Words with Power* was published. In both books, Frye pursued the idea that the basis of faith is imaginative, not doctrinal, that myths and metaphors are the verbal forms taken by the divine proclamation that comes from God to human beings. Literature may incorporate "our ideological concerns, but it devotes itself mainly to the primary ones, in both physical and spiritual forms: its fictions show human beings in the primary throes of surviving, loving, prospering, and fighting with the frustrations that block these things."

Only months after the publication of *Words with Power*, Frye entered the hospital to be treated for cancer. He died suddenly of heart failure in January 1991 at the age of seventy-eight.

Essential to Frye's intellectual focus throughout his career was a crucial insight: that the Bible, understood as the word of God, was accessible only through the human imagination. At the youthful age of twenty-two, he wrote a letter to Helen Kemp that offers an eloquent summation of what even then he regarded as the substance of his life: "I propose spending the rest of my life ... on various problems connected with religion and art. Now religion and art are the two most important phenomena in the world, or rather the most important phenomenon, for they are basically the same thing. They constitute, in fact, the only reality of existence."

HON. E. C. MANNING
PREMIER
1943-1968

Ernest George Fosbery (1874–1960)
Hon. E. C. Manning
1950, oil on canvas, 128 x 101 cm
Courtesy: Collection of the Government of Alberta
Photographer: K. J. Clark

inset: National Archives of Canada / C-87204

Ernest Manning

1908–1996

*"Manning always held the view that both God and the people had some say…
and he was not about to argue with either."*

Lloyd Mackey

Ernest Manning is best remembered as Alberta's premier from 1943 to 1968—the longest-serving premier in the Commonwealth—and as the host of *Canada's National Bible Hour* for nearly half a century. These dual roles exemplify his practice of integrating Christianity with every area of his life. He was prudent and careful in politics, always practicing Christian-based reconciliation and conflict resolution. Many Albertans were aware that his first call had been to the Christian ministry. Politics was a diversion. But Manning always held the view that both God and the people had some say in how long he would be premier—and he was not about to argue with either.

Manning grew up near Rosetown, Saskatchewan, where, as a curious teenager wanting to connect with the outside world, he acquired a three-tube radio kit. On that radio, he heard an early WILLIAM "Bible Bill" ABERHART Christian radio broadcast from the Calgary Prophetic Bible Institute (CPBI). Aberhart's compelling preaching persuaded Manning to commit his life to Christ. Years later, Manning was fond of recalling that ploughing the fields on his father's farm worked well for his scripture study. The furrows were long, and he could get a fair amount of memory work done before having to turn the tractor around.

In 1927, Manning enrolled in CPBI, where he met his future wife, the institute's pianist, Muriel Preston, who later served as the *National Bible Hour*'s musical coordinator. Aberhart saw in the young Manning a person who could greatly help him. Soon, Manning became Aberhart's assistant at CPBI and also helped him found the Social Credit Party, which won the 1935 Alberta election. Appointed provincial secretary, Manning succeeded to the premiership on Aberhart's death in 1943.

The Great Depression left Alberta virtually bankrupt in the late thirties and early forties. Manning's premiership signalled the beginning of policies to pay down the province's debt and restore its fiscal credibility. That process was well under way by 1947, when Alberta's first major oil strikes occurred.

Manning presided over a corruption-free government known for its populism and its fiscal conservatism. His careful stewardship of the province's oil reserves and revenues and his skill in working with the oil industry's corporate leaders built his reputation for integrity. A relationship of trust, developed through a shared Christian faith, led Manning and J. Howard Pew of Sun Oil to agree on development plans for the vast Athabasca tar sands in northern Alberta. When oil revenues brought Alberta into unprecedented prosperity, Manning's government invested extensively in health care, educational, and social programs.

Manning's understanding of the Scriptures gave him an appreciation of human need as enunciated by proponents of the social gospel. But unlike the premier of neighbouring Saskatchewan, Baptist minister TOMMY DOUGLAS, Manning did not espouse a socialistic doctrine. Rather, he encouraged strong individual, corporate, and religious initiatives in addressing social issues. Manning believed that government was there to motivate and give direction, not to intervene and carry the load. Many of Manning's views on health care and social issues were shaped as he and Muriel lovingly raised their eldest son, Keith, who had suffered oxygen deprivation at birth. The premier constantly emphasized that government spending on social programs was no substitute for individual, family, and community attention to human need.

On his radio broadcasts, Manning emphasized the individual side of faith. It was thus consistent for him to stress less government and more individual responsibility. His emphasis was on the life-changing effect of a commitment to Jesus Christ. And he wanted his listeners to understand that their parents, church, or good works could not make them Christians. As individuals, they were responsible for their own spiritual condition and destiny.

In a 1967 book, *Political Realignment*, Manning coined the phrase "social conservatism," which he described as the marriage of private enterprise and social responsibility. The book created a climate for key strategy shifts in the federal Progressive Conservative Party. Later, its concepts would be vital to his son Preston's advancement of Reform ideology.

After retiring as premier Ernest Manning established, with Preston, a firm that became known as Manning Consultants Limited. It engaged in community development, mainly in northern Alberta's Slave Lake region. Much of its work involved encouraging the corporate sector to create good communities and mediating between oil companies and native groups. During this time, Ernest Manning also served thirteen years in the Canadian Senate. He advocated electing members to that body, rather than having them appointed by the prime minister.

At Ernest Manning's funeral in February 1996, Reform Party of Canada leader Preston Manning suggested that his father's last political words could well be: "Do not let internal discord do to Canada what wars, depressions, and hard times were unable to do. Continue to build!" Those words were to be an inspiration to the younger Manning, who, sixteen months later, became the leader of the official opposition in the House of Commons.

Ernest Manning's radio preaching—which spanned forty-six years—blended evangelical pietism with an emphasis on the messages of the Bible's prophetic books. He spoke often of the need for national spiritual revival and urged Christians to live in the light of Jesus' imminent return. It was his radio work that gave him a national profile, particularly with respect to his Christian faith. At its peak, the *National Bible Hour* was estimated to have six hundred thousand listeners from across Canada each week—more than comedian Jack Benny had in his heyday!

In addition, Manning was a founder of the Fundamental Baptist Church in Edmonton. He was also active in such Christian organizations as the Gideons (a service group whose members distribute Bibles in hotels, hospitals, schools, and prisons) and the Evangelical Fellowship of Canada. During the last five years of his life, he and Muriel, having moved to Calgary, worshipped at that city's First Alliance Church. In retirement, he served on the boards of several corporations and organizations, including Canadian Pacific Airlines and the Canada West Foundation, all the while operating a dairy farm near Edmonton.

Strength, commitment, and reason marked Ernest Manning's presence in Alberta. Whether in matters of faith, politics, business, or family, he emphasized the values of hard work, high ethical standards, compassion, and a reliance on the goodness and grace of God. His political foes admitted that—almost without peer—he epitomized honesty and integrity in government.

Ernest Manning was always careful to communicate that he could not have done so without the work of God in his heart and life.

Let us give all our strength to this quest for unity, generosity, faith and loyalty. Let us first seek faith, faith in God above everything, faith in Christ and in his Church; and loyalty to our religious, moral, and cultural heritage. Let us show our faith not only with our lips but with our hearts and minds as well. Let us be loyal not so much to the traditions of our past as to their spirit, for only thus can our faith be open to the inspiration of the present and directed to the promise of the future.

—George Vanier (1888–1967)
Governor-General of Canada 1959–1967

Epilogue

Psalm 88 proclaims that righteousness cannot be done in the land of forgetfulness any more than wonders may be seen in the midst of darkness. Again and again in the Scriptures, God calls his people to remember. In fact, remembrance serves as a measuring rod of faithfulness throughout the Bible.

Governor-General GEORGES VANIER reflected a belief in the relationship between remembrance and faith when he expressed his hopes for Canadian families in 1964:

> Let us give all our strength to this quest for unity, generosity, faith and loyalty.
> Let us first seek faith, faith in God above everything, faith in Christ and in his
> Church; and loyalty to our religious, moral, and cultural heritage. Let us show our
> faith not only with our lips but with our hearts and minds as well. Let us be loyal not
> so much to the traditions of our past as to their spirit, for only thus can our faith be
> open to the inspiration of the present and directed to the promise of the future.

Yet, studies continue to reveal that Canadians do not recall their history. Many high school students can identify neither past nor present national leaders and are unable to construct even a rudimentary chronology of this country's legacy. The Dominion Institute's 1997 Canada Day History Survey assessed over 1,100 youth from across the country on a "basic Canadian history quiz." The average score? Just thirty-four percent.

During Citizen and Heritage Week 1998, the federal government distributed 90,000 glossy brochures to Canadian schools. The brochure identified the individual on our five dollar bill as Louis St. Laurent instead of Sir Wilfred Laurier! Such absurd faux pas are the brunt of many a joke. But the situation is hardly humorous. The ignorance of most Canadians about our past has trapped us in a recalcitrant present. Priest and historian LIONEL GROULX believed that when "a generation forgets its history, or turns its back upon it; such an act is a betrayal of history."

Canada: Portraits of Faith relates the life stories of men and women whose impact upon this nation remains evident today. The diversity of their interests and influence is given continuity through a common faith. A faith that, although expressed and practiced very differently, began when each personally sought the Lord. A faith that changed them, and Canada, forever. A faith, moreover, that modern-day Canadians would do well to understand and emulate.

Authors

Northrop Frye

Dr. Joseph Adamson teaches English and comparative literature at McMaster University. He is the author of *Wounded Fiction: Modern Poetry and Deconstruction* (1988); *Northrop Frye: A Visionary Life* (1993); and *Melville, Shame, and the Evil Eye* (1997). He is also one of the editors engaged in the forthcoming publication of *The Collected Works of Northrop Frye*.

Henry Alline

Dr. Jack Bumsted received his doctorate from Brown University in 1965. He has taught at Tufts, McMaster, and Simon Fraser Universities and is currently at St. John's College in Winnipeg, where he is the director of the Institute for the Humanities. Professor Bumsted has published many articles on the history of early North America, especially eighteenth-century New England and Maritime Canada, and on evangelical pietism, including the book *Henry Alline, 1748–1784* (1971).

John Robson

Dr. Robert Burkinshaw is a professor in and the chairman of the Department of History and Political Science and the dean of the Faculty of Social Sciences and Education at Trinity Western University. He is also the author of *Pilgrims in Lotus Land: Conservative Protestantism in British Columbia, 1917–1981* (1995).

William Howland

The Reverend Peter Bush is a teaching elder at Knox Presbyterian Church in Mitchell, Ontario. The child of missionary parents, he has lived in Lebanon and Iran. He earned his bachelor's and master's degrees in Canadian history at Queen's University, Kingston.

William Black

Dr. Don Chapman is a professor of adult education at the University College of the Fraser Valley in Abbotsford, British Columbia. He has taught at various postsecondary institutions, including the University of Alberta, the University of New Brunswick, and Concordia University in Montreal. He received his doctorate from the University of Alberta in 1986. His research interests include the religious roots of Canadian adult education. As it happens, Chapman is a direct descendant of William Black's sister, Sarah.

George Monro Grant
George Parkin Grant

Dr. William Christian received his bachelor and master of arts degrees from the University of Toronto and, in 1970, earned his doctorate in political philosophy from the London School of Economics. He teaches in the Department of Political Studies at the University of Guelph. He is best known for his work on Canadian intellectual history, especially on Canadian political parties, and on Harold Innis and particularly George Parkin Grant, of whom he wrote a critically acclaimed, best-selling biography.

William Dawson
Timothy Eaton
Joseph Scriven
Leonard Tilley

Michael Clarke serves as the president of Reel to Real Ministries. He is a faculty fellow for Summit Ministries and a public policy consultant to Focus on the Family. His research interests include popular culture, bioethics, politics, and history.

William Bompas

Dr. Kenneth Coates is the dean of arts at the University of New Brunswick, Saint John, and **Dr. William R. Morrison** is professor of history at the University of Northern British Columbia. They have written a number of books together, most recently *The Alaska Highway in World War II: The U.S. Army of Occupation in Canada's Northwest* (1992); *The Forgotten North* (1992); *Working the North: Labor and the Northwest Defense Projects, 1942–1945* (1994); and *The Historiography of the Provincial Norths* (1996). They are preparing a new biography of Bishop William Bompas.

Pauline Vanier

Deborah Cowley writes regularly for the international editions of *Reader's Digest*, involving research in Europe, Africa, and the Middle East. She has also worked as a travel writer, as a television scriptwriter, and as a broadcaster with CBC Radio. She became a personal friend of Pauline Vanier during the Vaniers' term at Government House and made regular visits to l'Arche in France to help Pauline with her voluminous correspondence. After Pauline Vanier's death, Cowley and her husband, George, collaborated in writing *One Woman's Journey: A Portrait of Pauline Vanier* (1994).

Georges Vanier

George Cowley served for over thirty years as an officer in the former Canadian Department of External Affairs (now the Department of Foreign Affairs). In 1965, he was appointed attaché to then governor-general Georges Vanier. He and his wife became close personal friends of the Vanier family. He served as consultant to Robert Speaight's definitive biography, *Vanier: Soldier, Diplomat and Governor General* (1970), and coedited, with Michel Vanier, *Only to Serve: Selections from Addresses of Governor General Georges P. Vanier* (1970).

Robert McAlister

James Craig received his master of arts degree in theology from the University of St. Michael's College, Toronto School of Theology, in 1995. He served as a pastor and as a Bible college teacher and has written extensively on Christian curriculum. He works at the national headquarters of the Pentecostal Assemblies of Canada in missions research and communications.

Letitia Youmans
Agnes Macphail

Dr. Terry Crowley is a professor of history at the University of Guelph and the editor of *Ontario History* magazine. In 1996, he contributed "The French Regime to 1760" to Oxford University Press's *A Concise History of Christianity in Canada*.

Marie-Madeleine de Chauvigny de La Peltrie
Marie Guyart de l'Incarnation
Jeanne Mance

Dr. Françoise Deroy-Pineau is the author of various social and historical biographies of Canadian pioneers, including *Madeleine de La Peltrie: Amazone du Nouveau monde* (1992); *Marie de l'Incarnation, Marie Guyart, femme d'affaires, mystique, mère de la Nouvelle-France* (1989); and *Jeanne Mance, de Langres à Montréal, le passion de soigner* (1995). Her doctoral dissertation on the social network of Marie de l'Incarnation, presented at the University of Montreal in 1996, is soon to be published. (Madame Deroy-Pineau's articles were translated by Barry Whatley, B.A., M.Div. and then revised by the editorial board.)

Egerton Ryerson

Dr. Goldwin French is a professor emeritus at Toronto's Victoria University, where he served as president from 1973 to 1987. Previously, he taught at Hamilton's McMaster University, from 1947 to 1970, where he was the chairman of the History Department from 1964 to 1970. He is the author of *Parsons and Politics* (1962); has contributed to many historical journals, encyclopedias, and dictionaries; and held the office of editor in chief of the *Ontario Historical Studies Series* from 1971 to 1993.

Charles Pandosy

Ted Gerk is the director of Life InterNET (http://www.interlife.org), an organization dedicated to disseminating information over the Internet on bioethical issues. He is a board member of Life Decisions International and of the National Society of Hope and is the communications director of the Pro-Life Society of British Columbia. He is also a member of the American Historical Society of Germans from Russia and of the American Association for the Advancement of Slavic Studies. Gerk lives in Kelowna, British Columbia, with his wife Marina and their nine children.

John Buchan

Dr. George Grant, Ph.D., D.Lit., is the director of the King's Meadow Study Center and the chancellor of Bannockburn College, both in Franklin, Tennessee. He also serves as the president of the Covenant Classical School Association in Concord, North Carolina. He is the author of nearly four dozen books in the areas of history, biography, politics, literature, and social criticism. Dr. Grant is a descendant of the early Scottish pioneers of Nova Scotia. He lives with his wife and children in the United States.

Oswald J. Smith

Dr. John David Hull is the senior pastor of The Peoples Church, founded by Oswald J. Smith and referred to as "the world's leading missions church." John speaks each Sunday to over half a million regular television viewers on *The Peoples Worship Hour* and is a regular guest speaker at world missions conferences throughout Canada and the United States.

Henri Bourassa
Lionel Groulx
Louis-François Laflèche

Preston Jones is a doctoral student at the University of Ottawa. His dissertation explores the relationship of the Bible to Canadian culture in the late nineteenth century. He has published papers in numerous academic and popular publications, including *Quebec Studies*, the *Journal of the National Library of Wales*, and *Books and Culture: A Christian Review*.

Hugh Crossley
John Hunter

Kevin Kee is completing a doctorate in history at Queen's University, Kingston. He has written on various aspects of Canadian and American popular Protestantism from the early 1800s to the middle of the twentieth century. His dissertation focuses on a number of key Canadian evangelists and evangelistic movements, including Crossley and Hunter, Oswald J. Smith, the Oxford Group, and Charles Templeton.

William Case

The Reverend J. William Lamb is a minister of the United Church of Canada and a past president of the Canadian Methodist Historical Society. Besides numerous articles and papers, he has written *William Losee, Ontario's First Methodist Missionary*; *Bridging the Years: A History of Bridge Street United/ Methodist Church, Belleville, 1815–1990*; and, with Mary Beacock Fryer and Larry Turner, *The Meaning of These Stones: The Life and Times of Wall Street United Church, Brockville, Ontario*.

Ernest Manning

Lloyd Mackey is the author of *Like Father, Like Son* (1997), the story of Ernest and Preston Manning. A British Columbia journalist for over thirty years, Mackey specializes in writing on religion, politics, and business. He is the founder of *Christian Info News*, a monthly tabloid circulated in 1,300 B.C. churches, and the director of the Institute for Christian Newspapering.

Marshall McLuhan

Philip Marchand received his bachelors and masters degrees in English literature from the University of Toronto, where he studied modern poetry under Marshall McLuhan. An award-winning journalist, Marchand is now books columnist for the *Toronto Star*. He is the author of *Marshall McLuhan: The Medium & the Messenger* (1989; forthcoming 1998) and will also have a collection of essays on Canadian literature published in spring 1998.

George Brown

Vincent Marquis has taught history and social sciences at Redeemer Christian High School in Ottawa for seventeen years. He holds degrees in history and education. He is a conference speaker on Canada's Christian history and Christian worldview and has authored the book *A Truly Loyal Subject, George Brown and Confederation* (1997).

Tommy Douglas

Ian McLeod, a former news reporter, is the coauthor (with his father, Dr. Tom McLeod) of *Tommy Douglas: The Road to Jerusalem* (1987). McLeod's three-hour documentary on Canada's Social Gospel movement was heard on CBC Radio's *Ideas* in 1985. His second book, *Under Siege: The Federal New Democrats in the Nineties*, was published in 1994. McLeod lives in Victoria, British Columbia.

Oliver Mowat

Dallas K. Miller, Queen's Counsel, is a lawyer in private practice and has been a member of the Law Society of Alberta since 1985. Much of his work includes defending the right of parents to direct the education of their children as senior counsel for the Home School Legal Defence Association of Canada. He is also active in encouraging people of faith to become involved in the political process and to engage in public policy development.

John Strachan

Dr. John Moir is a professor emeritus of the University of Toronto, where he was a professor of history until 1989 and an adjunct professor at Knox College and the Ontario Institute for Studies in Education. He has been the president of several historical societies and is the author or editor of over one hundred articles, encyclopedia entries, and books, chiefly about Canadian religious history.

Eliza Case
Barbara Heck
Jane Wilson

Dr. Elizabeth Gillan Muir is a graduate of Queen's University and of Harvard University and holds a doctorate in religious studies from McGill University. She lectures in Canadian studies at the University of Waterloo and is on the national executive staff of the United Church of Canada. Among her published works are *Petticoats in the Pulpit* (1991) and *Changing Roles of Women within the Christian Church in Canada* (1995).

William Duncan

Peter Murray received a B.C. Book Prize nomination for *The Devil and Mr. Duncan* (1985). After thirty years as a newspaperman in Vancouver and Victoria, he began writing Pacific Northwest histories. His other books include *The Vagabond Fleet: A Chronicle of the North Pacific Sealing Schooner Trade*; *From Amor to Zalm: A Primer on B.C. Politics and its Wacky Premiers*; *Homesteads and Snug Harbours: The Gulf Islands*; and *Home from the Hill: Three Gentlemen Adventurers*.

Albert B. Simpson

Dr. Darrel Reid holds a doctorate in history from Queen's University. Between 1986 and 1994, he served in information and research capacities with the Institute of Intergovernmental Relations and the School of Policy Studies, Queen's University. In 1994, he became the director of policy and research for the Reform caucus in Ottawa and in 1996 became the chief of staff to Preston Manning, the leader of the Reform Party of Canada. Reid now serves as Canadian president of Focus on the Family.

Henry Bird Steinhauer

Gayle Simonson is a freelance writer. She has published articles on a variety of topics, but she specializes in the development of environmental education materials. She is an active member of Southminster-Steinhauer United Church in Edmonton.

Marguerite Bourgeoys

Patricia Simpson, a member of the Congrégation de Notre-Dame de Montréal, has been the codirector of the Marguerite Bourgeoys Centre since 1992 and is the author of *Marguerite Bourgeoys and Montreal, 1640–1665* (1997). Previously, she taught English and humanities at Montreal's Marianoplis College from 1965 to 1990.

Peter Jones

Dr. Donald B. Smith is a professor of history at the University of Calgary. His research interests include native peoples, the early Canadian west and French Canadians in the Canadian west, and the Canadian north. He is the author of *Sacred Feathers: The Reverend Peter Jones (Kahkewaquonaby) and the Mississauga Indians* (1987) and has published many other works on the native peoples of Canada and on French-speaking groups in western Canada.

Jean de Brébeuf

Michael Solowan received his bachelor of arts in communication from Trinity Western University and has worked in media and public relations in higher education and for the federal government of Canada. He is a researcher and administrative assistant at Reel to Real Ministries (Canada) Society.

William Aberhart
Wilfred Grenfell

Dr. John G. Stackhouse, Jr., is the Sangwoo Youtong Chee professor of theology at Vancouver's Regent College. He is also the author of *Canadian Evangelicalism in the Twentieth Century: An Introduction to Its Character* (1993) and *Can God Be Trusted? Faith and the Challenge of Evil* (1998).

Margaret Burwash
Nathanael Burwash

Dr. Marguerite Van Die is a member of the Department of History and of Queen's Theological College, Queen's University. She is the author of *An Evangelical Mind: Nathanael Burwash and the Methodist Tradition in Canada, 1839–1918* (1989), and has contributed articles to historical journals, collected essays, dictionaries, and encyclopedias. She is the codirector of the Queen's University project Religion and Politics in Canada and the USA, funded by the Pew Charitable Trusts.

Paul de Chomedey de Maisonneuve

Dominique Vinay is a doctoral student in French sixteenth century civilization. Her research has led her to study in the Universities of Montreal, Tours (France), Salamanca (Spain), and Chicago. She is completing research on her dissertation in Paris, where she is also working on updating Grente's *Dictionnaire de XVIe siècle* (Dictionary of the Sixteenth Century).

Nellie McClung

Dr. Randi R. Warne teaches at Mount St. Vincent University in Halifax. She received her doctorate in religion and culture at the University of Toronto in 1988. Her *Literature as Pulpit: The Christian Social Activism of Nellie L. McClung* (1993) won the Dissertation Prize of the Canadian Corporation for Studies in Religion as the best dissertation on religion between 1988 and 1993. Warne has given Chatauqua presentations on McClung in Canada and the United States since 1989.

Matthew Begbie

David R. Williams, Queen's Counsel, is an adjunct professor and writer in residence for the University of Victoria's Faculty of Law. A lawyer since 1949, he was appointed Queen's Counsel (B.C.) in 1969. Williams is an award-winning author of many books in the areas of history and law, including . . . *The Man for a New Country: Sir Matthew Baillie Begbie* (1977).

Further Reading

Perhaps the greatest challenge facing each contributing author to *Canada: Portraits of Faith* was in writing of their subjects in only one thousand words. This limitation allows a mere glimpse into each subject's life. For this reason, authors were asked to suggest three further sources of information on each subject. Although these sources in no way represent an exhaustive bibliography, they will assist you as you begin to examine your favourite subjects.

William Aberhart

William Aberhart, *Outpourings and Replies*, ed. David R. Elliott (Calgary: Historical Society of Alberta, 1991).

David R. Elliott and Iris Miller, *Bible Bill: A Biography of William Aberhart* (Edmonton: Reidmore Books, 1987).

Lewis H. Thomas, ed., *William Aberhart and Social Credit in Alberta* (Toronto: Copp Clark, 1977).

Henry Alline

James Beverley and Barry Moody, eds., *The Life and Journal of the Rev. Mr. Henry Alline* (Hantsport, NS: Lancelot Press, 1982).

J. M. Bumsted, *Henry Alline, 1748–1784* (Toronto: University of Toronto Press, 1971).

George Rawlyk, *Ravished by the Spirit: Religious Revivals, Baptists, and Henry Alline* (Montreal: McGill-Queen's University Press, 1984).

Matthew Begbie

Edgar Fawcett, *Some Reminiscences of Old Victoria* (Toronto: William Briggs, 1912).

Frederic W. Howay and E. O. S. Scholefield, *British Columbia from the Earliest Times to the Present* (Vancouver: S.J. Clarke Publishing Co., 1914).

David Ricardo Williams, ... *The Man for a New Country: Sir Matthew Baillie Begbie* (Sidney, B.C.: Gray's Publishing Ltd., 1977).

William Black

Arthur Betts, *Bishop Black and His Preachers* (Sackville, N.B.: Tribune Press, 1976).

William Black, "The Journal of Mr. William Black, in his visit to Newfoundland," *The Arminian Magazine* 15 (1792), available from http://www.mun.ca/rels/meth/texts/black/black2.html.

Peter Penner, *The Chignecto 'Connexion'* (Sackville, N.B.: United Church, 1990).

William Bompas

K. M. Abel, *Drum Songs: Glimpses of Dene History* (Montreal: McGill-Queen's University Press, 1993).

W. C. Bompas, *Northern Lights on the Bible* (London: J. Nisbet, n.d.).

H. A. Cody, *An Apostle of the North: Memoirs of the Right Reverend William Carpenter Bompas, D.D.* (Toronto: Musson, 1908).

Henri Bourassa

Joseph Levitt, *Henri Bourassa and the Golden Calf* (Ottawa: Les éditions de l'Université d'Ottawa, 1969).

Joseph Levitt, *Henri Bourassa on Imperialism and Bi-Culturalism, 1900–1918* (Toronto: Copp Clark, 1970).

Robert Rumilly, *Henri Bourassa: La vie Publique d'un Grand Canadien* (Montreal: Les éditions Chantecler ltée., 1953).

Marguerite Bourgeoys

Simone Poissant, *Marguerite Bourgeoys*, trans. Frances Kirwan (Montreal: Bellarmin, 1982).

Elizabeth Rapley, *The Dévotes: Women and Church in Seventeenth-Century France* (Montreal and Kingston: McGill-Queen's University Press, 1990).

Patricia Simpson, *Marguerite Bourgeoys and Montreal, 1640–1665* (Montreal: McGill-Queen's University Press, 1997).

Jean de Brébeuf

Jean de Brébeuf, *The Huron Relation of 1635* (Midland, Ontario: Martyr's Shrine, 1972).

J. R. Miller, *Skyscrapers Hide the Heavens: A History of Indian-White Relations in Canada* (Toronto: University of Toronto Press, 1991).

E. J. Pratt, *Brébeuf and His Brethren* (Toronto: Macmillan, 1966).

George Brown

J. M. S. Careless, *Brown of the Globe*, 2 vols. (Toronto: Macmillan, 1959, 1983).

Sir Alexander Mackenzie, ed., *The Life and Speeches of the Honourable George Brown* (Toronto: Globe Printing, 1882).

Vincent Marquis, *A Truly Loyal Subject, George Brown and Confederation* (Russell, Ontario: The Home Works, 1997).

John Buchan

John Buchan, *Memory Hold the Door* (London: Hodder & Stoughton, 1940).

Andrew Lownie, *John Buchan* (London: Constable, 1995).

Susan Tweedsmuir, *John Buchan by His Wife and Friends* (London: Hodder & Stoughton, 1947).

Margaret Burwash

Margaret Proctor Burwash Papers (United Church of Canada/Victoria University Archives, Toronto).

Nathanael Burwash Papers (United Church of Canada/Victoria University Archives, Toronto).

Johanna M. Selles, *Methodists & Women's Education in Ontario, 1836–1925* (Montreal: McGill-Queen's University Press, 1996).

Nathanael Burwash

Nathanael Burwash Papers (United Church of Canada/Victoria University Archives, Toronto).

Michael Gauvreau, *The Evangelical Century: College and Creed in English Canada from the Great Revival to the Great Depression* (Montreal: McGill-Queen's University Press, 1991).

Marguerite Van Die, *An Evangelical Mind: Nathanael Burwash and the Methodist Tradition in Canada, 1839–1918* (Montreal: McGill-Queen's University Press, 1989).

Eliza Case

Peter Jones, *Life and Journals of Kah-ke-wa-quo-na-by (Rev. Peter Jones), Wesleyan Missionary* (Toronto: Anson Green, 1860).

Elizabeth Gillan Muir, *Petticoats in the Pulpit: The Story of Early Nineteenth-Century Methodist Women Preachers in Upper Canada* (Toronto: The United Church Publishing House, 1991).

Letitia Youmans, *Campaign Echoes: The Autobiography of Mrs. Letitia Youmans, the Pioneer of the White Ribbon Movement in Canada* (Toronto: William Briggs, 1893).

William Case

John Carroll, *Case and His Cotemporaries* [*sic*], 5 vols. (Toronto: 1867–77).

Goldwin S. French, "William Case," in *Dictionary of Canadian Biography* vol. VII (Toronto: University of Toronto Press, 1985).

Donald B. Smith, *Sacred Feathers: The Reverend Peter Jones (Kahkewaquonaby) and the Mississauga Indians* (Lincoln: University of Nebraska Press, 1987).

Marie-Madeleine de Chauvigny de La Peltrie

Marie de l'Incarnation, *Correspondance*, ed. Guy-Marie Oury (Paris: Saint-Pierre de Solesmes, 1971).

Guy-Marie Oury, *Madame de La Peltrie et ses fondations canadiennes* (Quebec City: Presses de l'Université Laval, 1974).

Reuben Gold Thwaites, *The Jesuit Relations and Allied Documents*, vols. 1635–1636, 1642–1643, and 1671–1672 (Cleveland: 1901).

Paul de Chomedey de Maisonneuve

Jean-Rémi Brault, *Les Origines de Montréal* (Montreal: la société de Montréal, 1993).

Guy LaFleche, ed., "Le missionaire, l'apostat, le sorcier," in *Relation de 1634 de Paul Le Jeune* (Montreal: Presses de l'Université de Montréal, 1973).

Louise-Martin Tard, *Chomedey de Maisonneuve, le pionnier de Montréal* (Montreal: XYZ, 1994).

Hugh Crossley

Hugh T. Crossley, *Practical Talks on Important Themes* (William Briggs, 1895).

John Webster Grant, *A Profusion of Spires: Religion in Nineteenth-Century Ontario* (Toronto: University of Toronto Press, 1988).

Kevin B. Kee, "The Heavenly Railroad: An Introduction to Crossley-Hunter Revivalism," in *Aspects of the Canadian Evangelical Experience*, ed. G. A. Rawlyk (Montreal: McGill-Queen's University Press, 1997).

William Dawson

Rankine Dawson, ed., *Fifty Years of Work in Canada, Scientific and Educational* (London: Ballantyne, 1901).

Michael Gauvreau, *The Evangelical Century: College and Creed in English Canada from the Great Revival to the Great Depression* (Montreal: McGill-Queen's University Press, 1991).

Susan Sheets-Pyenson, *John William Dawson: Faith, Hope and Science* (Montreal: McGill-Queen's University Press, 1996).

Tommy Douglas

Thomas H. McLeod and Ian McLeod, *Tommy Douglas: The Road to Jerusalem* (Edmonton: Hurtig, 1987).

Doris French Shackleton, *Tommy Douglas* (Toronto: McClelland & Stewart, 1975).

Robert Tyre, *Douglas in Saskatchewan: The Story of a Socialist Experiment* (Vancouver: Mitchell, 1962).

William Duncan

J. W. Arctander, *The Apostle of Alaska* (New York: Fleming H. Revell, 1910).

Peter Murray, *The Devil and Mr. Duncan: A History of the Two Metlakatlas* (Victoria: Sono Nis Press, 1985).

Jean Usher, *William Duncan of Metlakatla: A Victorian Missionary in British Columbia* (Ottawa: National Museums of Canada, 1974).

Timothy Eaton

John Bassett, *Timothy Eaton* (Toronto: Fitzhenry and Whiteside, 1982).

Joy L. Santink, *Timothy Eaton and the Rise of His Department Store* (Toronto: University of Toronto Press, 1990).

William Stephenson, *The Store that Timothy Built* (Toronto: McClelland & Stewart, 1969).

Northrop Frye

Joseph Adamson, *Northrop Frye: A Visionary Life* (Toronto: ECW Press, 1993).

Northrop Frye, *The Great Code: The Bible and Literature* (Toronto: Academic Press, 1982).

Northrop Frye, *The Double Vision* (Toronto: University of Toronto Press, 1991).

George Monro Grant

George Monro Grant, *Ocean to Ocean* (Toronto: James Campbell & Son, 1873).

William Lawson Grant and Frederick Hamilton, *George Monro Grant* (Edinburgh: T. C. & E. C. Jack; Toronto: Morang, 1905).

D. B. Mack, "George Monro Grant: Evangelical Prophet" (Ph.D. diss., Queen's University, 1992).

George Parkin Grant

William Christian, *George Grant: A Biography* (Toronto: University of Toronto Press, 1993).

George Grant, *Lament for a Nation: The Defeat of Canadian Nationalism* (Ottawa: Carleton University Press, 1965; reprint, 1997).

George Grant, *Selected Letters*, ed. William Christian (Toronto: University of Toronto Press, 1996).

Wilfred Grenfell

Wilfred T. Grenfell, *A Labrador Doctor* (Boston and New York: Houghton Mifflin, 1919).

Wilfred T. Grenfell, *What Christ Means to Me* (London: Hodder & Stoughton, 1926).

Ronald Rompkey, *Grenfell of Labrador: A Biography* (Toronto: University of Toronto Press, 1991).

Lionel Groulx

Lionel Groulx, *Mes Mémoires*, 4 vols. (Montreal: Fides, 1974).

Benoît Lacroix, ed., *Lionel Groulx* (Montreal: Fides, 1967).

Susan Mann Trofimenkoff, *Abbé Groulx: Variations on a Nationalist Theme* (Toronto: Clark Copp Publishing, 1973).

Marie Guyart de l'Incarnation

Jean Comby, *L'itinéraire mystique d'une femme, Marie de l'Incarnation, Ursuline* (Montreal: Bellarmin, 1993).

Marie de l'Incarnation, *Écrits spirituels et historiques* (Paris: Albert Jamet, 1985).

Françoise Deroy-Pineau, *Marie de l'Incarnation, Marie Guyart, femme d'affaires, mystique, mère de la Nouvelle-France* (Paris: Robert Lafont, 1989).

Barbara Heck

Eula C. Lapp, *To Their Heirs Forever* (Belleville: Mika Publishing Co., 1977).

Elizabeth Gillan Muir, *Petticoats in the Pulpit: The Story of Early Nineteenth-Century Methodist Women Preachers in Upper Canada* (Toronto: The United Church Publishing House, 1991).

W. H. Withrow, *Barbara Heck, A Tale of Early Methodism* (Toronto: William Briggs, n.d.).

William Howland

Desmond Morton, *Mayor Howland: The Citizen's Candidate* (Toronto: A. M. Hakkert Ltd., 1973).

Desmond Morton, "The Crusading Mayor Howland," *Horizon Canada* 2, no. 23 (1985).

Lindsay Reynolds, *Footprints: The Beginning of the Christian and Missionary Alliance in Canada* (Toronto: The Christian Missionary Alliance, 1982).

John Hunter

John Webster Grant, *A Profusion of Spires: Religion in Nineteenth-Century Ontario* (Toronto: University of Toronto Press, 1988).

Kevin B. Kee, "The Heavenly Railroad: An Introduction to Crossley-Hunter Revivalism," in *Aspects of the Canadian Evangelical Experience*, ed. G. A. Rawlyk (Montreal: McGill-Queen's University Press, 1997).

Lynne S. Marks, *Revivals and Roller Rinks: Religion, Leisure and Identity in Late Nineteenth Century Small Town Ontario* (Toronto: University of Toronto Press, 1996).

Peter Jones

Peter Jones, *Life and Journals of Kah-ke-wa-quo-na-by (Rev. Peter Jones), Wesleyan Missionary* (Toronto: Anson Green, 1860).

Peter Jones, *History of the Ojebway Indians; With Especial Reference to Their Conversion to Christianity* (London: A.W. Bennett, 1861).

Donald B. Smith, *Sacred Feathers: The Reverend Peter Jones (Kahkewaquonaby) and the Mississauga Indians* (Lincoln: University of Nebraska Press, 1987).

Louis-François Laflèche

André Labarrière-Paulé, ed., *Louis-François Laflèche* (Montréal: Fides, 1970).

Robert Rumilly, *Monseigneur Laflèche et son temps* (Montréal: Éditions B.D. Simpson, 1945).

Nive Voisine, *Louis-François Laflèche, deuxième éveque de Trois-Rivières* (Saint-Hyacinthe: Edisem, 1980).

Agnes Macphail

Terry Crowley, *Agnes Macphail and the Politics of Equality* (Toronto: James Lorimer & Co., 1990).

Kenneth McNaught, *A Prophet in Politics: A Biography of J. S. Woodsworth* (Toronto: University of Toronto Press, 1959).

Margaret Stewart and Doris French, *Ask No Quarter: A Biography of Agnes Macphail* (Toronto: Longmans, Green, 1959).

Jeanne Mance

Pierre Dhombre, *Jeanne Mance, Foundress of Hôtel-Dieu and Co-Foundress of Montréal* (Montreal: Saint-Joseph, 1992).

J. K. Foran, *Jeanne Mance: Her Life* (Montreal: Herald Press, 1931).

Guy-Marie Oury, *Jeanne Mance et le rêve de M. de la Dauversière* (Paris: Chambray-lès-Tours, 1983).

Ernest Manning

Lloyd Mackey, *Like Father, Like Son* (Toronto: ECW Press, 1997).

Ernest C. Manning, *Political Realignment: A Challenge to Thoughtful Canadians* (Toronto: McClelland, 1967).

Preston Manning, *The New Canada* (Toronto: Macmillan, 1992).

Robert McAlister

James D. Craig, "Out and Out for the Lord," in "James Eustace Purdie: An Early Anglican Pentecostal" (master's thesis, University of St. Michael's College, 1995).

James D. Craig, *Robert Edward McAlister: Canadian Pentecostal Pioneer* (Mississauga, Ontario: PAOC Archives, 1987).

Thomas William Miller, *Canadian Pentecostalism: A History of the Pentecostal Assemblies of Canada* (Mississauga, Ontario: Full Gospel Publishing House, 1994).

Nellie McClung

Carol Hancock, *No Small Legacy* (Winfield, B.C.: Wood Lake Books, 1986).

Candace Savage, *Our Nell: A Scrapbook Biography of Nellie L. McClung* (Saskatoon: Western Producer Prairie Books, 1979).

Randi R. Warne, *Literature as Pulpit: The Christian Social Activism of Nellie L. McClung* (Waterloo: Wilfred Laurier University Press, 1993).

Marshall McLuhan

Philip Marchand *Marshall McLuhan: The Medium & the Messenger* (Boston: Ticknor & Fields, 1989; reprint, with revisions, Cambridge, MA: The MIT Press, forthcoming 1998).

Marshall McLuhan, *Understanding Media* (Cambridge, MA: The MIT Press, 1964).

Marshall McLuhan, *The Gutenberg Galaxy* (Toronto: University of Toronto Press, 1962).

Oliver Mowat

C. R. W. Biggar, *Sir Oliver Mowat: A Biographical Sketch* (Toronto: Warwick Brothers & Rutter Ltd., 1905).

Ramsay Cook, *Provincial Autonomy, Minority Rights and the Compact Theory, 1867–1921* (Ottawa: Macmillian, 1969).

Donald Swainson, ed., *Oliver Mowat's Ontario* (Toronto: Macmillian, 1972).

Charles Pandosy

Kay Cronin, *Cross in the Wilderness* (Toronto: Mission Press, 1960).

Edward J. Kowrach, *Charles Pandosy, O.M.I., A Missionary of the Northwest* (Fairfield: Ye Galleon, 1992).

Denys Nelson, "Father Pandosy, O.M.I.," *Second Annual Report of the Okanagan Historical and Natural History Society* (Vernon, B.C.: 1927; reprint, 1975).

John Robson

Olive Fairholm, "John Robson and Confederation," in *British Columbia and Confederation*, ed. W. George Shelton (Victoria: University of Victoria, 1967).

Frederick W. Howay and E. O. S. Scholefield, *British Columbia from the Earliest Times to the Present* (Vancouver: S.J. Clarke Publishing Co., 1914).

James Morton, *In the Sea of Sterile Mountains: The Chinese in British Columbia* (Vancouver: J.J. Douglas, 1974).

Egerton Ryerson

Goldwin S. French, *Parsons and Politics* (Toronto: Ryerson, 1962).

R. D. Gidney and W. P. J. Millar, *Inventing Secondary Education: The Rise of the High School in Nineteenth-Century Ontario* (Montreal: McGill-Queen's University Press, 1990).

Charles B. Sissons, *Egerton Ryerson: His Life and Letters*, 2 vols. (Toronto: Clarke Irwin, 1937).

Joseph Scriven

L. F. Clarry, "Joseph Scriven" (handwritten memoir of Scriven's life held by the United Church Archives in Toronto, 1921).

Foster Meharry Russell, *What a Friend We Have in Jesus* (Belleville: Mika, 1981).

Joseph Scriven, *Hymns and Other Verses* (Peterborough: James Stephens, 1869).

Albert B. Simpson

David F. Hartzfeld and Charles W. Nienkirchen, eds., *The Birth of a Vision: Essays on the Ministry and Thought of Albert Benjamin Simpson* (Regina: Canadian Theological Seminary, 1986).

A.E. Thompson, *A. B. Simpson: His Life and Work* (Harrisburg: Christian Publications, 1920).

A.W. Tozer, *Wingspread: A. B. Simpson: A Study in Spiritual Altitude* (Harrisburg: Christian Publications, 1943).

Oswald J. Smith

Lois Neely, *Fire in His Bones* (Wheaton: Tyndale House, 1982).

Oswald J. Smith, *The Passion for Souls* (Burlington, Ontario: G.R. Welch, 1938).

Oswald J. Smith, *The Story of My Life* (Burlington, Ontario: G.R. Welch, 1962).

Henry Bird Steinhauer

Gerald Hutchinson, "Early Wesleyan Missions," *Alberta Historical Review* 6, no. 4 (1958).

Isaac K. Mabindisa, "The Praying Man: The Life and Times of Henry Bird Steinhauer" (Ph.D. diss., University of Alberta, 1984).

Gayle Simonson, "The Prayer Man," *The Beaver* (Oct./Nov. 1988).

John Strachan

A. N. Bethune, *Memoir of the Right Reverend John Strachan, D.D., LL.D., First Bishop of Toronto* (Toronto: Henry Rowsell, 1870).

J. L. H. Henderson, ed., *John Strachan: Documents and Opinions* (Toronto: McClelland & Stewart, 1969).

J. L. H. Henderson, *John Strachan 1778–1867* (Toronto: University of Toronto Press, 1969).

Leonard Tilley

James Hannay, *The Life and Times of Sir Leonard Tilley, Being a Political History of New Brunswick for the Past Seventy Years* (Saint John, N.B., 1897).

James Hannay, "Sir Leonard Tilley," in *The Makers of Canada*, vol. X (Toronto: Morang, 1912).

J. Castell Hopkins, "The Hon. Sir Samuel Leonard Tilley," in *Canada: An Encyclopædia of the Country*, vol. I (Toronto: Linscott, 1898).

Georges Vanier

George Cowley and Michel Vanier, eds., *Only to Serve: Selections from Addresses of Governor General Georges P. Vanier* (Toronto: University of Toronto Press, 1970).

Robert Speaight, *Vanier: Soldier, Diplomat and Governor General* (Toronto: Collins, 1970).

Jean Vanier, *In Weakness, Strength: The Spiritual Sources of Georges P. Vanier* (Toronto: Griffin House, 1969).

Pauline Vanier

John Cowan, *Canada's Governors-General: Lord Monck to General Vanier* (Toronto: York, 1965).

Deborah Cowley and George Cowley, *One Woman's Journey: A Portrait of Pauline Vanier* (Ottawa: Novalis, 1994).

Jane Wilson

"The Doctrines and Discipline of the British Primitive Methodist," *Connexion* (York: W.J. Coates, 1833).

Jane Agar Hopper, *Primitive Methodism in Canada 1829–1884* (Toronto: William Briggs, 1904).

Elizabeth Gillan Muir, *Petticoats in the Pulpit: The Story of Early Nineteenth-Century Methodist Women Preachers in Upper Canada* (Toronto: The United Church Publishing House, 1991).

Letitia Youmans

Sharon Anne Cook, *"Through Sunshine and Shadow": The Woman's Christian Temperance Union, Evangelicalism, and Reform in Ontario, 1874–1930* (Montreal: McGill-Queen's University Press, 1995).

Jan Noel, *Canada Dry: Temperance Crusades before Confederation* (Toronto: University of Toronto Press, 1995).

Letitia Youmans, *Campaign Echoes: The Autobiography of Mrs. Letitia Youmans, the Pioneer of the White Ribbon Movement in Canada* (Toronto: William Briggs, 1893).

In addition, almost every author recommended the at present thirteen-volume series *Dictionary of Canadian Biography* (University of Toronto Press, 1966–), especially as a starting point for studying subjects who died in 1910 or before.

Family Prayer

A family gathers together to pray. A doll lies where it was dropped as a mother hurriedly collects her two smallest children to kneel beside her, asking the Lord for the grace to make it through another day. Grandfather clasps his cane with gnarled hands, remembering when he prayed with his wife beside him. Along the window bench the two older children whisper hushed secrets back and forth: save the "daily bread," the table is empty. In the centre of it all, the father looks expectantly for his family's prayer to be answered. Sunlight streams through the window signifying the divine light of God touching each family member.

God does hear our prayers. He illuminates our thoughts, providing warmth and comfort as we commune with Him. *Family Prayer* was painted in 1890 by Canadian artist George Agnew Reid (1860–1947). It hangs in Victoria College at the University of Toronto. This beautiful painting captures the intimate warmth of a family united in faith.

Limited-edition prints of this inspired and touching work are available. Each is hand numbered and printed on acid-free paper of the highest quality.

Dimensions: 44.5 x 56 cm (17.5" x 22")
Cost: $110 (GST, shipping, and handling included)

Cheque or money order payable to
HSLDA of Canada
#2-3295 Dunmore Road, SE
Medicine Hat, Alberta T1B 3R2

Credit card orders: (403) 528-2704